MW01165698

The Satanic War on the Christian Vol.4 The Protection from Satan & Demons

FIRST PRINTING

Billy Crone

Cover Design:
CHRIS TAYLOR

To my sister, Heather.

If ever there was two people,
who knew firsthand
the ravages of spiritual warfare,
It would be you and me.

Prior to salvation,
both of us,
at various times,
have danced with the devils,
played their games,
and sang their songs.

We ingested their poison,
believed their lies,
and even tried to end these lives,
multiple times.

But God did what only He can do.
He rescued us from the dominion of darkness,
He saved us from the clutches of the evil one.
He set us free through Jesus Christ.

Thank you for not only putting up with me,
and for being a wonderful sister here on earth,
but for now, being a fellow soldier of Christ,
fighting the good fight,
in this greatest battle of all,
The Satanic War on the Christian.

Don't ever give up Heather,
We know who wins.

I love you.

Contents

Preface

Why are so few Churches making an impact on the world today? Why are so many believers living defeated lives? Why do so many Christians talk about having a victorious Christian life, yet so few seldom ever do? The answer lies in the greatest spiritual war of all time, The Satanic War on the Christian.

But we have a problem, a big problem in the Church today. You see, you would think that the knowledge and mastery of spiritual warfare would be commonplace among the Christian community. After all, our Lord Jesus Christ took on and defeated the devil himself. But unfortunately, waging war against the enemy of our souls is one of the least talked about topics in the Church today, for a couple of reasons. One reason is because some in the Church have detrimentally taken spiritual warfare to an unhealthy extreme. The result is that the moment you try to talk about spiritual warfare in Christian circles, most people think you're some sort of a weird lunatic. Then, as if that wasn't bad enough, we have the second extreme to deal with. Well over half of all professing Christians today don't even believe that our greatest archenemy, the devil, even exists. No wonder we're losing the fight! Yet in the midst of our sad skepticism, spiritual warfare really is something we all have to deal with every single day here on earth. And unless we get a proper balanced handle on it, we will simply continue to be beaten to shreds spiritually.

Thus, I have written this book, without all the hyper fanaticism, showy sensationalism, or dry theological jargon and simply focused on getting down to the nuts and bolts of the greatest war of all time, the war against the children of God and the forces of hell. It is penned with a powerful concoction of practical information and personal application for personal victory, while clearly exposing the lies, traps, and pitfalls of the very forces of evil. It is my prayer that this book will not only clearly unveil this deadly invisible war and expose the seductive weapons the devil uses to keep the Church from becoming a mighty army for God, but that it will also provide the practical tools needed for the personal spiritual victory that our Lord Jesus Christ has already won for us.

One last piece of advice. When you are through reading this book then will you please READ YOUR BIBLE? I mean that in the nicest possible way. Enjoy, and I'm looking forward to seeing you someday!

Billy Crone
Las Vegas, Nevada
2018

Part 4

The Protection Against Satan & Demons

Chapter Twenty-One

Protection from Satan and Demons Part 1

"It started out just like any other typical morning in January. The people were busy scurrying around with the usual activities trying to keep warm and productive. The adults went off to the fields or other various places of employment and the children went about their usual daily chores. Why, it appeared to everyone it was just going to be another ho hum day in this far east country. But all that was to change in a matter of seconds.

Suddenly an 8.0 earthquake struck with such a force that the ground suddenly rose up and formed new hills. Then it sank in abruptly and became new valleys. In other areas, a stream burst forth in an instant, or the ground broke up and new gullies appeared. Then houses, temples and city walls collapsed crushing anything and everything in their path.

But that was just the beginning. Since the people were surrounded by several high plateaus that were filled with layers of silt, the quake triggered one of the deadliest landslides of all time. So even if the people managed to escape being crushed by a building they were doomed by a raging river of mud.

And when the screams and cries finally subsided, the damage was assessed. An entire region of this country had been absolutely destroyed. A 520-mile-wide area was obliterated and, in some counties, 60% of the population was annihilated. In just a matter of minutes, 830,000 people had been totally snuffed

out. The year was 1556. The disaster was, the Shaanxi Earthquake."[1]

How many of you have heard of the Shaanxi Earthquake? Okay, maybe a couple. But how many of you would agree it was one of the greatest disasters of all time, right? But with all due respect to those who lost their lives in the Shaanxi Earthquake, what if I were to tell you I know of a disaster that makes that earthquake look like a game of patty cake? And what if I were to tell you that this disaster didn't occur in just one place and one country at one time, but it's going on right now today all over the world and it's been leaving a trail of death and destruction for centuries. I'm talking once again about *the satanic War on the Christian.*

Whether you see it, feel it, believe it or not, the moment you got saved you entered a spiritual war against a demonic host whose sole purpose is to destroy you and extinguish your testimony for Jesus Christ. And what's wild is that most wars go on for a few years or even longer. But *the satanic War on the Christian* has been going on for the last 2,000 years non-stop and it's sending people straight to hell! YET how many people, even Christians, will openly discuss the longest war in mankind's history? *The satanic War on the Christian,* that has destroyed more lives than all the wars put together? What we have seen is that the devil will actually trick you and I into giving up in the fight against sin, getting us all discouraged, so we'll act like a bunch of modern-day traitors! HOW? By getting us to not understand the positive reasons why God allows us to be tempted with sin. He's not the author of it, but He's so powerful He'll use even what the enemy throws at us for bad and turn it around for good. We saw that some of those positive reasons from God, was **To Humble Us**, **To Strengthen Us**, and **To Bless Us**. We get to give the enemy an uppercut when we say yes to Jesus and no to sin!

Now so far, we've seen if you're ever going to win a war, then the **1st thing** you must do is **Know Who Your Enemy Is**…

Then we saw the **2nd thing** you need to know is **What Your Enemy is Like**, their character, amen? It's common sense, right?

Then we saw the **3rd thing** you need to know is **The Tactic of Your Enemy,** what they're up to, what's their goal and why are they here.

Then we saw the **4th thing** you need to know is **The Destruction of Your Enemy,** what price you pay when you DON'T take this seriously.

Then we saw the **5th thing** you need to know is **The Temptation of Your Enemy,** how he's out there trying to get us to sin against God.

But that's not the only positive things God does for us when it comes to dealing with the devil and demons, and spiritual warfare!

The **sixth thing** we need to deal with if we're going to stop getting beat up and duped all over the place as Christians in *this satanic War on the Christian* is **The Protection FROM Our Enemy**.

You see, folks, believe it or not, God has not left us hanging high and dry in this Great Cosmic War with satan and his demons. Are you kidding me? He's actually given us His full-blown protection and weaponry to stand our ground and be victorious in all situations every single time! It's called The Armor of God! But hey, don't take my word for it. Let's listen to God's.

Ephesians 6:10-20 "Finally, be strong in the Lord and in His mighty power. Put on the full armor of God so that you can take your stand against the devil's schemes. For our struggle is not against flesh and blood, but against the rulers, against the authorities, against the powers of this dark world and against the spiritual forces of evil in the heavenly realms. Therefore, put on the full armor of God, so that when the day of evil comes, you may be able to stand your ground, and after you have done everything, to stand. Stand firm, then, with the belt of truth buckled around your waist, with the breastplate of righteousness in place, and with your feet fitted with the readiness that comes from the gospel of peace. In addition to all this, take up the shield of faith, with which you can extinguish all the flaming arrows of the evil one. Take the helmet of salvation and the sword of the Spirit, which is the Word of God. And pray in the Spirit on all occasions with all kinds of prayers and requests. With this in mind, be alert and always keep on praying for all the saints. Pray also for me, that whenever I open my mouth, words may be given me so that I will fearlessly make known the mystery of the gospel, for which I am an ambassador in chains. Pray that I may declare it fearlessly, as I should."

So here we see the infamous text that we've already seen a couple of times before in our study and it's dealing with the armor of God. And now we're going to begin the process of tearing it apart, so we don't miss the blessing of why Paul has it here at the end of this Chapter. And as we're going to see, it's not by chance, it's very, very important. But this passage deals with God's Mighty Power that is available to us every single day as Christians to deal with temptation and spiritual warfare and we'll see God's plea for us to be strong in it. In fact, it actually says, "be constantly strengthened" day in and day out and "put it on now, once and for all." But we'll get to that later. It also exposes the reality of real live, wicked, evil, demonic forces, that daily seek to take us out in a hierarchal structure. They take their attacks on us seriously, in a uniformed fashion, unlike us. It also reveals piece by piece the supernatural equipment that God gives to us to experience His victory, that He's already given to us, so we can stand firm in Christ in the day of evil, when, not if, it comes. But as you can see, God has not left us hanging high and dry when it comes to dealing with spiritual warfare! Not at all! He's given us His armor! It's not my armor, it's not your armor, it's not armor you buy at Walmart and falls apart later! Praise God it's not! It's His armor, the actual armor of God that defeats the enemy every single time! God never loses! Do you get it? It's His armor and He give it to us! That means we can't lose if we just do what He says, put it on, and understand how to use it! Therefore, if we're going to experience this victory that God's already given to us with His armor, then let's make sure we get it right, amen? Let's not gloss over this and tear it apart piece by piece for all it's worth.

The **1st thing** we see about the Armor of God is that **It's Designed for War**.

The **1st way** we see it's designed for war is the **Context of the Scripture**.

You see, when Paul is writing this section about the armor of God to the Ephesian Church, it just so happens to be placed at the end of the Book. How many of you can figure that out without any help? That's not by chance. In fact, when you take a look at the context of where it's placed in the Book at the back end, it sends a clear message that it's designed for war.

Ephesians 1-3	Ephesians 4-6
Spiritual Wealth	Spiritual Walk
Theology	Ethics
Position of the Believer	Practice of the Believer
Identity	Obligation
God Sees Us in Christ	World Should See Christ in Us
The Privilege	The Practice
Christian Doctrine	Christian Duty
Revelation	Responsibility
Christian Blessings	Christian Behavior
Our Heritage in Christ	Our Life in Christ
Work of Christ	Walk of the Christian
Christ's Work in Us	Christ's Work Through Us
Heavenly Standing	Earthly Walk[2]

And this is the point. After Paul deals with the Believers position in Chapters 1-3 and then deals with the Believers practice and responsibility to that position in Chapters 4-6, he then ends with the Believers warfare. Because it's common sense! Think about it folks! Anytime you truly begin to live for Christ and make a difference in this wicked world system by our Christ-like behavior, sharing the Gospel, letting other people know the way out through Jesus Christ. You're going to get it! You've entered into a war! The enemy is going to come at you every single day with guns blazing full force and they'll do anything they can just to get you to stop doing that, living the Christian life! The phrase I use is, "Anytime you want to do something truly significant for Christ, you're going to pay a significant price!" You're going to have warfare! So, Paul knows this, and he ends the Chapter by telling us how to deal with spiritual warfare affectively that will come your way when you live like this. A godly life in Christ. A Christian who knows their position and practices is on a collision course with the enemy as this man shares.

"The committed Christian and satan are on a collision course. It is inevitable that your life will intersect with the forces of Hell as you live for God. There is absolutely no question about that. It's only a question as to how that manifests itself and what specifics may occur.

In fact, it's rather constant as well. The adversary works hard and effectively. He works powerfully against the child of God. Paul is saying this: if you are a true Christian as defined in chapter 1, chapter 2 and chapter 3, and if you are living the way a true Christian should live as defined in chapter 4, 5 and 6, then you can be sure of one thing and that is that you are going to run right into the enemy.

If we're walking in humility and unity, not in the vanity of our mind as the Gentiles. If we're putting on the new man. If we're walking in love, not lust. If we're walking in light, not darkness. If we're walking in wisdom, not foolishness. If we're not drunk with wine but filled with the Spirit.

If we're not singing the world's songs but psalms and hymns and spiritual songs, and if rather than being proud and individualistic we are submitting ourselves one to another, and if we are submitting as wives should to husbands as to the Lord, and if husbands are loving their wives as Christ loved the church, and if children are obeying their parents and parents are nurturing and rearing their children to the things of God, and if employees and employers have right relationships biblically and with Spirit-filled impact, then believe me, we will counter the system. We will run against the grain.

It is impossible to live in the manner that Ephesians outlines without having conflict with Satan. It's impossible."[3]

In other words, you're headed for war! And that's not the only time that the Apostle Paul and the New Testament writers warn us of this harsh battle reality. It's all over the place if you do the study.

We're Soldiers for Christ

- **1 Corinthians 9:7** "Who serves as a **soldier** at his own expense? Who plants a vineyard and does not eat of its grapes? Who tends a flock and does not drink of the milk?"
- **Philippians 2:25** "But I think it is necessary to send back to you Epaphroditus, my brother, fellow worker and fellow **soldier**, who is also your messenger, whom you sent to take care of my needs."
- **2 Timothy 2:3** "Endure hardship with us like a good **soldier** of Christ Jesus."
- **2 Timothy 2:4** "No one serving as a **soldier** gets involved in civilian affairs – he wants to please his commanding officer."

- **Philemon 1:2** "To Apphia our sister, to Archippus our fellow **soldier** and to the church that meets in your home."

We War for Christ

- **Romans 7:23** "But I see another law at work in the members of my body, waging **war** against the law of my mind and making me a prisoner of the law of sin at work within my members."
- **2 Corinthians 10:3** "For though we live in the world, we do not wage **war** as the world does."
- **1 Peter 2:11** "Dear friends, I urge you, as aliens and strangers in the world, to abstain from sinful desires, which war against your soul."

We have the Weapons of Christ

- **2 Corinthians 6:7** "In truthful speech and in the power of God; with **weapons** of righteousness in the right hand and in the left."
- **2 Corinthians 10:4** "The **weapons** we fight with are not the **weapons** of the world. On the contrary, they have divine power to demolish strongholds."

We Battle for Christ

- **James 4:1** "What causes fights and quarrels among you? Don't they come from your desires that **battle** within you?"

We Struggle for Christ

- **Romans 15:30** "I urge you, brothers, by our Lord Jesus Christ and by the love of the Spirit, to join me in my **struggle** by praying to God for me."
- **Ephesians 6:12** "For our **struggle** (a wrestling contest between two entities is decided when the victor is able to hold his opponent down with his hand upon his neck) is not against flesh and blood, but against the rulers, against the authorities, against the powers of this dark world and against the spiritual forces of evil in the heavenly realms."
- **Philippians 1:30** "Since you are going through the same **struggle** you saw I had, and now hear that I still have."
- **Hebrews 12:4** "In your **struggle** against sin, you have not yet resisted to the point of shedding your blood."

We Fight for Christ

- **1 Corinthians 9:26** "Therefore I do not run like a man running aimlessly; I do not **fight** like a man beating the air."
- **2 Corinthians 10:4** "The weapons we **fight** with are not the weapons of the world. On the contrary, they have divine power to demolish strongholds."
- **1 Timothy 1:18** "Timothy, my son, I give you this instruction in keeping with the prophecies once made about you, so that by following them you may **fight** the good **fight**."
- **1 Timothy 6:12** "**Fight** the good **fight** of the faith. Take hold of the eternal life to which you were called when you made your good confession in the presence of many witnesses."
- **2 Timothy 4:7** "I have fought the good **fight**, I have finished the race, I have kept the faith."

And that's why Ephesians 6:10-20 carries the same War Verbiage.

- Be strong in the Lord (v10)
- Put on the Armor of the Lord (v11)
- Take Your stand against the enemy (v11)
- Our struggle against the enemy (v12)
- Stand Your Ground (v13)
- Stand firm (v13)
- Put on the Belt of Truth (v14)
- Breastplate of Righteousness (v14)
- Feet fitted Gospel of Peace (v15)
- Grab the Shield of Faith (v16)
- Helmet of Salvation (v17)
- Sword of the Spirit (v17)
- Pray to the Commander (v18)
- Be alert (v18)
- Obey without Fear (v19-20)
- CONCLUSION: Sounds like we're in a WAR!!!![4]

Now you know why I say, "Anytime you want to do something truly significant for Christ, you're going to pay a significant price!" You're going to go to war! You're going to have to fight, struggle, battle, and go to war as a good soldier of Christ! And that's why Paul says here in essence to the Ephesian

Church, and to us today, you better get the Armor on and you better use the weapons God gives you, so you can stand your ground, amen? It's coming! Oh, but that's not all.

The **2nd way** we see the Armor of God is designed for war is in the **Catastrophes of the Churches**.

When Paul is writing this Book to the Ephesians dealing with the armor of God and the war we're in, if we start living for Christ. He's writing to a real live Church with real live Christians that existed at that time, the Ephesus Church, just like you and I today. And believe it or not, God tells us how they fared after getting this letter from Paul telling them you better buck up and get the armor on because somebody's out there to take you out. We see this in the Seven Churches mentioned in the Book of Revelation, Chapters 2-3. Paul wrote to the Ephesian Church in approximately 60-62 AD and John wrote the Book of Revelation in approximately 95-96 AD. So, you do the math and we're going to see how the church of Ephesus and others fared after about 30 years have passed from Paul's initial warning. As we're going to see, only 2 out of the 7 survived. 5 Failed!

The **1st Church** that failed to heed Paul's advice on how to deal with the War were in is **Ephesus**.

This just blows me away because Ephesus is the Church to whom the Book of Ephesians was addressed to first and mentions the armor of God. But they didn't listen.

Revelation 2:2-4 "I know your deeds, your hard work and your perseverance. I know that you cannot tolerate wicked men, that you have tested those who claim to be apostles but are not and have found them false. You have persevered and have endured hardships for My Name and have not grown weary. Yet I hold this against you: You have forsaken your first love." Now each one of these 7 Churches could be a sermon in and of itself, but I don't have time to totally go down deep. So, let me just give you a brief breakdown of each one so we can see where they went wrong, so we don't make the same mistake.

Ephesus is simply the Church that lost its first love. That is, they stopped loving Jesus like they used to when they first got saved. As we saw in other studies, this wasn't an accident it was a deliberate choice. One day they decided, no, I'm not going to love Jesus like I used to. Oh, they knew all the right stuff, nobody could beat these guys at a doctrinal test, they had great leadership, they were orthodox, they wouldn't put up with false teachers or false teachings, they persevered, they kept at it. But they chose to stop loving Jesus and started going through the motions. It was just dry stale orthodoxy, punching in your religious time clock, looking good on the outside, saying all the right stuff, doing all the right stuff, but you stopped loving Him and He sees the whole thing. One guy puts it this way.

"This is the church where love died. Orthodoxy and activity without love. This is dangerous because you cannot be effective for God apart from loving the Lord with all your heart, soul, mind and strength.

Ephesus had turned their hot hearts for Christ in for cold orthodoxy. They were simply becoming those who carried out a very biblical ministry without passion.

And I warn you that if we ever get to the place where what we do is an orthodox performance without love, that's step one and Satan has a foothold.

When you come to the place where the honeymoon ends, and you don't do what you do out of an overwhelming love for Jesus Christ you're in real trouble. If you're serving the Lord Jesus Christ as an orthodox performance rather than a passionate love for Him, then you've missed it. You've totally missed it, all together.

So, look at your own life. Is the enthusiasm for Christ there, or is the thrill gone? Is it a fair description of your Christian life to say, "Well, I just kind of do it. I don't have the same love I used to have."

Listen, if you love anything in this world more than you love Jesus Christ you've lost your first love. If you love yourself, your family, your leisure, money, success – anything – you've lost it...you're in real trouble.

You need to get back to how it used to be. Get back on your knees. Get back to the Book. Get back to witnessing. Get back to fellowship. Get back to prayer. Get back to sharing and praising the Lord. Why?

Because unless you do…the same thing will happen to you.

The Church in Ephesus died, they went out of existence. Great, evangelical, orthodox, historic, monumental Church went out of existence because it lost its first love."[5]

And this is the one passage on the Armor of God which was first written, yet even they didn't survive the war. Don't kid yourself Christian if you don't think it could happen to you! If any of those things mentioned is true of you today, you better turn around today! You better get right with God, put the armor on and start standing firm in Christ if you're ever going to survive the war!

The **2ⁿᵈ Church** that failed to heed Paul's advice on how to deal with the War we're in is **Pergamum**.

Now what we're going to see is that it all spills downhill. Once you lose your first love for Jesus it just gets worse as you go. And that's what we see with Pergamum.

Revelation 2:13-15 "I know where you live – where satan has his throne. Yet you remain true to My name. You did not renounce your faith in Me, even in the days of Antipas, my faithful witness, who was put to death in your city – where satan lives. Nevertheless, I have a few things against you: You have people there who hold to the teaching of Balaam, who taught Balak to entice the Israelites to sin by eating food sacrificed to idols and by committing sexual immorality. Likewise, you also have those who hold to the teaching of the Nicolaitans."

So, in essence what you see here with Pergamum, is that once you lose your first love for Jesus, you have got to love something, and so that love gets transferred to the world. This is the compromising Church. They compromised by intermingling with the world. The teaching of Balaam was to get the Israelites to intermarry with the pagans and follow their practices. And the teaching of the Nicolaitans was just wholesale immorality. So, this Church went ape after the world and let the world come in as this guy shares.

"The Church at Pergamum began to court the world. They began to indulge themselves in worldly things. They let the world in.

They were violating 2 Corinthians 6, "What fellowship has light with darkness. What harmony has Christ with Belial?" They were to "come out from among them and be separate and touch not the unclean thing," but they let the world come in.

They were doing what the world wanted them to do. They were aping the world. And so, it is with American Christianity. We too have become very smug and content and almost subcultural, rather than confronting the world we're just kind of waltzing along with the system, trying to accommodate it.

We believe we can win them by becoming what they are. It's amazing to me, how the Church in America today is going all out, whole hog, to ape the world. They do it in so many ways.

If the world's view of the family changes, the Church accommodates it. If the world's view of the woman changes, the Church accommodates it. If the world's view of the homosexual changes, the Church accommodates it, and we get on the bandwagon and do everything the world does.

We want to identify with it and it's just shocking! The Church becomes materialistic because the world is materialistic. The Church becomes preoccupied with entertainment because the world is preoccupied with entertainment.

Oh, the message is still the same, we preach Christ and yet the compromise begins to eat away like termites at the foundation.

How does satan attack a Church? First, it's very subtle. We lose our first love. And then all of a sudden we begin to compromise with the world because the easiest thing to lead you into compromise is a lack of love for God."[6]

Again, it all spills downhill. Pergamum didn't survive the war either. And don't kid yourself Christian it you don't think it could happen to you! If any of those things mentioned in there is true of you today, you better turn around today! You better get right with God, put the armor on and start standing firm in Christ if you're ever going to survive the war!

The **3rd Church** that failed to heed Paul's advice on how to deal with the War we're in is **Thyatira**. Let's see what happened to them.

Revelation 2:19-20 "I know your deeds, your love and faith, your service and perseverance, and that you are now doing more than you did at first. Nevertheless, I have this against you: You tolerate that woman Jezebel, who calls herself a prophetess. By her teaching she misleads my servants into sexual immorality and the eating of food sacrificed to idols."

Now we see an even further progression of what happens to a Church or a Christian individually when you stop loving Jesus. You not only compromise with the world and let the world in, you start to tolerate sin. This is what this Church was doing with a woman teacher who called herself a prophetess who was leading people astray. They not only knew she was doing it, but they allowed it, they tolerated it! This is a tolerating Church. And once you start tolerating sin in the Church, you're headed for destruction, as this man shares.

"If the Church in Pergamum married the world, the Church in Thyatira is celebrating their anniversaries. This is the church that tolerates sin. Ephesus lost their first love. Pergamum compromised with the world. Thyatira was tolerant of sin. The floodgate was open, and they just allowed sin to come in, and have its heyday.

There were people committing fornication there. Sounds like the Corinthian Church doesn't it? And by the way, they went out of existence too.

But here came this woman and she was seducing and involving them in the idol worship of the day, sexual activity, and so here were these people just having a great time, getting involved in the filth and the rot of the world.

They committed adultery. Why? Because the believer is married to Christ and fooling around with idols and sexual activity is a form of adultery. Here is the Church that tolerates sin.

An elder told me about a Church that he was in, in the past, that two elders and their wives exchanged wives in the Church. The Church thought it shouldn't do anything about that because it might upset the congregation.

This is Thyatira. A Church that tolerates sin.

Thyatira remains

Beloved, there are so many Churches that do this. They just don't want to deal with sin. They just don't want to confront anybody. They say, 'You mean you discipline people in your Church?' We do. Because the Bible says to.

'Oh, we don't want to get into any of that because we might make…' You start tolerating sin, compromising with the world, and it just descends."[7]

Man is that so true. When you don't discipline, you're tolerating sin! You know it's going on, you know it's wrong, but you refuse to do anything about it! This is why Pergamum didn't survive the war either. And don't kid yourself Christian if you don't think it could happen to you! If any of those things mentioned in there is true of you today, you better turn around today! You better get right with God, put the armor on and start standing firm in Christ if you're ever going to survive the war!

The **4th Church** that failed to heed Paul's advice on how to deal with the War we're in is **Sardis**. Let's see what happened to them.

Revelation 3:1 "I know your deeds; you have a reputation of being alive, but you are dead."

Wow! Short and sweet and straight to the point from the Lord. What happens when you stop loving Jesus and start compromising with the world and start tolerating sin? You end up dead like Sardis, like this man shares.

"You start with a loss of love, and then pretty soon when you don't love the Lord anymore you're willing to compromise. You compromise a little bit and pretty soon your compromise becomes a tolerance of sin and sin floods in the Church and you go right from Thyatira into Sardis, the dead Church.

Why? Because when sin completely takes over a Church, the spiritual life is choked out and what you have left is a dead Church. Like Samson, you're moving around alright, you just don't have any strength. The life is gone.

And so, a Church that tolerates sin becomes a degenerate Church, a dead church, and a dead Church is a corpse.

All Sardis had left was form, like the the rhyme of the ancient mariner, corpses man the ship, dead men pull the oars, and dead men steer the vessel. The thing was going, functioning - just everybody was dead.

This is when the church becomes a group of activities, a series or programs. You have your classes and you have your little groups and you have your activities for the kids and for the young people and for the adults, and everybody's very busy, and the fleet's rolling, and the people are coming.

It's just that there's no life there. God's not there. 'Ichabod' is written. The glory is departed. Sardis went out of existence because Sardis was a degenerate, dead church."[8]

And so, it happens today. When your life or your Church is full of sin, the life of Christ is not there. You're like an episode of the Walking Dead. You call yourself a Christian, but you're actually a Religious Zombie. This is why Sardis didn't survive the war either. And don't kid yourself Christian it you don't think it could happen to you! If any of those things mentioned in there is true of you today, you better turn around today! You better get right with God, put the armor on and start standing firm in Christ if you're ever going to survive the war!

The **5th Church** that failed to heed Paul's advice on how to deal with the War we're in is **Laodicea,** it's the worst one of all.

Revelation 3:15-16 "I know your deeds, that you are neither cold nor hot. I wish you were either one or the other! So, because you are lukewarm – neither hot nor cold – I am about to spit you out of My mouth."

Wow! This Church made Jesus want to puke! Why? Because they were neither hot nor cold! They were basically a good-for-nothing Church! All show no substance! And that's the last place you want to be as this man shares.

"Laodicea is the apostate church. The church that is no church at all. They were neither cold nor hot. They were not interested, not even concerned, indifferent to the Gospel, no pretense at all, just unmoved and uninterested. This is playing Christianity, and this is Liberalism today.

Under the guise of Christianity, they deny the Bible, deny the deity of Jesus Christ, deny all of the great tenants of the Christian faith and yet say they are Christian churches. They're hypocrites. They're phony. And a phony Church is no Church at all.

Oh, you started out so good. You started out like the Ephesian Church did but the descent comes and pretty soon you've got nothing left. I've been in auditoriums in this country that seat 4,000 people, and on a Sunday morning there's 150 liberals huddled in the front and that's it.

This happens to thousands and thousands of Churches around the world. They go out of existence, because they went Apostate like Laodicea and it all started when you stopped loving Jesus. "[9]

And this is what I believe God is warning us about in the letters to the Seven Churches and we see His constant pleas for us to put the Armor of God **on** once and for all and keep it on and start standing firm in the Church. WHY? Because this is real! Unless you take this seriously and put on the Armor of God, don't kid yourself, we're in a war, you or your Church will descend into apostasy every single time! It all spills downhill. Take this seriously! And lest you think Churches or Professing Christians can't go Apostate, let me give you a few examples that I am aware of.

"I was in Scotland preaching and a man came up to me and he introduced his name and said, 'My name is Mr. Reverend Cecil Mills.' He said, 'I am a minister, and I have been for many years.' He said, 'Is your father named Jack MacArthur? And I said, 'Yes.'

He said, 'Your father came to Ireland at least 30 years ago,' and he said he came with two other men to hold a revival in Ireland, in Belfast, and all-around Ireland. And he said, 'At that meeting, I went to hear your father, and I received Jesus Christ and dedicated my life to the ministry.' And he said, 'I am a pastor now because of the Lord using your father, and I just wondered if it was indeed your father. And would you do me a favor and tell him that when you see him?'

And I said, 'I will.' And he said, 'Let me ask you a question.' He said, 'Where is your father, now?' I said, 'Oh he's pastoring, ministering, teaching the Word, like he always has.' He said, 'Is he still faithful to the Word?' And I said, 'Yes, he's still faithful to the Word, still carrying on, still standing.' He said, 'Good.'

He said, 'What happened to the other guy with him, Chuck?' I said, 'Oh, he became an apostate, denied the faith, forsook the truth, denied the Word of God.' He said, 'Oh, oh.' He said, 'That's so sad. He had so much potential.'

He said, 'What ever happened to the second guy?' I said, 'Oh, he died an alcoholic.' He said, 'Oh no.' I said, 'Yes, he did.'

I don't relish telling you that, but you want to know something? Three men went to Ireland 30 years ago, and they did it all. And lots of people have done it all, but when the battle is over, and the dust clears, they're not all standing, you see? They're not all standing.

I got a letter this week from a lady. She said, 'You know, I've been to your Church for several years, and I've been very involved,' but she said, 'I'm leaving because I've decided to marry a non-Christian.' Having done it all, she is not standing anymore.

Listen. There are lots of people who did it all – pastored a church, taught a class, had a bible study, led people to Jesus Christ, but when the battle got hot and the smoke cleared, they were down. You know why? They didn't have the armor on – they didn't take it serious."[10]

I've seen this in my own acquaintances. One of my first friends in the Lord who took me under his wing and helped me get my first internship, even discipled me, has now left the Protestant faith and became a Catholic. Another person who was one of the few people who dared witness to me when I was involved in New Age, has now gone into New Age themselves. Past interns, past congregants that I've pastored over the years, are no longer following Christ, but are in this world, indifferent and frankly dead. Did they lose their salvation? No, because you can't. Rather, their Apostasy is a sign they never had it in the first place. I didn't say that God did.

1 John 2:19 "They went out from us, but they did not really belong to us. For if they had belonged to us, they would have remained with us; but their going showed that none of them belonged to us."

Not everybody is standing firm when the dust clears from the battle, from the war we're in as a Christians. Why? Because they didn't put the Armor on and the truth became known. They became a plastic Christian with a plastic Jesus, like this guy, and the Church is full of them!

A man is sitting on a park bench. "Hey, I'm Ryan, I'm a Christian (he claims to be a Christian) and this is my story. Growing up I never missed going to church, (my parents made me go to church). When I was twelve I accepted Christ as my savior (I guess I got "saved") I was even baptized (I was even dunked in some water). It undoubtedly was a very important decision (It apparently was a meaningless decision). It even affected how I lived in high school (It made no difference on how I lived in high school)

I mean, don't get me wrong I had fun on the weekends (I got drunk most weekends). I had a girlfriend (I had sex often). I was a normal high school kid. College was one big blur (one big party) but I did make it to church out of obedience (I did make it to church out of guilt).

After school I married a great girl. She has been a great influence on me. (I've been a terrible husband for her). Life's been good (Life's been a struggle). I have a house, three kids (debt, lots of responsibility). I couldn't ask for more. (I thought life would be so much more).

I mean sure, I worry about my future (I'm panicked about my future). My marriage could be better. (My marriage is falling apart). And I need to spend more time with my kids. (I don't spend time with my kids). But things will be alright (Things are not alright).

I have my faith (I have no faith). You may not hear me talk about it a lot (That's why you don't hear me talk about it). It's just because it's personal. (It's non-existent). But don't worry for me, my Jesus is real (My Jesus is plastic). [11]

Looks to me like somebody didn't take the war we're in seriously, how about you? As it was in the early Church, so it is today. You better get on the armor and start standing firm in Christ! This is serious stuff. Only 2 Churches out of the 7 succeeded. *Smyrna* and *Philadelphia* which unfortunately I don't have time to get into in great detail. But briefly *Smyrna* was the "persecuted Church." No fake Christians were there because persecution keeps the Church clean. When your life is on the line you don't fake belonging to Jesus. Fake Christians, on the other hand run, they don't stand for Jesus, because they're trying to save their hide. And *Philadelphia* was the Soul Winning Church. They didn't have time to get worldly and compromise and sin, they were too busy with an outward focus reaching the world for Christ away from sin. So, what does it look like when a Church or a Christian has the Armor of God on and they're willing to suffer for Christ and preach Christ to anyone they meet, like Smyrna and Philadelphia? Well simple. You look like Mr. Genor. No Plastic Christian here!

A number of years ago in a Baptist church in Crystal Palace, Southern London, the Sunday morning service was closing, and a stranger stood up in the back and raised his hand and said, "Excuse me Pastor, can I share a little testimony?" The Pastor looked at his watch and said, "You have three minutes."

This man proceeded, "I just moved into this area, I used to live in another part of London. I came from Sydney, Australia, and just a few months back I was visiting some relatives. I was walking down George Street, you know where George street is? It runs from the business hub out to the rocks of the colonial area. And he said, "A strange little white-haired man stepped out of a shop doorway and put a pamphlet in my hand and he said, 'excuse me sir, are you saved, if you died tonight are you going to Heaven?'

I was astounded by those words. No one had ever told me that. I thanked him courteously and, on the way back to Heathrow, on British Airlines, this puzzled me. I called a friend that lived in this new area, where I am living now, and thank God he was a Christian and he led me to Christ. I'm a Christian and I want to fellowship here." I just love testimonies like that. Everyone applauded and welcomed him into the fellowship.

That Baptist pastor flew to Adelaide the next week and ten days later in the middle of a three day series in a Baptist Church in Adelaide, a woman came to him for counseling to establish where she stood with Christ and she said, "I used to live in Sydney and just a couple months back I was visiting friends in Sydney, doing some last minute shopping down George Street and a strange little white-haired man stepped out of a shop doorway, offered me a pamphlet and said, 'excuse me mam, are you saved, if you died today would you go to Heaven?' She said I was disturbed by those words but when I got back to Adelaide I knew this Baptist Church was on the next block from me and I sought out the Pastor and he led me to Christ, so sir I am telling you, I am a Christian.' Now this London Pastor was now very puzzled. Twice within a fortnight he heard the same testimony.

He then flew to preach in a Mt. Pleasant Baptist Church in Perth and when his teaching series was over, the senior elder of that church took him out for a meal and he said, 'mate how did you get saved?' He said, 'I grew up in this church from the age of 15 through the Boy's Brigade. Never made a commitment to Jesus, just jumped onto the bandwagon like everyone else. And because of my business ability, grew up to a place of influence. I was on a business outing in

Sydney just three years ago and an obnoxious, spiteful, little man stepped out of a shop doorway, offered me religious pamphlet, cheap junk, and accosted me with a question. 'Excuse me sir, are you saved and if you were to die tonight would you go to Heaven?'

'I tried to tell him I was a Baptist Elder, but he wouldn't listen to me.' He said, 'I was seething with anger all the way home on Quantas to Perth. I told my Pastor, thinking he would sympathize with me and my Pastor agreed, he had been disturbed for years knowing that I didn't have a relationship with Jesus and he was right, so my Pastor led me to Jesus just three years ago.'

Now this London preacher flew back to the UK and was speaking at the Kisik Convention in the Lake district. He threw in these three testimonies. At the close of his teaching session, four elderly Pastors came up and said we got saved between 25 and 35 years ago respectively through that little old man on George St. giving us a tract and asking us that question.'

He then flew the following week to a similar convention as Kisik in the Caribbean to missionaries. And he shared the testimonies and at the end of his teaching session, three missionaries came up and said, 'We got saved between 15 and 25 years ago respectively, through that little man's testimony and asking us that same question on George Street in Sydney.

Coming back to London he stopped outside of Atlanta, Georgia to speak at a Naval Chaplains convention. After three days of revving up these Naval Chaplains, over a thousand of them, the Chaplain General took him out for a meal. And he said, 'How did you become a Christian?' He said, 'Well, it was miraculous. I was on the United States Battleship and I lived a reprobate life. We were doing exercises in the South Pacific and we docked in Sydney harbor for replenishments.

We hit Kings Cross with a vengeance. I got blind drunk, I got on the wrong bus, got off on George Street and as I got off the bus, I thought it was a ghost. This elderly white-haired man jumped in front of me, pushed a pamphlet in my hand and said, 'Sailor, are you saved? If you died tonight would you go to Heaven?'

He said, 'The fear of God hit me and immediately I was shocked sober, and I ran back to the battleship, sought out the chaplain, and he led me to Christ.

And I soon began to prepare for the ministry under his guidance. And here I am in charge of over a thousand chaplains, so we are bent on soul winning today. That London preacher, six months later, flew to a Convention of five thousand missionaries in a remote part of Northeastern India and at the end, the Indian missionary in charge, a humble little man, took him home to his humble little home for a simple meal.

He said, 'How did you, as a Hindu, come to Christ?' He said, 'I was in a very privileged position, I worked for the Indian Diplomatic Mission and I traveled the world and I am so glad for the forgiveness of Christ and His blood covering my sin because I would be very embarrassed if people found out what I had gotten into.

One bout took me to Sydney and I was doing some last-minute shopping, carrying toys, clothes and parcels for my children walking down George Street and this courteous little white-haired man stepped out in front of me, offered me a pamphlet and said, 'Excuse me sir, are you saved, and if you were to die tonight, would you go to Heaven?' I thanked him very much, but this disturbed me. I got back to my town, I sought out my Hindu priest and he couldn't help me, but he gave me some advice.

He said, 'Just to satisfy your curious mind, nothing else, go and talk to the missionary in the mission house at the end of the road. And that was great advice because the missionary led me to Christ and I left Hinduism immediately and then began to study for the ministry. I then left the diplomatic service and by God's grace I am in charge of all these missionaries and we are winning hundreds of thousands of people to Christ.'

Well eight months later that Chrystal Palace Baptist minister was ministering in Sydney. He said to the Baptist Minister, 'Do you know of a little man, an elderly little man who witnesses and hands out tracts on George Street,' and he said, 'I do, his name is Mr. Genor. But I don't think he does it any more, he is too frail and elderly.'

The man said, 'I want to meet him.' Two nights later they went around to his little apartment, they knocked on the door, and this tiny frail little man opened *the door. He sat them down and made them some tea. He was so frail that he was slopping tea into the saucers as he shook. As he sat with them, this London preacher told him all the accounts over the previous three years.*

This little man sat with tears running down his cheek. He said, 'My story goes like this. I was on an Australian warship. I lived a reprobate life. In a crisis I really hit the wall and one of my colleagues who I really gave literal hell was there to help me. He led me to Jesus and the change in my life was night to day in 24 hours.

I was so grateful to God that I promised God that I would share Jesus in a simple witness with at least ten people a day. As God gave me strength, sometimes I would be so ill I couldn't do it, but I made up for it at other times. I wasn't paranoid about it, but I have done this for over 40 years. In my retirement years the best place was on George Street.

There were hundreds of people. I got all kinds of rejections, but a lot of courteous people took the tracts. In the 40 years of doing this, I've never heard of one single person coming to Jesus until today.' I would say that would have to be commitment. That has to be shear gratitude and love for Jesus to do that. Not hearing of any results.

Margarita did a little count, that's 146,100 people that that simple little non-charismatic Baptist man influenced somehow to Jesus. And I believe what God was showing that Baptist Minister was the tip of the iceberg. Goodness knows how many more have been arrested for Christ doing huge jobs out in the mission field.

Mr. Genor died two weeks later, and can you imagine the rewards he went home to inherit. I doubt if his face would ever appear on Charisma Magazine. I doubt if there would ever be a write up in Billy Graham's Decision Magazine as beautiful as those magazines are. Nobody except a little group of Baptists in Southern Sydney knew about Mr. Genor.

But I will tell you his name was famous in Heaven. Heaven knew Mr. Genor and you can imagine the welcome, the red carpet, and the fanfare he went home to when he arrived in glory![12]

Why? Because he fought the good fight all the way to the end like a good soldier of Christ. He preserved His walk with Christ like Smyrna and Philadelphia by not letting suffering get him down and he kept sharing the gospel every single day until he went home. True Christianity. He had his armor on and thus he was victorious. No plastic Christians here. No apostates. No deadness. He fought the good fight all the way to the end, just like the Apostle Paul and he went off to receive his reward. And so, if we too are going to have the same kind of welcome in heaven today, don't kid yourself, we better do the same thing today. Why? Because we're in a war. It's not going to be easy. It's going to be a battle. The Scripture is clear. Do what God says to do now. Get the Armor on and start standing for Christ. Ask yourself, "Based on your behavior right now when the dust settles, where will you be?" Standing firm, or an Apostate. What you do with God's protection from the enemy will determine your destiny. Make sure you have the Armor on, amen? Its high time, we the Church, stop being ignorant of the devil's schemes.

There's a war going on, and it's not just abroad, its right here in our own country. It's a cosmic battle for the souls of men and women all around us. The stakes are high, and millions of lives are at risk. And if we're ever going to win this war then the American Church needs to once again shine for Jesus Christ. People, this is no time to be an Unprotected Christian! Wake up! The alarm has sounded. We are under attack, *The satanic War on the Christian.* Don't let the enemy get you! Amen?

Chapter Twenty-Two

The Protection from Satan and Demons Part 2

"Some say it came from a tropical monkey while others say it was a government planned disease released upon the public. But wherever it came from, these are the facts; Right now, tens of millions of people have it worldwide and millions more get it every single year.

In fact, in 1998 alone, the combined wars in Africa killed 200,000 people, but this virus killed 10 times more than that. And now, many of the infections are being spread via heterosexual contact through the blood, the body fluids, or even breast milk. It's everywhere and anyone can get it.

Deaths due to HIV/AIDS per million persons in 2012

- 0
- 1–4
- 5–12
- 13–34
- 35–61
- 62–134
- 135–215
- 216–458

And it all starts with a simple headache that turns into a fever, but soon leads to a case of sore muscles and a stomachache. In fact, most people think it's merely a case of the flu, but it's not. The killer virus is there, multiplying in your body slowly destroying your immune system.

And the next thing you know, this disease is full blown whereupon a person's last days are spent dying from a multitude of ways such as pneumonia, skin cancer, tumors, or apparently one of the disease's favorite ways to kill you, that of eating your brain alive.

You might live for several years or you might die in a few days and with medication you might be able to slow it down, but it's still just a matter of time. You're going to die. Why? Because there is no cure!

KNOW, PREVENT, CARE, CURE.

MEET AN EXTRAORDINARY COALITION OF AIDS ACTIVISTS WHO HAVE COME TOGETHER TO RAISE VITAL AWARENESS AND ADDRESS THE DESTRUCTIVE STIGMA ASSOCIATED WITH HIV/AIDS.

The year is 2018. In the 90's it was the leading cause of death. The killer disease is of course, the AIDS Virus."[1]

Now, how many of you have heard of the AIDS Virus? Okay, I think we all have. But how many of you believe it was one of the greatest disasters of all time, right? But with all due respect to those who lost their lives with the AIDS Virus, what if I were to tell you I know of a disaster that makes the AIDS Virus look like a mild case of acne? And what if I were to tell you that this disaster didn't occur in just one place and one country at one time, but it's going on right now today all over the world and it's been leaving a trail of death and destruction for centuries. I'm talking once again about *the satanic War on the Christian.* We Christians don't battle here and there occasionally. We go to war, every single day. Whether you see it, feel it, believe it or not, the moment you got saved you entered a spiritual war against a demonic host whose sole purpose is to destroy you and extinguish your testimony for Jesus Christ. Therefore, in order to stop getting duped and beat up all over the place, we're going to continue in our study, *The satanic War on the Christian.*

Now so far, we've seen if you're ever going to win a war, then the **1ˢᵗ thing** you must do is **Know Who Your Enemy Is**…

Then we saw the **2ⁿᵈ thing** you need to know is **What Your Enemy is Like**, their character, amen? It's common sense, right?

Then we saw the **3ʳᵈ thing** you need to know is **The Tactic of Your Enemy,** what they're up to, what's their goal and why are they here.

Then we saw the **4ᵗʰ thing** you need to know is **The Destruction of Your Enemy,** what price you pay when you DON'T take this seriously.

Then we saw the **5ᵗʰ thing** you need to know is **The Temptation of Your Enemy,** how he's out there trying to get us to sin against God.

 In the last chapter we saw the **6ᵗʰ thing** you need to know is **The Protection from your enemy.**

And there we saw God has not left us hanging high and dry in this Great Cosmic War dealing with satan and demons. Are you kidding me? He's actually given us His full-blown protection and amazing weaponry to stand our ground and be victorious in all situations every single time! It's called The Armor of God!

The **1ˢᵗ thing** we see about the Armor of God is that it's **Designed for War**.

We saw that in two ways. In the context of the Scripture, how many times does the Bible have to say we're in a battle? In the Catastrophes of Churches, not everybody is left standing when the dust settles from the battle we're in. Some actually go Apostate, they show their true colors, they're fake, they go out of existence like the 5 out of 7 Churches in the Book of Revelation. Why? Because they didn't put the Armor on. They didn't take it seriously. They didn't heed the warning that it's designed for war! And the same thing will happen to you and me today if we're not careful! But that's not all.

The **2nd thing** we see about the **Armor of God** is that **It's Designed for Victory**.

Now, as we saw before, it's not my armor, it's not your armor, it's not the armor you buy at Walmart and falls apart three days later! Praise God that it's not! It's GOD's armor, the actual *Armor of God* that defeats the enemy every single time! Why? Because God never loses! Therefore, that means we can't lose if we just do what He says, put it on, leave it on, and understand how to use it! Why? Because it's Designed for Victory! It's not there to make us look good, it's not a fashion statement, it's designed to make us win! And that's good news! But hey, don't take my word for it. Let's listen to God's.

Ephesians 6:10-13 "Finally, be strong in the Lord and in His mighty power. Put on the full A*rmor of God* so that you can take your stand against the devil's schemes. For our struggle is not against flesh and blood, but against the rulers, against the authorities, against the powers of this dark world and against the spiritual forces of evil in the heavenly realms. Therefore, put on the full armor of God, so that when the day of evil comes, you may be able to stand your ground, and after you have done everything, to stand."

So here we see the reason why we need to put on the *Armor of God*. It gives us the ability to stand strong in the mighty power of God. It gives us the ability to effectively struggle and come out on top in our war against the evil ones, every single day when they come at us, not if. It gives us the ability to stand our ground and not buckle or break under pressure when the dust clears from the battle that we're in. In short, the *Armor of God* is Designed for Victory! How many of you guys can figure that out without any help? Now, for those of you who can't, let me see if I can help you out today.

The **1st way** we see that the *Armor of God* is Designed for Victory is in **The Need for Victory**.

And this is what we see in verse 12.

Ephesians 6:12 "For our struggle is not against flesh and blood, but against the rulers, against the authorities, against the powers of this dark world and against the spiritual forces of evil in the heavenly realms."

So here we see the reason why God is providing this victory for us via His Armor, in the first place. Why does He give us His armor? Why are we to stand strong in His mighty power? Why are we to put the Armor on and leave it on? Because our struggle isn't just against flesh and blood. In other words, it's not just natural, it's supernatural. It's not just people, its demons. Real live demons! It's *against* (key word there) all kinds of demonic powers, demonic entities, that work *against* us in a hierarchal structure. And that shouldn't surprise us when you see how angels are classified in Scripture.

CLASSIFICATIONS OF ANGELS

- Seraphim – (Isaiah 6)
- Cherubim – (Genesis, Exodus, 1&2 Samuel, 1&2 Kings, 1&2 Chronicles, etc.)
- Angels – (Old & New Testament)
- Archangels – (1 Thessalonians 4, Jude1)
- Rulers/Principalities/Powers – (Ephesians 6)
- Authorities/Powers/World Forces – (Ephesians 6)
- Powers of this Dark World/Rulers of the Darkness of this World/Forces of Darkness – (Ephesians 6)
- Spiritual Forces of Evil in the Heavenly Realms/Spiritual Wickedness in High Places/Forces of Wickedness in Heavenly Places – (Ephesians 6)

But as you can see, demons are not only real, but they really are split up in a hierarchal structure, as Paul mentions here in Ephesians 6. This is whom in which we have to deal with. Therefore, we need the Armor on for Victory. You have got your rulers or principalities, you have got your authorities or powers, you have got your world forces of darkness, forces of evil and spiritual wickedness in heavenly places, etc. etc. This is who's against us. It's not a game. Our battle is not against flesh and blood. It's real live actual demonic forces working against us in a hierarchal fashion. And the sooner we realize that the better, as this man shares.

DEMON FORCES EVERYWHERE

"Notice the use of the word 'against' that separates each of the categories. You have principalities. You have powers. You have rulers, and you have wicked spirits, literally. These are simply categories of demon beings.

Paul says, 'We are fighting a superhuman foe, highly and intensely organized.'

In God's governmental order, God had the angels organized. God created all the angels at one time. They were created differently, just like people are different, angels are different. There are all different kinds of angels, and that means demons have distinctions too.

In fact, I believe that behind the scenes, ruling the world, are demon forces. People are always asking, 'Do you believe there is a sort of a worldwide conspiracy going on? And do you believe there are demons in high places?'

Of course! There is absolutely no doubt in my mind that there is a global conspiracy in which demons are involved in high places working the world to their own ends. There's no question about that. I know demons are behind the systems of the world. I know the Old Testament says the gods of the nations are demons.

There's no question in my mind that demons were behind Hitler, and no question in my mind that demons were very active in other world rulers such as Napoleon, Alexander the Great, and on and on and on, we could go. Satan is the prince of this world, and I believe he has infiltrated the world with the network of world rulers that are demonic, and I think the way the world is going – it is going because of demonic influence.

I remember talking to a young man who had come out of the occult, and he was very highly involved in this thing, and had reached high, high levels and he was getting all kinds of opportunities to get in on some high-level information. And they were teaching him in one particular point how the demon network worked and how demons were involved in all these things.

They gave him the name of certain demons that were involved in the United Nations and certain demons that were occupying themselves in various continents and in various countries, and he told me things that were literally *beyond my comprehension. There is no doubt about the fact that this is a reality, Biblically.*

And so, what we're saying is this, we are in a warfare against us and it is very sophisticated. There are high-ranking and powerful demons who are principalities and powers. There are others who have found themselves to be occupying places of world leadership as they literally indwell the world rulers.

And so, the battle lines are drawn. It is against this incredible force that we fight. We are pitted against an enemy that is beyond us. We can't see. We can't touch. We can't outthink, outwit, that is deceiving, that is lying, that is powerful, supernatural, superhuman. And that's where the battle lies.

And the sooner you realize it the better off you're going to be."[2]

Or as Paul would say, "You better get that Armor on and leave it on, now! Why? Because there is a need for victory here! There really is an invisible force of supernatural evil beings determined to disrupt, discourage, deceive, discomfort, disarm, dissatisfy, dissuade, distract, disappoint, disgruntle, dishearten, dishevel, distress, disqualify, disquiet, dispossess, disturb, disunite and destroy Christians and Churches! Paul is in essence telling us you need to wake up! There is a need for victory! The enemy is not only real, and not only really out there, but they really are working against us in an organized fashion causing great damage. Why? Because the enemy is not dumb. He knows the power of a unified organized effort, that's what he does! That's why he's so effective! That's why his evil gets spread so easily! Evil works together! Demons work together in an organized fashion! This is what Paul is saying here. Therefore, is it any wonder the enemy works so hard at getting us Christians and the Church to do the exact opposite to be divided, to be disorganized in disarray. No way that's not by chance. He knows exactly what he's doing! He's getting us to do the exact opposite of what he knows works all too well, being unified. And if you don't think he does that, you might want to listen to this interview.

INTERVIEW WITH THE DEVIL

A man walks into the room, "Well hello, satan." He puts his hand out to shake but pulls it back real fast. Satan says, "hello yourself." Then after the hand is pulled back he says, "Every time, it happens, every time." And laughs. The man says, "I wish I could say I'm glad to see you, but I can't."

Satan says, "The feelings mutual, so we're good." The man asks him, "Can you put away that cookie, we are fasting." Satan says, "Hey, you want to go halvsies on this, you're fasting, I had no idea?" The man says, "No, no, no. you know what I'm going to say to you?" Satan replies," "Yeah, get thee behind me or something like that."

The man asks, "I was curious, when it comes to the church, what's your strategy?" Satan answers, "I'm growing to like the church, honestly, you know, they stay mad at each other half the time, they hate each other, they hate half the world. You know I sit back and watch the fights like the rest of the world. You see what I'm talking about?" The man asked, "So you're pretty good at division of the church, how is it that you pull this off?"

Satan answers, "The easiest way is to just make someone think that they are right, that they are completely and totally right. Another big thing is Bible versions. Everyone knows, myself included, King James is the only way to go. It's what I have in my personal library. I don't read it, let's set the record straight on that. I don't read it, but you wouldn't find me reading one of those other hippie versions of the Bible with their street language, hip hop Jesus stuff. You give me a scenario and I can make someone fight about it."

The man then asks, "How about politics?" Satan answers, "Easy, Christians are all Republicans and we've known that from day one." The man then asks, "How about music?" Satan answers, "The music is too loud, do I have five people singing, can we really sing secular music in the church. Come on! This is kids play here!" The next question asked, "How about entertainment?"

Satan answers, "Did you see what I did to Disney? I'm the king, I rest my case. I can't let the church be united. You've heard the phrase, 'A kingdom divided against itself can't stand." The man answers, "It's in the Bible." Satan asks, "It's in the Bible? Wow, that's embarrassing. Can we? I'm sorry." The man asks, "Satan, have you ever attended a board meeting?" He answers, "Absolutely, every Tuesday. If you've never seen a Deacon just straight up cuss in church at another Deacon, it's a sight to behold."[3]

Yeah it is. And I've been at some of those meetings, unfortunately, where the enemy is having a heyday. And we laugh at this because it's so true. Why? Because not all of our battles are against flesh and blood! There's real live evil supernatural forces out there working through people and sometimes in people to cause disruption, disorder, and disunity in the Church. Why? Because the enemy doesn't want us to do what he does. He knows if we ever get unified like him and his evil cohorts then great things can be accomplished for Christ. And he doesn't want that, so he gets us to do the exact opposite to our own detriment, like this story reveals.

STORY SPOONS IN HEAVEN

"An executive died and went to heaven. There he found all former executives separated into two groups. The failures in one hall and the successful in the other.

Around mealtime he entered the hall of those who failed and was surprised to find the occupants thin and hungry-looking.

When the angels began to serve dinner, large platters of delicious food were placed at the table, but before anyone was seated, another angel came along and strapped a long iron spoon to each executive's arm.

The long handle of the spoon was fastened to the wrists and biceps, making it impossible to bend the arm. As a result, none was able to lift the spoon to his mouth.

Walking over to the hall of those who had succeeded, he was surprised to find them well fed and healthy.

Dinner was already on the table and an angel had just finished strapping the long iron spoons to the arms of the diners. Each executive then dipped his spoon into the food and fed the man across from him."[4]

When the Church stops being selfish and self-centered (which is at the heart of satanism by the way) and starts feeding one another, loving one another, taking care of each other, you know, being the family of God, then we are unified. When we are unified, it's not only healthy for us and keeps us from becoming starved, frail, and ineffective Christians, but we grow strong and healthy and we start working together doing great things for Jesus. This is what Paul is saying. Not all of our battles are against flesh and blood. These real live supernatural forces are real and really work together. So, should we, if you find that we aren't, then you can bet these "rulers, authorities, powers of this dark world and spiritual forces of evil in the heavenly realms" are working against you! Even though we have the power and weaponry in Christ to defeat all the evil attacks, the enemy gets us to split up and use that power and weaponry on each other to our own detriment. We damage ourselves not him.

Galatians 5:15 "If you keep on biting and devouring each other, watch out or you will be destroyed by each other."

When the Church is divided we destroy each other. But when the Church is unified, it's healthy and great things can happen. The enemy knows it, he does it himself. So, we need to realize this is one area he will always attack us. He will try to get us to bite and devour, divide and conquer, yell and scream even though the whole time we should be conquering him. That's why there's a need for victory here. That's why God gives us His Armor. And the sooner we realize this, the better, as this person shares.

IGNORANCE OF SPIRITUAL WARFARE

"Too many Christians have failed to realize that they are engaged in this titanic spiritual struggle of the ages, and that they were 'drafted' into God's army the moment they were saved by grace through faith.

The Church is not a cruise ship, the Pastor is not the master of ceremonies, it's not a showboat, it's a battleship.

We're called to see satan's strongholds crumble under the power of heaven's artillery. We do not have the luxury of neutrality. We must engage in the fight. To be ignorant of our calling and the magnitude of this great struggle is a dangerous ignorance.

We are at spiritual war! A truce will never be called. God's will for his saints is not that we merely survive, but that we thrive in total victory."[5]

How? By putting the Armor on and doing what He says to do! Amen? But that's not all.

The **2ⁿᵈ way** we see that the Armor of God is Designed for Victory is in **The Solution for Victory**.

Now we're going to see what He says to do. The solution for victory over this real live daily assault against the devil and his demons working together in unison against us. That's what we see in these passages.

Ephesians 6:10-11,13 "Finally, be strong in the Lord and in His mighty power. Put on the full armor of God so that you can take your stand against the devil's schemes. Therefore, put on the full armor of God, so that when the day of evil comes, you may be able to stand your ground, and after you have done everything, to stand."

So here we see God's command to appropriate His solution for this spiritual battle that we're in every single day. Notice the solution is tucked in not just before, but right after verse 12 that shows us who we're battling against. Completely surrounding verse 12 that defines the objects of the battle. God now tells us the solution to overcoming that battle. And it's two things, stand strong in God's mighty power and put on the full armor of God. That's it! Not scream at a demon, shout at the devil, call out a spirit of so and so and bind them. Just stand strong in God's mighty power and put on the full armor of God. That's it! And this is important because we have all kinds of people doing all kinds of other things than what God says to do and they're getting whooped on! The only command given in the Scripture for dealing with satan is to "stand" and "resist." That's it. Not scream at a demon, shout at the devil, call out a spirit of so and so. Just stand and resist.

1 Peter 5:8-9 "Be self-controlled and alert. Your enemy the devil prowls around like a roaring lion looking for someone to devour. Resist him, standing firm in the faith, because you know that your brothers throughout the world are undergoing the same kind of sufferings."

James 4:7 "Submit yourselves, then, to God. Resist the devil, and he will flee from you."

Ephesians 6:13 "Therefore put on the full armor of God, so that when the day of evil comes, you may be able to stand your ground, and after you have done everything, to stand."

That's it, just "stand" and resist." No gimmicks. No screaming. No buy my techniques or go to a spiritual guru because you just don't have that power. Just "stand" and "resist." In fact, what's really interesting, is that the words "stand" and "resist" in those three passages are all the same Greek word, "antihistemi." It's the same word we get our English word, "Antihistamine" from that's used to speak of a medicine we take for allergies to "block" or "anti" the histamines or those things that cause allergy symptoms. This is what "antihistemi" in the Greek means, "to block, to set oneself against, to oppose, to resist, to withstand." That's it. No screaming. No shouting. None of that stuff!

Is that what we do to get rid of our allergies? We scream at the hay fever? We call out those dust mites and name them by name? We rebuke the spirit of pollen and bind what has fallen all around us? NO! Not only would that NOT get rid of your allergies it would be a complete waste of time, let alone you'd be looking pretty goofy! Rather, you take the medicine, the solution, the antihistamine, and let it do its work! That's it! And so, it is with spiritual warfare! You don't scream at a demon. You don't call out the devil. You don't rebuke the spiritual strongholds all around you. You just take the medicine, the solution, the *Armor of God*, and let it do its work. Why? Because it blocks, it opposes, it antihistemis, and sets itself against the enemy, who cannot penetrate. That's why James says when you do this, when you follow God's solution, he, the devil will flee from you, just like your allergies, they go away. That's it! This is God's medicine for spiritual warfare. But notice, God then defines that we are to stand and resist in what? Not your own strength. Not in somebody else's technique. But in the what? In the mighty power of God. It's the Greek words, "ischus kratos." It's not just "kratos" or "power, force, or strength." But it's "ischus kratos," "mighty power" "mighty force" "mighty strength." The emphasis is on a "mind blowing strength!"

This is God's amazing power that He gives to Christians to defeat the enemy every single time! This is His solution. It's a guaranteed victory because it's backed by God's amazing mighty undefeatable power of God! The enemy can't withstand it. He can't defeat it. He can't and never will prevail against it ever! WHY? Because this is God's mighty power at our disposal and nobody can beat that! And I want to show you why.

The **1st way** we see God's mighty Power is in His **Demonstration of Miracles**.

Matthew 8:27 "The men were amazed and asked, what kind of man is this? Even the winds and the waves obey Him!"

Now according to our text here, the disciples were absolutely blown away by Jesus behavior here. Why? Because they saw firsthand that Jesus, God, had the power to control the wind and the waves! And that's just the tip of the iceberg! All throughout the Gospels we see Jesus performing all kinds of miracles! I don't have time to get into them, but we see He walked on water, He healed the sick, He cured the blind, He raised the dead, He saved wretches like you and me, now that's a miracle! You're a miracle!" You prove the power of God! But folks, I don't know about you, but I'd say that anyone who could command the winds and waves, walk on water and raise the dead, and save a bunch of wretches like us might be just a little bit powerful, how about you?

The **2ⁿᵈ way** we see God's mighty Power is in His **Destroying of satan**.

1 John 3:8 "He who does what is sinful is of the devil, because the devil has been sinning from the beginning. The reason the Son of God appeared was to destroy the devil's work."

Now according to our text here, one of the biggest reasons why Jesus came to this earth was not only to save us from our sins, but to also come and destroy the one who instituted sin, satan. The Bible is clear folks. Other passages tell us Jesus stripped the devil of his power. The Lord exposed him, shattered him, defeated him on the cross. And because of that the devil's currently on death row awaiting his final sentence in the Lake of Fire. And only gets to do what God allows him to do. His gig is up! This is why he's so furious in the last days! Now folks, I don't know about you, but I'd say that anyone who could reduce the devil to a pipsqueak of a rat, and put him on a chain might be just a little bit powerful, how about you?

The **3ʳᵈ way** we see God's mighty Power is in His **Defeating of Death**.

1 Corinthians 15:55,57 "Where, O death, is your victory? Where, O death, is your sting?" thanks be to God! He gives us the victory through our Lord Jesus Christ."

Now according to our text here, the great news about Jesus going to the cross was not only that He forgave us of all our sin, He not only defeated the devil, but He also defeated death itself! In fact, so much so has Jesus defeated death that He reassures us to never ever, ever, be afraid of death, that is, if you're a Christian. And this is great news because if we're honest, everyone's afraid of something in life. For some it's elevators, for some it's spiders, for some it's chicken, but we won't go there will we! But there's one fear that is not only the greatest of all, but it's universal for all. And that's the fear of death. But once again this is the great news of the gospel. Jesus not only destroyed the devil, but He defeated death! Through the cross of Christ, mankind's darkest hour has now become his entrance into eternal light! And it's only the Christian who is genuinely freed from this fear of death that we all have. And folks, I don't know about you, but I'd say that anyone who could reduce death to a beautiful transition into eternal bliss, might be just a little bit powerful, how about you?

The **4th way** we see God's mighty Power is in His **Display of Creation**.

Romans 1:18-20 "The wrath of God is being revealed from heaven against all the godlessness and wickedness of men who suppress the truth by their wickedness, since what may be known about God is plain to them, because God has made it plain to them. For since the creation of the world God's invisible qualities – His eternal power and divine nature – have been clearly seen, being understood from what has been made, so that men are without excuse."

According to our text, one of the most obvious ways to show us that God not only exists, but that He's All-Powerful, is by looking at His what? His creation, right? What He has made! You see, God not only created the world, so we'd have a place to live but, hello, He created the world so we'd come to a knowledge of Him. And folks, once you start looking at this world we live in, you're not only going to see that God must exist, but you're going to see that He's incredibly powerful! "ischus kratos" mighty power! In fact, let me show you what I mean by taking a look at just a piece of the universe that God brought into existence.

THE UNIVERSE INSIDE & OUT

The video begins with a lady laying on her back on the ground looking up at the sky. The camera starts to raise higher above her. She gradually gets smaller; the camera is 1 meter above her. It keeps going up higher. 10 meters, 100 meters. Now you see the neighborhood that she is lying in.

And it goes higher. 1 Kilometer. Now you are seeing the city in which she lives. And it keeps going higher. Now we are 10 kilometers above her and we are looking at the state she is in. and the camera keeps going higher. 1000 kilometers. Now we see part of the Country she is in. And it keeps going higher. 10 thousand, 100 thousand kilometers, now you see a tiny dot that is the earth and another dot that is the moon.

And it keeps going higher. 1 million kilometers, 10 million kilometers, now we see Mars, Venue and Mercury and how they are spaced around earth. And it keeps going higher. 1 billion kilometers. Now we see Saturn Jupiter, Uranus, the Sun and even some Asteroids.

And it keeps going higher. 10 Billion Kilometers. Pluto, Voyager 1. 100 Billion Kilometers, Eris, Sedna, dwarf planets. 1 trillion kilometers, Comets. 1 light year. The Sun is all we see. At 10 light-years we see Alpha centauri, Sirius and Procyon. At 100 Light-years we now see Vega an Capella. At 1 thousand light years we see Orion Nebula, Pleiades, and Hyades cluster.

At 10 thousand light years we see Scutum-Centaurus Arm, Sagittarius arm, Orion Spur and Perseus arm. At 100 Thousand light years we see Cold gas, Stellar disk and Magellanic clouds. And we keep going higher. At 1 million light years we see Leo II, Ursa minor dwarf, Draco Dwarf, Barnard's galaxy.

At 10 million light years we see the Milky Way, Andromeda Galaxy and Ursa Major group. At 10 Billion Light years there is nothing. We pause and head back to earth. We are finally back to the girl laying in the yard, but we go lower. At 10 centimeters we see her smiling face. At 1 Centimeter we see her Iris and her Pupil. At 1 Millimeter we see her Iris, Pupil and Retina.

At 100 Micrometers we see her white blood cells. And lower we go. To 10 Micrometers to see her White blood cells and Red Blood cells. At 1 Micrometer we see her Chromosomes. At

100 Nanometers we see her DNA 10-nmfiber. At 10 Nanometers we see DNA double helix, 1ˢᵗ and 2ⁿᵈ polymer. At 100 picometers we see two 1s-orbitals, two 2s-orbitals, Four 2p-orbitals.

At 10 Picometers there is 1s-orbital spin down an 1s-orbital, spin up. At 100 Femtometers we see Atomic Nucleus. At 10 Femtometers we see Newtron and Proton. At 1 Femtometer we see Down Quark, Up quark, Down quark and then we start rising again to find her laying on the yard again with her pretty smiling face.[6]

I don't know about you, but I'd say somebody had to be pretty powerful to create all that, how about you? In Ephesians 1 Paul says when God was doing it He flung it down like it was no big deal. Like you're just casually tossing something down. I don't know about you, but I'd say that anyone who could casually throw the world and the whole universe into existence, might be just a little bit powerful. And this is what God is telling us, is the solution to dealing with spiritual warfare! This is the power we have available at our finger tips! This is the power the enemy cannot defeat! He cannot win and never will! It's God's mighty power! The same power He used to do all those miracles, destroy the works of satan, defeat death itself, display all of creation, is the same power available to us! No wonder we don't have to freak out and be afraid! Just do what He says to do. Follow His solution.

Ephesians 6:10-11,13 "Finally, be strong in the Lord and in His mighty power. Put on the full armor of God so that you can take your stand against the devil's schemes. Therefore, put on the full armor of God, so that when the day of evil comes, you may be able to stand your ground, and after you have done everything, to stand."

You don't scream at a demon. You don't call out the devil. You don't rebuke the spirit of this or the spirit of that. You just stand in the armor of God and in His mighty power and the devil will flee from you! That's the solution. People, its high time we the Church stop being ignorant of the devil's schemes. There's a war going on and it's not just abroad but its right here in our own country. It's a cosmic battle for the souls of men and women all around us. The stakes are high, and millions of lives are at risk. And if we're ever going to win this war then the American Church needs to once again shine for Jesus Christ. People, this is no time to be an Unprotected Christian! Wake up! The alarm has sounded. We are under attack, *the satanic War on the Christian*. Don't let the enemy get you! Amen?

Chapter Twenty-Three

The Protection from Satan and Demons Part 3

"It started out just like any other typical day in this wonderful mountain paradise. Birds were singing, tourists were hiking, animals of various kinds were frolicking and playing, enjoying another sunny day in this nature preserve. But all that was to change in a matter of seconds.

Suddenly, at precisely 8:32am on a Sunday morning, an earthquake struck beneath this mountain which allowed the partly molten, highly pressurized gas and steam to suddenly explode causing the entire north face of this mountain to disappear.

It exploded with such force that it actually produced the largest landslide ever recorded traveling at a speed of 155 mph destroying everything in its path.

Soon it was carrying trees, rocks, giant boulders, and even a mixture of hot lava that dumped into nearby lakes and streams for as far as 13 miles away clogging them up with debris for some 24 square miles. In fact, some of the lakes were still covered with trees and debris 30 years later.

But that was just the eruption out of the side. The eruption also blew huge ash column 15 miles straight into the air in just 10 minutes time and continued on for the next 10 straight hours with a force of 26 megatons.

In fact, so high and so much debris was being blown upward from this eruption that it actually covered 11 different states in the United States

And when all was said and done, half the mountain was gone, hundreds of square miles were reduced to wasteland, 57 people were killed along with 1000's of animals and it caused over 3 billion dollars' worth of damage.

In fact, it has even been declared as the most disastrous volcanic eruption in all of U.S. history.

The year was 1980. The deadly eruption is of course, Mount St. Helens."[1]

Now, how many of you have heard of the Mount Saint Helens eruption before? Okay, I think we all have. But how many of you know that it was one of the greatest disasters of all time, right? With all due respect to those who lost their lives with the eruption of Mount Saint Helens, what if I were to tell you I know of a disaster that makes that Mount St. Helens look like a scratch on the arm? And what if I were to tell you that this disaster didn't occur in just one place and one country at one time, but it's going on right now today all over the world and it's been leaving a trail of death and destruction for centuries.

I'm talking once again about *the satanic War on the Christian.* These are the facts. We Christians don't battle here and there once in a while. We go to war, every single day. Whether you see it, feel it, believe it or not, the moment you got saved you entered a spiritual war against a demonic host whose sole purpose is to destroy you and extinguish your testimony for Jesus Christ. And what's wild is that most wars go on for a few years or even longer. But *The satanic War on the Christian* has been going on for the last 2,000 years non-stop and it's sending people straight to hell! And what's wild is most people will readily talk about all the other wars throughout history and all their atrocities, and rightly so, we even have the History Channel, we need to talk about them! Yet, how many people, even Christians, will openly discuss the longest war in mankind's history, *the satanic War on the Christian,* that has destroyed more lives than all the wars put together? Therefore, in order to stop getting duped and beat up all over the place, we're going to continue in our study, *the satanic War on the Christian.*

Now so far, we've seen if you're ever going to win a war, then the **1st thing** you must do is **Know Who Your Enemy Is**…

Then we saw the **2nd thing** you need to know is **What Your Enemy is Like**, their character, amen? It's common sense, right?

Then we saw the **3rd thing** you need to know is **The Tactic of Your Enemy,** what they're up to, what's their goal and why are they here.

Then we saw the **4th thing** you need to know is **The Destruction of Your Enemy,** what price you pay when you DON'T take this seriously.

Then we saw the **5th thing** you need to know is **The Temptation of Your Enemy,** how he's out there trying to get us to sin against God.

And the **last two times** we saw the **6th thing** you need to know is **The Protection FROM Your Enemy**.

There we saw God has not left us hanging high and dry in this Great Cosmic War dealing with satan and demons. Are you kidding me? He's actually given us His full-blown protection and amazing weaponry to stand our ground and be victorious in all situations every single time! It's called The Armor of God!

So far, we've seen the **1st thing** about the Armor of God that **It's Designed for War** and last time **It's Designed for Victory**.

It's not my armor, it's not your armor, it's not the armor you buy at Walmart and falls apart three days later! Praise God that it's not! It's GOD's armor, the actual armor of God that defeats the enemy every single time! Why?

Because God never loses! Therefore, that means we can't lose if we just do what He says, put it on, leave it on, and understand how to use it! Because it's Designed for Victory! And we saw that in two ways, in the Need for Victory, we're surrounded by real live demonic forces seeking to take us, therefore we need victory and the Solution for Victory. What do you do when you experience spiritual warfare. Simple. Two things stand strong in God's mighty power and put on the full armor of God. That's it! Not scream at a demon, shout at the devil, call out a spirit of so and so and bind them. Just stand strong in God's mighty power and put on the full armor of God. That's it! And that's where we left off last time. The question is, "How do you, practically, be strong in the mighty power of God? Great question! It works well with my notes! Let's go back to that text that tells us how.

Ephesians 6:10-13 "Finally, be strong in the Lord and in His mighty power. Put on the full armor of God so that you can take your stand against the devil's schemes. For our struggle is not against flesh and blood, but against the rulers, against the authorities, against the powers of this dark world and against the spiritual forces of evil in the heavenly realms. Therefore, put on the full armor of God, so that when the day of evil comes, you may be able to stand your ground, and after you have done everything, to stand."

So here we see again God's command to appropriate His solution for this spiritual battle that we're in every single day. As we saw, it's tucked in, not just before, but right after verse 12, that shows us who we're battling against. Completely surrounding verse 12 that defines the objects of the battle. God now tells us the solution to overcoming that battle. It's like a spiritual warfare sandwich. It was two things, stand strong in God's mighty power and put on the full armor of God. That's it! Remember mighty power was "ischus kratos." Not just "kratos" or "power, force, or strength." But it's "ischus kratos," "mighty power" "mighty force" "mighty strength." The emphasis is on a "mind blowing strength!" And this is the same kind of amazing power available at our fingertips in Christ to deal with spiritual warfare that Paul was referring to as far back as Ephesians Chapter 1.

Ephesians 1:18-22 "I pray also that the eyes of your heart may be enlightened in order that you may know the hope to which He has called you, the riches of His glorious inheritance in the saints, and His incomparably great power for us who believe. That power is like the working of His mighty strength, which He exerted in Christ when He raised Him from the dead and seated Him at His right hand in the heavenly realms, far above all rule and authority, power and dominion, and every title that can be given, not only in the present age but also in the one to come. And God placed all things under His feet and appointed Him to be head over everything for the Church."

That's the power Paul is saying we have available at our finger tips later in Chapter 6! The same power that God used to do all His miracles, destroy satan, defeat death, display all of creation, is the same power available to us. This is the power the enemy cannot defeat! He cannot win and never will! No wonder we don't have to freak out and be afraid! Amen? Just do what He says to do. Follow His solution. Put on the whole Armor of God, be strong in His mighty power, take your stand, resist the devil, and he will flee from you! So, the question is, "How do you be strong in the mighty power of God? Simple. You do what the Greek tells you to do as we saw last time. It actually says, "to be constantly strengthened" day in and day out and "put it on now, once and for all." In other words, every day you need to be constantly strengthened in God's power.

Once the Armor is on leave it on, but God's power is something you need to be strengthened in every day! How? By daily Bible reading, daily prayer, daily witnessing, daily singing/listening to God-honoring worship music, daily fellowshipping with godly Christians. You know, all the things we call the Christian basics! Why? Because when you're reading the Bible where's your mind? On the things of God. When you're praying, where's your mind? On the things of God. When you're listening/singing to God-honoring worship music where's your mind? On the things of God. When you're fellowshipping with godly Christians where's your mind? On the things of God. All these are ways we fulfill another Christianese phrase we call abiding in Christ! And when we abide in Christ and He in us we have His power!

John 15:5-6 "I am the vine; you are the branches. If a man remains in Me and I in him, he will bear much fruit; apart from me you can do nothing. If anyone does not remain in Me, he is like a branch that is thrown away and withers; such branches are picked up, thrown into the fire and burned."

How many times do we get burned in spiritual warfare let alone bearing Christian fruit because we don't listen to Jesus. He simply says if we remain or abide in Him, we bear much fruit and things are going to be great. Conversely, Jesus says "Apart from Me you can do nothing." In other words, don't abide in Me, don't remain in Me, don't read your Bible, don't pray, don't sing or listen to

God-honoring music, or fellowship with godly Christians, and you're going to get burned! Why? Because you have no power! You're unplugged from the Vine! The problem is we've allowed the enemy to trick us into unplugging ourselves from Christ, to not abide in Him to not daily receive His power to effectively stand in our struggle against spiritual warfare. How? By getting us to not engage in all these daily activities, what we call the Christian basics! Why? Because he knows getting unplugged from Christ is the path to a powerless Christian life!

The enemy is not dumb. He knows He can't defeat God's power and he knows he can't take God's power from us, so he gets us to simply not utilize it. To not tap into it. It's like the glow in the dark socks my son got one time. We were so excited. We went into the room and closed the door, and nothing happened. Apparently, the trick is you have to charge them up. You have to place them near a lightbulb first for a substantial amount of time before they start glowing. And so, it is that we Christians spiritually need to do the same. We need to become glow in the dark saints, not glow in the dark socks, in this dark and dying world. I didn't say it. Paul did.

Philippians 2:14-15 "Do everything without complaining or arguing, so that you may become blameless and pure, children of God without fault in a crooked and depraved generation, in which you shine like stars in the universe."

How do you shine like stars in the universe in this dark and depraved world? By doing everything without complaining or arguing. Well how do you get the power to do that? By daily getting charged up next to the Light, abiding in Christ. How? By daily Bible reading, daily prayer, daily witnessing, daily singing/listening to God-honoring worship music, daily fellowshipping with godly Christians. That's how you draw near Him. That's how you get charged up! Unfortunately for most of us our spiritual batteries are so low we sound and look kind of freaky.

CHARGED BATTERIES IN A TOY

The commercial starts with the announcer stating, 'What have we here? We have all sorts of stuff. This is an older Vtech, kind of small, a Sing n Smile Pals. It is older, meaning it's not a new one. So, let's turn it on." He picks up the toy. It has the numbers, 1,2,3,4 with a rabbit, a dog, a cat and a duck on it. It also has the musical numbers, A, B, C, D, and E on it. He clicks the on button and it starts playing the little tune, 'Mary had a little lamb.' He proceeds to spin the little ball on the edge and as it turns the toy plays, 'A, B, C, D, E, F, G', the alphabet song. He says, "Let's press the duck." The duck goes 'duck, quack, quack.' "So that lights up, now the kitty." The kitty goes, 'cat, meow, meow'. "And the dog." He presses the little dog and it says, 'Dog, wolf, wolf.' "And the rabbit." And the rabbit says, 'Bunny, boing, boing.' When the announcer starts pushing the number buttons, they go 'green circle, yellow star, red square and orange triangle.' He then goes to the alphabet keys. For each key he pushes it says that letter. He pushes all the buttons and animals one last time. He says, "Pretty neat." And then turns off the toy.

NO CHARGE BATTERIES IN A TOY

Again, the Announcer explains that this toy is a Vtech Sing n Smile Pals toy. He pushes the little duck and it only groans. He then pushes down on the little kitty and it only groans. It actually sounds like a mooing cow in a pasture. The little dog doesn't sound much better. The batteries are all run down, and these little animals are just barely making a noise.

Every day we have no spiritual energy because we never charge our spiritual batteries by abiding in Christ and we wonder why every day we lose the spiritual battle we're in! Here comes the enemy again and we're so weak all we can do is make a feeble noise! POW! CRACKLE! AWAY! FROM! ME! But it's not supposed to be this way! This is His plea to us here in Ephesians 6! God's given us everything we need in Christ! Don't fall for the enemy's trap! "Be constantly strengthened" day in and day out, in His mighty power. Abide in Christ! Get powered up! Make sure your spiritual batteries are always at peak performance! WHY? Because we're in a war and you're going to need God's mighty power if you're going to stand strong.

YOU'RE IN GOD'S ARMY NOW

"If you think as a believer in Jesus Christ that you are NOT in a spiritual war, then you are deceived and/or ignorant! When you got saved, you personally became a target! No more mister nice guy. You are on the satanic hit list.

And if you're really a Christian and you're really living and walking with Jesus Christ, they're coming after you. There is 'no discharge in this war.' While you and I are alive in this world the devil will be there with his evil ones; and he will fight us to the end, he will fight us to our deathbed.

It is a mighty conflict; BUT I can be 'strong in the Lord and in the power of his might.' I can clothe myself with 'the whole armor of God.'

And so that's the question. Are you ready for the battle? Are you on the alert, are you on your feet? Or are you just indulging in your weaknesses and whims and fancies, and pitying yourself, and grumbling and complaining about this and that problem or situation?

Rise up Christian, shake them off, stand on your feet, be a man! Realize that you are a member of the mighty regiment of God, fighting the battle of the Lord and destined to enjoy the glorious fruits of victory throughout the countless ages of eternity.

Have you heard the trumpet call? 'Be strong in the Lord and in the power of his might. Put on the whole armor of God.'

YOU ARE IN THE ARMY NOW! GOD'S ARMY! Be a man and fight!"[2]

And that's brings us to the **3rd way** we see that the Armor of God is Designed for Victory is in **The Mistake for Victory**.

And this is exactly what the enemy wants. He wants us to make a crucial mistake! Either don't put the armor on, let alone keep it on, OR he gets us to use some other so-called man-made technique for dealing with spiritual warfare other than what God says to do. Let's revisit what God says to do.

1 Peter 5:8-9 "Be self-controlled and alert. Your enemy the devil prowls around like a roaring lion looking for someone to devour. Resist him, standing firm in the faith, because you know that your brothers throughout the world are undergoing the same kind of sufferings."

James 4:7 "Submit yourselves, then, to God. Resist the devil, and he will flee from you."

Ephesians 6:13 "Therefore put on the full armor of God, so that when the day of evil comes, you may be able to stand your ground, and after you have done everything, to stand."

That's it, just "stand" (in God's power) and resist." No gimmicks. No screaming. No buy my techniques. No going to a spiritual guru because you just don't have that power unlike them. No following this 18-step plan, just "stand" and "resist." And as we saw before, the words "stand" and "resist" in those three passages are all the same Greek word, "antihistemi." It's the same word we get our English word, "Antihistamine" that's used to speak of a medicine we take for allergies to "block" or "anti" the histamines or those things that cause allergy symptoms. This is what "antihistemi" in the Greek means, "to block, to set oneself against, to oppose, to resist, to withstand." That's it. No screaming. No shouting. None of that stuff! That's not how we get rid of our allergies. We don't scream at the hay fever. We don't call out those dust mites and name them by name. And we don't rebuke the spirit of pollen and bind it that has fallen all around us? NO! Not only would that not get rid of your allergies it would be a complete waste of time, let alone you'd be looking pretty goofy! Rather, you take God's medicine, His solution, His antihistamine, and let it do its work! "Stand" and "resist."

This is precisely what the enemy gets us not to do! Instead of "standing" and "resisting" which works every single time because it's backed by God's power and His amazing armor. He gets us to listen to so-called Deliverance Ministries and their man-made techniques that not only does not deliver but leads to further problems. One guy puts it this way.

DANGERS OF DELIVERANCE MINISTRIES

"When believers go on the offensive against satan they are stepping out of their legitimate bounds, by becoming involved in situations which the lord has never intended for them.

This offensive type of response was described by Peter as characteristic of false teachers (2 Peter 2:10,11).

Often this opens the door to demonic oppression in the believer's life."[3]

In other words, it makes it worse, not better!

And the 1st **way** so-called Deliverance Ministries makes things worse for people spiritually is they say **Christians Can Be Possessed.**

And that's why they have to do what they do because they got to get those demons out of Christians. But as we saw earlier in our study, this is not true!

1 Corinthians 3:16 "Don't you know that you yourselves are God's temple and that God's Spirit lives in you?"

John 14:23 "Jesus replied, "If anyone loves Me, he will obey My teaching. My Father will love him, and We will come to him & make Our home with him.""

If God the Spirit, and God the Father, and God the Son has made their home in me as a Christian and I have become their temple then there's no way in the world I can even become demon-possessed again! I can be externally oppressed as a Christian, but I can never be possessed because God isn't going to scooch over in His Temple and make room for a demon! Second, I don't have to be afraid even of their external attacks.

1 John 4:4 "You are from God, little children, and have overcome them; because greater is He Who is in you than he who is in the world."

2 Timothy 1:7 "For God hath not given us the spirit of fear; but of power, and of love, and of a sound mind."

We don't have to be afraid of the devil, or satanists, or any of their activity. If you belong to Jesus, the devil can't touch you, without God's permission, as even this former devil worshipper found out. So, I don't need to be delivered from a demon. I can't have a demon if I'm a Christian!

The **2nd way** so-called Deliverance Ministries makes things worse for people spiritually is they say **Possessed Christians Go to Church Services**.

And they usually cite this passage out of context.

Luke 4:31-35 "Then He went down to Capernaum, a town in Galilee, and on the Sabbath began to teach the people. They were amazed at His teaching, because His message had authority. In the synagogue there was a man possessed by a demon, an evil spirit. He cried out at the top of his voice, 'Ha! What do you want with us, Jesus of Nazareth? Have you come to destroy us? I know who you are – the Holy One of God!' 'Be quiet!' Jesus said sternly. 'Come out of him!' Then the demon threw the man down before them all and came out without injuring him.'"

Well, there you have it. Christians who are possessed go to Church services, and that's why we need these deliverance ministries to deliver us from these Christians possessed with demons. What!? Nice try! Talk about twisting Scripture! First of all, this guy is not a Christian because he's in a Jewish synagogue not a Christian Church. Second, these people are meeting on a Saturday Sabbath (because they're Jews not Christians) unlike Christians who meet on Sundays. And third, the Church wasn't even born yet in the timing of this passage. That didn't happen until Acts Chapter 2 much later in the timing. In fact, Jesus hadn't even gone to the cross yet when this event occurred! So, no, I don't need your deliverance ministries according to this passage.

The **3rd way** so-called Deliverance Ministries make things worse for people spiritually is they say **The Bible Says We Need to Bind & Bind & Lose Demons**.

No, it doesn't! But they cite this passage out of context as well.

Matthew 16:19 "I will give you the keys of the kingdom of heaven; whatever you bind on earth will be bound in heaven, and whatever you lose on earth will be loosed in heaven."

Well there you have it. Total proof as to why we Christians need to call out demons, scream at the devil and bind them and loose them blah blah blah. Are you kidding me? This is one of the most abused Scriptures in the Bible!!!! First of all, in the context this passage has absolutely nothing to do with demons, let alone binding them and casting them out! It's actually dealing with Church Authority. It follows Peter's statement contextually that Jesus was the Christ and Jesus responded by saying that, "On this rock I will build my Church." That's it! No talk of demons, no mentioning demons anywhere in there, let alone binding or losing them. In fact, the words there "binding and loosing" literally mean "forbidding and permitting" again speaking of Church Authority, not demonic warfare. "The expressions "bind" and "loose" were common to Jewish legal phraseology meaning to declare something forbidden or to declare it allowed. Jesus' words in the context meant that Peter would have the right to enter the kingdom himself, that he would have general authority symbolized by the possession of the keys, and that preaching the gospel would be the means of opening the kingdom of heaven to all believers and shutting it against unbelievers. The book of Acts shows us this process at work. By his sermon on the day of Pentecost (Acts 2:14-40), Peter opened the door of the kingdom for the first time."[4]

And to those that didn't believe it, it was shut. That's it. That's the "binding or losing" or "forbidding and permitting" going on here! And by the way even if you wanted to say it referred to binding a demon then why in the world would you so-call "bind" the thing and then turn right around and "loose" it! Hello! McFly! The reason it sounds so goofy is because that's not what it means! Yet, that doesn't keep these Deliverance Ministries from trying. Here's a list of 25 things you need to do if you need to get rid of a demon according to these Hucksters.

25 DELIVERANCE MINISTRY TECHNIQUES

- Make sure your own heart is clean.
- I pray about deliverance ministry assignments.
- Have a team of intercessors praying in another room.
- Pray for the gifts of the Spirit to be in operation.
- Pray in tongues.
- Plead the blood of Jesus.
- Fast before the session.
- Ask the Lord to reveal the strongholds.
- Don't cast out devils alone.
- Study Scripture.
- Warn the one who is getting ministered to in advance that they will be tempted to run.
- Ask the one being ministered to if it's OK to touch them before the session begins.
- Designate one person as the leader.
- Submit any words of knowledge, discerning of spirits or other prophetic insight to the leader so they can use them at the right time.
- Ask the person if they know what the issues are.
- Have the person seeking deliverance forgive anyone.
- Don't get distracted by the manifestations.
- Bind them.
- Try to be safe.

- You can't always cast out all the demons in one session. A person can only take so much.
- Try to be led by the Holy Spirit.
- Pray for protection for yourselves, your family and friends.
- Break and bind all retaliatory attacks.
- Never share publicly what happens in a deliverance session.
- Have a trashcan and Kleenex on hand.[5]

And all God says is two things, if you're experiencing spiritual warfare, "stand" (in His Mighty power) and "resist." That's it! And that's just one Deliverance Ministry. Everybody's got their own giant list of what you're supposed to do. But you might be wondering about that last technique there, "Have a trash can or Kleenex on hand." What's up with that? Well, believe it or not, you're going to need it during their so-called services.

DELIVERANCE CHURCH SERVICE

ABC Nightline News Reports:

Terry Moran: Demonic possession, the idea that evil spirits of the devil can move into human bodies and somehow occupy us is not just the stuff of horror films, in fact, to hear the Pastor we hear tonight tell it, we all have our demons, a statement that might not sound so controversial until we see how he goes about getting rid of them.

I visited his congregation for our series 'Beyond Belief.' At the Agape Bible Fellowship in East Aurora, a small town outside of Buffalo, an extraordinary ministry is taking place. Pastor John Goguen: "Our church service is normal. We open in prayer, we sing praise songs, we open the word of God, most importantly."

At first glance that seems about right. On a recent Saturday we visited Agape and it seemed like any other church in any other town. But the paper towels and shopping bags stacked neatly in the back of the room are a clue that something is different here. When they are brought out it's a sign that the fireworks are about to begin.

Pastor Goguen: "Most of our services are just a normal Baptist service until we get to the end when we tackle the believers." And when Pastor John says tackles he means it literally. Agape Bible Church is a deliverance church where they say they expel demons through prayer. "It begins quietly, but they lead with incessant yawns and then sometimes they will lead with what appears like burps or they will lead with actual mucus.

Some of this is painful. It's just that demons are trying to leave under the authority and the power of the Lord Jesus Christ." By nine o'clock the room is filled with screams, moans, writhing bodies. Diane Coller says deliverance has changed her life. She says, "It comes right up. It's such a cleansing feeling. It's a relief to know that you are getting rid of these demons. It's just amazing what the Lord can do to get rid of these demons in me." And if it looks a little off-putting Pastor John says that is the point.

Pastor John says, "People have to get over the hump. This looks foolish, this looks like something I didn't do in church on Sunday. This looks weird. But God uses it, we find, to humble people. For them to finally admit that they may not know everything. And before God, to be honest and say I need help." For these believers, Pastor John's ministry helps with everything, sins of the flesh, adultery, drunkard, drug addicts, to the surrender to the occult.

Pastor John: "I break any and all curses to sicknesses." In the pulpit he says, "All muscle spasms, cramps, restless legs, all the demons that are in the muscles, hemorrhoids." He says, "If you are breathing, you've got them. If you're not breathing don't worry about it. Everybody's got them, it's the question of how many have you got." Everybody's got them he says including himself.[6]

Wow! How would you like to have that guy as your Pastor with all due respect??? A Church service where so-called Christians yawn, burp and spit up demons in a bag? That behavior is about as sad as this story.

LAKE STUPID

"In Oklahoma there's a lot of Indian tribes, and a long time ago there was an Indian tribe on either side of a lake. Sometimes they would have their tribal meetings together there.

And it was during this time, as the story goes, that a very handsome young Indian man met a very beautiful young Indian girl from the other tribe and they fell for each other, head over heels.

But they didn't get to see each other too much because they were on either side of the lake. So, they started a little romantic tradition just between each other.

Every night this young man would stand at the edge of the lake on his side and he would call out an Indian love call across the water of the lake. And sure enough, soon he would hear her voice coming back to him in beautiful melody.

And that is what they did every night. He would call her, and she would call back to him. Well one time, during the course of their relationship, it was the end of January, it was freezing, it was snowing, messy, and he's there and he calls out his love call, and he hears her voice and he just couldn't stand it.

"I know it's cold, it's difficult, but I'm young, I'm strong, I'm virile, and I can do this." So, he dived into the lake to swim across to his beloved.

But he got about half way out there and he got so cold, he realized that I'm not going to make it. It was too far to go back and too far to go on to her.

So, he lifted himself up out of the water and with his last breath he called out one last time his Indian love and sank beneath the water and drowned.

So, the tribes got together, and they felt they needed to recognize what this young man had done so that people in the future would look back and remember what he did. And so, they decided to name the lake after Him.

They called it, 'Lake Stupid.'[7]

Folks don't kid yourself. If you're trying to yawn up a demon, burp out a demon, spit up a demon, or any of these other so-called endless man-made techniques from deliverance ministries to deal with spiritual warfare. You're swimming in Lake Stupid! That's about as blunt as I can be! And if you want a way to stay out of Lake Stupid then quit hanging around people that are swimming around in Lake Stupid. Just do what God says when it comes to spiritual warfare, "Stand" and "resist." That's it! Put on the Armor of God and leave it on! Amen? Its high time we, the Church, stop being ignorant of the devil's schemes. There's a war going on and it's not just abroad but its right here in our own country. It's a cosmic battle for the souls of men and women all around us. The stakes are high, and millions of lives are at risk. And if we're ever going to win this war then the American Church needs to once again shine for Jesus Christ. People, this is no time to be an Unprotected Christian! Wake up! The alarm has sounded. We are under attack, *The satanic War on the Christian.* Don't let the enemy get you! Amen?

Chapter Twenty-Four

Protection from Satan and Demons Part 4

"It all began just like any other average workday day in this bustling desert city. People were leaving for lunch, eager to get a bite to eat, when all of a sudden, one of the largest explosions in history was about to take place right under their feet at a local chemical plant.

It all started with a few seemingly innocent sparks from a welding torch inside of the company building, but in just 4 minutes time, it created a fire that spread so rapidly that it caused 3 massive explosions. And what explosions they were!

This plant just happened to be storing the exact same kind of chemical used in solid fuel rocket boosters that were used in the Space Shuttle Challenger that exploded just two years prior!

In fact, the explosions were so big that they actually measured 3.5 on the Richter scale and was compared to the same force of a 1-kiloton air-blast nuclear detonation, and basically, as you might guess, the plant disappeared.

But that was just the immediate area. The impact was felt for miles away. Shockwaves destroyed nearby buildings in its wake, destroyed cars, downed power lines, windows were shattered, walls were cracked, doors were blown off their hinges, and structures were impacted as far as 10 miles away.

And when the smoke and dust had finally cleared, the explosions killed 2 people, injured 370 others and created $100 million dollars' worth of damage in just a matter of seconds.

It was the largest domestic, non-nuclear explosion ever recorded in history.

The year was 1988. The explosion is of course, the PEPCON Disaster in Henderson, Nevada."[1]

How many of you had heard of the PEPCON disaster in Henderson before? Okay, I think we all have. But how many of you would say it was one of the greatest disasters of all time, right? But with all due respect to those who lost their lives in the PEPCON disaster, what if I were to tell you I know of a disaster that makes the PEPCON explosion look like a mild case of desert erosion? And what if I were to tell you that this disaster didn't occur in just one place and one country at one time, but it's going on right now today all over the world and it has been leaving a trail of death and destruction for centuries. I'm talking once again about *the satanic War on the Christian.* Here are the facts. We Christians don't battle here and there once in a while. We go to war, every single day. Whether you see it, feel it, believe it or not, the moment you got saved you entered a spiritual war against a demonic host whose sole purpose is to destroy you and extinguish your testimony for Jesus Christ. How many people, even Christians, will openly discuss the longest war in mankind's history, that has destroyed more lives than all the wars put together? Therefore, we're going to continue in our study, *the satanic War on the Christian.*

Now so far, we've seen if you're ever going to win a war, then the **1st thing** you must do is **Know Who Your Enemy Is**…

Then we saw the **2ⁿᵈ thing** you need to know is **What Your Enemy is Like,** their character, amen? It's common sense, right?

Then we saw the **3ʳᵈ thing** you need to know is **The Tactic of Your Enemy,** what they're up to, what's their goal, why are they here.

Then we saw the **4ᵗʰ thing** you need to know is **The Destruction of Your Enemy,** what price you pay when you DON'T take this seriously.

Then we saw the **5ᵗʰ thing** you need to know is **The Temptation of Your Enemy,** how he's out there trying to get us to sin against God. .

And the **last three times** we saw the **6ᵗʰ thing** you need to know is **The Protection FROM Your Enemy**.

There we saw God has not left us hanging high and dry in this Great Cosmic War dealing with satan and demons. Are you kidding me? He's actually given us His full-blown protection and amazing weaponry to stand our ground and be victorious in all situations every single time! It's called The Armor of God!

And so far, we've seen the **1ˢᵗ thing** about the Armor of God and that is **It's Designed for War.**

The last two times *It's Designed for Victory.* It's not my armor, it's not your armor, it's not the armor you buy at Walmart and falls apart three days later! Praise God that it's not! It's GOD's armor, the actual armor of God that defeats the enemy every single time! Why? Because God never loses! Therefore, that means we can't lose if we just do what He says, put it on, leave it on, and understand how to use it! Why? Because it's *Designed for Victory*! And we saw that in three ways, in the *Need for Victory,* we're surrounded by real live demonic forces seeking to take us out, Ephesians 6:12, therefore we need victory, hello! And we also saw it in the **Solution for Victory** mentioned in verses 10-11,13 surrounding the problem in Verse 12. What do you do when you experience spiritual warfare?

Simple. Two things stand strong in God's mighty power and put on the full armor of God. That's it! Not scream at a demon, shout at the devil, call out a spirit of so and so and bind them. Just stand strong in God's mighty power and put on the full armor of God. That's it!

And that leads us to **the third thing** about the Armor of God and that is the **Mistake for Victory**.

Instead of doing what God says to do when dealing with spiritual warfare just stand strong in God's mighty power and put on the full armor of God. People unfortunately make the horrible mistake of listening to so-called Deliverance Ministries and their unbiblical man-made techniques that not only don't work but are a horrible witness to the lost! Even the lost know this behavior is a bunch of baloney! And I'm sorry, but when you think a Christian can be demon possessed, which is not true, and then you say you can yawn, burp or spit them up in a bag in your so-called Deliverance Church service, what did we see last time? You're swimming around in Lake Stupid! Get out of there! But it's not just ignorant, it's dangerous! Let's now continue to take a look at the fruit of these unbiblical practices of Deliverance Ministries and see what happens when you get it wrong!

DEATHS CAUSED BY DELIVERANCE MINISTRIES

- In a Milwaukee strip mall, several people gathered around Terrance Cottrell, an 8-year-old autistic child. Fervent in their intentions, yet misled in their methods, members of this deliverance Church laid hands on Terrance and began to pray that God would deliver him from the evil spirits that they believed were behind his condition. Two hours later, little Terrance lay dead, wrapped in a sweat-soaked sheet, while his mother and several church members frantically attempted to revive him. The coroner's report: suffocation. The boy's mother later told investigators that the minister had held Terrance on the floor with one hand on the boy's head and with his knee pressed into the boy's chest. The mother and another woman had each held one of his legs, while a third woman lay across his torso. But that's just the beginning of this type of "deliverance" ministry going bad.
- Pentecostal ministers in San Francisco pummeled a woman to death, attempting to drive out demons.
- A Korean Christian woman was trampled to death in Glendale, California, in a so-called exorcism.
- A 5-year-old girl died after being forced to swallow a mixture of ammonia and vinegar, in an attempt to drive out an evil spirit.
- A 17-year-old girl in Sayville, New York, was suffocated with a plastic bag, while her mother tried to destroy a demon inside her.
- The disturbing nature of these tragedies have led many to question the methods of those who practice deliverance ministry and reveal an ongoing state of

confusion in the Church regarding who the devil is, what he does, and how he can be stopped. Amazingly, few in deliverance ministry actually claim that their methods and theology are derived strictly from Scripture. "Sometimes we let our experience determine our theology," Eddie Smith admits. And the Smiths' experiences are often strange enough to make the stodgiest scholar rethink his doctrine, including one woman supposedly expelling demons through flatulence.

- Another so-called "deliverance" minister, Kim Daniels, attributes many issues in her deliverance ministry to two key factors, sympathetic magic and charismatic witchcraft. While Daniels admits that there is no direct reference to sympathetic magic in Scripture, she says: "Everything can't be put to Scripture. Napoleon sailed across the water, but you can't find that in the Word." She also attributes knowledge to special revelations that God has shown her.[2]

In other words she's going outside the Bible to get her information and you wonder why people are being killed and harmed with this bologna! Why? All because you didn't do what God said to do when it comes to spiritual warfare. Just stand strong in His mighty power and put on the full armor of God. That's it! Not all that other stuff! Don't make the same mistake as those Deliverance Ministries! But that leads us to the next practical question in our study, and that is, "How do you do that? How do you do that second part? Put on the full armor of God? I say that because we already saw that we practically do the first part, "stand strong in God's mighty power," by "abiding in Christ," every single day. We become those glow in the dark saints. By daily Bible reading, daily prayer, daily witnessing, daily listening/singing to God-honoring worship music, daily fellowshipping with godly Christians. You know, all the things we call the Christian basics! Why? Because that's how we get charged up with the power of God! That's how you practically stand strong in His mighty power. But how do you "practically" do the second part, put on the full armor of God? Well hey, great question! It works well with my notes! Let's go back to that text that tells us how. But hey, don't take my word for it. Let's listen to God's.

Ephesians 6:10-20 "Finally, be strong in the Lord and in His mighty power. Put on the full armor of God so that you can take your stand against the devil's schemes. For our struggle is not against flesh and blood, but against the rulers, against the authorities, against the powers of this dark world and against the spiritual forces of evil in the heavenly realms. Therefore, put on the full armor of God, so that when the day of evil comes, you may be able to stand your ground, and after you have done everything, to stand. Stand firm then, with the belt of truth buckled around your waist, with the breastplate of righteousness in place, and with your feet fitted with the readiness that comes from the gospel of peace. In addition to all this, take up the shield of faith, with which you can extinguish all the flaming arrows of the evil one. Take the helmet of salvation and the sword of the Spirit, which is the Word of God. And pray in the Spirit on all occasions with all kinds of prayers and requests. With this in mind, be alert and always keep on praying for all the saints. Pray also for me, that whenever I open my mouth, words may be given to me so that I will fearlessly make known the mystery of the gospel, for which I am an ambassador in chains. Pray that I may declare it fearlessly, as I should."

So here we see again, God's command to appropriate His solution for this spiritual battle that we're in every single day. There were two things, stand strong in God's mighty power and put on the full armor of God. Now let's start to focus on the second piece of God's solution. As we saw before, what the Greek actually says, in regard to the armor and putting it on, is that we are to, "put it on *NOW* and *ONCE* and *FOR ALL*." With the power we are to, "be constantly strengthened" day in and day out, but the armor is "a once and for all decision, with an urgency to do it now, don't delay. Whatever you do you better take this seriously, this is key!" Why? Because in our daily battle against satan and his evil emissaries, we not only need God's power, i.e. His strength, but we also need His supernatural military equipment to deal with the enemy as well. It's God's heavenly two bang punch in dealing with the devil and demons! So, He now reveals this supernatural equipment, piece by piece, that He gives to us to experience His victory that He's already given to us, so we can stand firm in Christ on the day of evil when, not if, it comes.

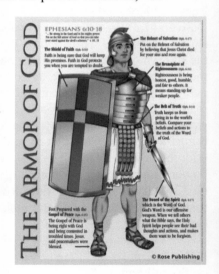

Which brings us to the **3rd thing** we see about the Armor of God that **It's Designed for Wear**.

This equipment from God, this armor, is not something to look at, it's not meant just to stare at, or stick on a shelf and collect dust. It's designed for wear. Daily wear, continual wear. You put it on! And again, the Greek says to put it on now and leave it on! Quick! Chop, chop! Don't delay! In fact, is also says, "to put on the full armor of God," literally "the *complete* armor of God" meaning you put on every single piece of it and leave it on and you better do it now! Not one piece, not half the armor, not a piece here and there when you get around to it, no, no, no! You need every single piece, all of it, right now, the complete package, the full uniform. You need this full uniform from God, His second solution if you're going to be able to come out on top, hold your ground, stand firm against the devil's schemes. And just like the army, when they give you a uniform, they expect you to wear all of it, all the time, especially in battle! It ain't for looks! It's for wear. For your protection!

And the **1st piece** we hurry up and put on, don't delay, with the Armor of God for His Victory is **The Belt of Truth**.

Ephesians 6:14a "Stand firm then, with the belt of truth buckled around your waist."

So here we see the first piece of supernatural military equipment. With it God gives us the ability to effectively struggle and come out on top in our war against the evil ones, every single day, when they come at us, not if. This is the first piece that gives us the ability to stand our ground and not buckle or break under pressure when the dust clears from the battle that we're in, it was called the belt of truth. And so that's the obvious big question, "What in the world is this Belt of Truth?" Well, as we're going to see, the supernatural equipment that's mentioned here in Ephesians 6 is paralleling the military uniform and equipment of a Roman soldier. Paul's simply using an analogy here. This makes sense because Paul is observing his surroundings for this analogy because most scholars believe that Paul wrote the Book of Ephesians while imprisoned in Rome around 62AD. He's surrounded by soldiers and that's what he sees. And so, let's take a look at what the Roman soldier would have looked like and why Paul chose this analogy for the armor of God in regard to the daily spiritual battle we're in.

ROMAN SOLDIERS ARMOR

"Did you know that at this very minute there is an unseen war going on? Today the devil has shot flaming arrows at you. Those arrows can be fought saying, 'don't do it, you'll fail, you always do. I know it's wrong but go ahead and do it. God will forgive you. Don't let them get away with that. Make them pay. These thoughts will destroy you." The good news is that God has given us this armor to protect us, fight back.

Ephesians 6:13-17 tell us, "Put on every piece of God's armor so you will be able to resist the enemy in the time of evil. Then, after the battle, you will still be standing firm."

Stand your ground putting on the Belt of Truth and the body armor of God's righteousness. For shoes put on the peace that comes from the good news so that you will be fully prepared. In addition to all of these, hold up the shield of faith, to stop the fiery arrows of the devil. Put on salvation as your helmet and take up the sword of the spirit which is the word of God. Do you have this armor on right now? The devil is ready for battle, are you?

Boy, that's the question isn't it? The devil is ready for battle each and every day, are you? This is why Paul is using this analogy of a Roman Solider and the armor that they wore. Why? Because it would be goofy to go into a battle without armor! In fact, it would be suicide! And this is what Paul is saying. We too are in a battle every day just like the Roman Soldier, only ours is spiritual, yet nonetheless real. And just as it would be insane for a soldier to engage in the fight without weapons, armor, uniform, so it is for us when it comes to the daily fight with satan and the demons. Get the armor on and get it on now! All of it! Don't be a goofball! It's a common every day analogy that everybody knew of and was familiar with, including Paul, there in prison, totally surrounded by them. but, again, the soldiers uniform and weaponry speak of a real reality, a real spiritual truth that we need to know today. And that's an important point. We know this armor is not a literal armor that we go down to the local Christian bookstore and purchase and put on. We don't go online and see what kind of deal you can get with free shipping included, hopefully they don't take too long, chop, chop! Or even going to your local military base, or commissary, or combat surplus store. NO! This armor is symbolic of a literal spiritual weapon, a literal truth, or a literal mindset we need to literally adorn every single day. It's part of a literal spiritual uniform. And we know this by the context. For instance, in verse 17 it says...

Ephesians 6:17 "Take the helmet of salvation and the sword of the Spirit, which is the word of God."

In other words, the sword of the spirit is the Bible. Sometimes the Bible tells us what the piece of armor represents, as in this case, other times we figure it out by the context and common sense Biblical interpretation rules. And so, it is with the first piece, The Belt of Truth. It's not a literal belt that we put on, but it speaks of a literal belt worn by the Roman Soldiers to teach us a literal spiritual truth that we need to mentally wear every day. So, let's take a look at what that belt was like for the Roman Soldier and to find out what it represents for us today.

The **1ˢᵗ thing** we see about The Belt of Truth is that **It Holds All Things Together**.

ROMAN SOLDIER'S BELT

"A Roman Soldier's belt, also known as a cingulum militare was a piece of ancient Roman military equipment in the form of a belt with metal fittings. The belt was broad and composed of sturdy leather and from it hung an overlapping skirt of leather straps almost like an 'apron' with decorative rivets.

It was worn with the tunic at all times and it formed the central piece of the soldier's armor holding all the rest of the equipment securely in place. From the belt hung specialized hooks and holders on which to secure the scabbard that contained the dagger ('pugio'), the quiver which held lances, and an apparatus on which to rest a large battle shield. Also, on the belt were clips with which to hold the breastplate in its proper place and even supplies of bread, oil and water were also on the belt."[3]

So, as you can see there's a lot going on with this belt. It was a multi-purpose belt. It's the ultimate tool belt, a lot of things were hung on it, necessary things. Things you needed in the midst of a battle. In fact, it was not only designed to carry things, but it held all things together.

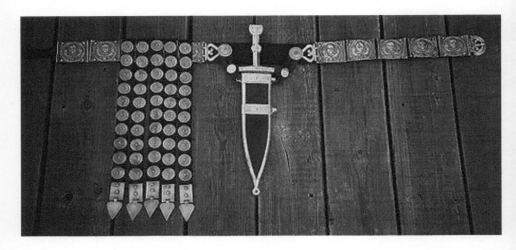

Without it, everything else fell apart. You had no place to hang your dagger, your lance, your shield, your breastplate, even your food supply. Without this belt you were in a mess. You were not equipped. The Roman Soldier was toast! They were not prepared. The belt held all things together. And Paul tells us that this belt of the Roman Soldier literally represented something in our spiritual battle with satan and demons. And it was the belt of what? You don't have to pray and fast about it, you don't have to go to a conference or buy a book, you don't have to wonder about it, he fills in the blank for us. It was the belt of truth. Now, the Greek word for truth is, "aletheia" and it simply means, "That which is objectively true in any matter, pertaining to God, the duties of man, moral and religious truth." Of course, Who is the truth and Who determines truth? God, Jesus.

John 14:6 "Jesus answered, I am the way and the truth and the life. No one comes to the Father except through Me."

And we all know the Bible is where God records that truth for us find out, discover, and read all about it, that's why Jesus later says this.

John 17:17 "Sanctify them by the truth; Your Word is truth."

In other words, the Bible is the truth. So, the truth is determined by God, it is God Himself (Jesus), and the Bible is the only book where we get that truth from. Now Paul says this is what this belt symbolizes. It's God's truth that we need to keep us from falling apart. God's truth holds all things together! It prepares us for battle. It gets us equipped so we don't lose the fight! One guy puts it this way.

WHY DO WE CLOTHE WITH TRUTH?

"To be clothed with God's truth simply means we are to be sincerely committed to the truth. In other words, I am totally sold out to who God is. I am totally sold out to what God has done. I am totally sold out to what God has said. I am yielded to Him. It is the truth, it is His truth, and I am now completely surrendered to Him and what He says about life.

You say, 'Where are you going with all this? Why is it armor? Why is it so important in warfare?' Listen, we live in a dark and deceptive world. Do you not realize this? The Bible says the devil deceives the whole world. That is actually in the present tense, which means the devil is constantly deceiving the whole world. This whole world is under the deception of darkness continually.

That's why God calls us to be a light in the midst of that darkness. That is what Ephesians teaches us. But if we are going to stand firm and fight in this darkness we must wear God's truth. Why? Because it's His armor to counteract the darkness and deception we daily face."[4]

The **2nd thing** we see about The Belt of Truth is that **It Has to Be Put on By Me**.

Paul goes on to say we don't just look at this belt of truth, we don't just stare at it, or hang it on the wall as a cool Christian decoration to impress your friends, he says to, "buckle it around your waist." Now, in the Greek it literally says that it's something that only the individual can do. In other words, no one can do it for you. "Buckling around" is the Greek word "peri-zon-numi" which is in the middle voice and it means this: "You yourself have to fasten on the belt, only you can wrap yourself around with the truth of God's Word, No one can do it for you." One guy puts it this way.

WHY MUST WE DO IT

"When Paul says, 'having girded your loins with truth' it is in the aorist middle participle. What it means is that I can't put it on for you. I can't make it happen. You can't make it happen with me.

It is a choice that we make constantly, constantly choosing to be affected, to be totally committed to that which God says, to His truth, to what He is, and that which He has done.

To be girded with truth means that I am sincerely, totally, wholly committed to truth. Obviously, that involves God's Word.

Therefore, I alone must choose every day to allow that truth to influence and totally surround my life."[5]

And that makes total sense. I can't read the Bible for you. You can't read it for me. I can't make you go to Bible studies or Church services to learn the Bible. And you can't for me. Oh, you might feel guilty about it and it's good to be invited. But the best-case scenario is when each individual takes their own initiative and makes themselves available for Bible study. Nobody has to twist their arm. And notice it's not once a week it's every day! Why? Because the battle is going on every day! Therefore, every day I need to get God's Truth on! Paul is basically saying if you want to be an effective soldier, you must take your own daily personal initiative to immerse yourself into God's Word!

The **3rd thing** we see about The Belt of Truth is that **It Indicates Seriousness**.

Other translations say not "buckling around" but "having your loins girt about with truth," or "girding your loins with truth." And when you look at Scripture and where this phrase occurs, it speaks of the person being serious towards the things of God. Loins or literally "hip" is the Greek word "osphus" and it referred to the general area of the body between the ribs and the thighs, basically the midsection that includes the hips, the small of the back, the waist, and the reproductive organs. That's why the Jews considered "osphus" "loins" as the place of the reproductive organs and we find phrases like "go forth from someone's loins" speaking of "being a descendant." The "loins" were in that area. But "girding the loins" also signified that a person was "ready for service" or "heavy battle." It describes a state of "seriousness" and "alertness."

Matthew 3:4 "And the same John had his raiment of camel's hair and a *leathern girdle about his loins*; and his meat was locusts and wild honey."

Nobody was more serious than John. John was a guy on a serious mission proclaiming the Messiah to any and all and so should we.

Luke 12:35 "*Let your loins be girded about* and your lights burning. And ye yourselves like unto men that wait for their Lord, when He will return from the wedding; that when He cometh and knocketh, they may open unto him immediately."

In other words, we are to be seriously ready and seriously serving the Lord and seriously eagerly awaiting His return as faithful believers.

1 Peter 1:13-16 "Wherefore *gird up the loins of your mind*, be sober, and hope to the end for the grace that is to be brought unto you at the revelation of Jesus Christ. As obedient children, not fashioning yourselves according to the former lusts in your ignorance: But as He which hath called you is holy, so be ye holy in all manner of conversation; Because it is written, be ye holy; for I am holy." In other words, we are to be seriously ready for action, our minds are seriously alert to all the wicked ways this world is daily, constantly, moment by moment trying to drag us back to a life of unholiness. We are seriously, daily, moment by moment, refusing these unholy temptations, and we are letting God mold us into His Holy character by His truth. In short, "girding up your loins" and certainly "girding your loins with truth" meant you were one serious Christian, seriously serving the Lord, you know His truth, you're surrounded in it, the darkness and deception won't get to you. And you're seriously ready to fight over it at any moment. One guy put it this way.

GIRDING THE LOINS SERIOUSNESS

"Now I don't know if you understand what the Apostle Paul is trying to say here but the analogy is beautiful. You see, if you don't know it yet, maybe you're not old enough yet, but your lower back is what really helps you to stand. And if you have trouble in your lower back, you are going to start bending and bowing and falling.

Years ago, I bought a little car to save gas and one day I came to the Church facility and got out of the car and when I did, I swung my body the wrong way. Something went out in my lower back and I fell on my hands and knees. I could not get up. I could not stand. Something happened in my lower back that brought me down.

Now the word "loins" here refers to that area of the back. And Paul is identifying a Roman soldier who wore not just a belt but a big wide belt. It not only carried their weapons on it, but it also protected their abdomen and lower back. You see, when they went into combat, it was hand to hand, they were constantly digging in and standing up. Something had to gird them. Something had to support and strengthen them and that's what the belt did.

And this is what Paul says, 'Listen, you are in a dark world. You are in a deceived world. When you get up on Monday morning and walk out to face it, you need your support belt on, God's Word, His Truth.' If you don't have the belt of truth on, forget the rest of the armor.

What we don't understand is, if we are not putting the Word of God, balancing out the error and deception that we are being pounded with every day, we already are misled and don't know it. Even on Sundays, we face it right in the Church. It is brought in. It is everywhere. It is all around us, people who are not surrendered to Jesus Christ and to His Word.

And how do you know when people are not surrendered to Jesus Christ and His Word, they don't have the belt of truth on? Simple. Just examine the attitude. The behavior. Examine your moods. Examine what you are going through. Examine your critical spirit. Examine your sarcastic attitude. Examine it. Where is it coming from?

The way you are thinking right now is determined by some standard in your life. If it is not the standard of God's truth, you have already lost your garment, you are already led astray, and you don't even know it. That is what Paul is saying. It is urgent. The Word has to be in your life.

No wonder you have grown weak in the back. No wonder you are trying to cower down. No wonder you have been knocked down. Only truth of God's Word can gird up your loins and cause you to stand against the wiles of the devil. And if I don't do it, it's my own fault. No one can do it for me. "[6]

Think about it. How many Christians are walking around with "spiritual backaches" simply because they don't have the belt of truth on? They don't get into God's Word? No wonder they're lumping around, limping around spiritually in pain all the time, because they don't have God's Truth cinched around them every day, supporting them spiritually wherever they go. They need to get serious again about God's Truth. I can't do it for you, you can't do it for me. But we all need to put the belt of truth back on, by our own initiative, every single day like a spiritual back brace and start getting rid of our spiritual problems, amen? That's what Paul is saying. Turn to somebody and say, "Put the belt on! It's time to get serious!"

The **4th thing** we see about The Belt of Truth is that **It Indicates Readiness**.

"Girding up the loins" also meant that you were ready to fight, you were ready for action. Your uniform is in place. Your belt is tightly cinched around you. All your armor is on, ready to go. You were ready to fight! Bring on the action! You're prepared. You're ready! And the key words there is tightly cinched around you. Because we all know, if your belt is loose, your pants what? They fall down! And so, it was with the belt of the Roman Soldier.

WHAT GIRDING THE LOINS SYMBOLIZED

"Girding the loins was a symbolic way of saying that one was standing firm or exercising self-control. The picture derived from the fact that Orientals would often tuck their long flowing robes in their belt around their loins, with a view to greater mobility for work, for travel, or for battle. One of the most famous illustrations of this custom is found in Exodus where Moses records God's instructions to Israel on the night of the Passover.

Exodus 12:11 *"Now you shall eat it in this manner: with your loins (Lxx=osphus) girded, your sandals on your feet, and your staff in your hand; and you shall eat it in haste – it is the LORD'S Passover."*

Thus, the girded one would be enabled to move unimpeded and be less likely to be hindered or tripped when traveling or in battle."[7]

Or in this case in Ephesians 6 it meant the soldier, the Christian was ready for battle. Nothing was going to impede him in the fight. Conversely a slackened belt meant one of two things. *One*, the soldier was going off duty, and for the Christian we are never given that liberty because the battle we are in never stops and it will never stop until we get to heaven. So, if you don't have the belt of truth on, stop going AWOL, stop goofing off, no wonder you're getting slaughtered. This is no day off. There never is a day off in this spiritual battle we're in, so get that thought out of your head. *Two*, a slackened belt, as was mentioned with the custom, meant that you were in danger of having your pants hanging down or falling down in the middle of the battle. And that's about as goofy as this song.

SONG PANTS ON THE GROUND

The scene opens on American Idol. The next contestant comes on the stage. As they look at the man he seems to be rather old. They ask his name and proceeds to tell them he wants to sing his song, 'Pants on the Ground." They look at him with questions in their eyes. Kind of stunned. They ask, "Pants on the ground?" He says, "Yes, Pants on the Ground. Are you ready?" They shake their heads and say, "Yes we are ready." General Larry Platt, Atlanta, Ga. Age 62 proceeds with his song. "Pants on the Ground, Pants on the Ground, looking like a fool with your pants on the ground. With gold in your mouth, hat turned sideways, pants on the ground." By now they are all laughing at him. He proceeds, "Looking like

a fool, walking down town, with your pants on the ground. Pants on the ground, pants on the ground, looking like a fool with your pants on the ground." Now the screen is showing a guy dancing in his bedroom but as he is bouncing around his pants are falling down. "With gold in your mouth, hat turned sideways, call yourself a cool cat, pants on the ground, pants on the ground" Then we see slides of all these different guys on the street with their pants falling off and their underwear is showing. "Gold in your teeth, hat turned sideways, pants on the ground, hey get your pants off the ground." Now the judges are laughing. They are shaking their heads with the music and the contestant keeps singing his song. They can't seem to get him to stop singing. A couple judges are still laughing while another is saying, "Ok, Ok, that's enough!" He finally stops singing. Simon asks him, "Larry, what was the name of your song?" Larry answers, "Pants on the ground." The judges are still laughing.

Why? Because you look like a fool when your pants are on the ground, right? And here's my point. This is what Paul is saying here with the belt of truth and our need to daily gird our loins with it. Christian, every single day, whether you realize it or not, when you don't get into God's Word every single day, spiritually you're walking around like those guys on the video. You're thinking you're cool, but you're really a spiritual fool with your pants on the ground! And lest you think I'm being overly dramatic with this analogy, the loosening of the belt so your opponent's pants would fall down, it was an actual battle tactic in history!

MCGEE ON CUTTING BELTS IN BATTLE

"Stand therefore." This is the fourth time Paul gives this exhortation to the believer. This is the only place that I find Paul laying it on the line and speaking like a sergeant. Earlier he said, "I beseech you," But now he gives the command to stand. Not only are we to be in standing position, but we are also to have on certain armor to protect ourselves.

www.alamy.com - C6FF6X

"Having your loins gird about with truth." In the ancient garment of that day, the girdle about the loins held in place every other part of the uniform of the soldier. It was essential. To tell you the truth, if the girdle was lost, you lost everything. The garments would fly open and the pants would fall down.

We see this routine in comedies and the people laugh to see a man trying to run or fight with his trousers drooping down. It looks funny in a comedy routine, but it is not funny in a battle.

A great battle in the past, we are told, was won by a clever general who told his men to cut the belts of their enemy while they were sleeping. The next morning the enemy troops were so busy holding up their trousers that they weren't able to shoot their guns, and, therefore, they lost the battle.

We are told to be girded with truth in the face of the enemy. Truth is that which holds everything together. What is truth? It is the Word of God. We need people whose loins are gird about with truth. They need to know the Word of God. Unfortunately, many folks are standing there about to lose their spiritual garments."[8]

In other words, their spiritual pants are on the ground. Why? Because they don't have the belt of truth on, God's Word. They never get into it. It's a rare occurrence. They expect somebody else to do it for them. They think Sundays are good enough, not realizing that's just icing on the cake, that doesn't keep your pants up every day of the week. As Paul says, you need to take this seriously, you need to get ready every single day before you leave the house, otherwise everything falls down, everything falls apart. Your attitude goes, your behavior goes, you're thinking goes, you get cranky critical, sarcastic, you don't have the power, energy, know how, you become a bad witness for Jesus and you begin to look, act, speak like the world. Why? Because you didn't get the Belt of Truth on! You didn't get into God's Word! Without it, everything else falls apart and I can't do it for you! How many times do you have to walk around with your pants on the ground before you get it! Pull them up! Get the truth on!

The **5th thing** we see about The Belt of Truth is that **It Indicates Victories**. Let's get back to the customs and mannerisms.

THE BELT WAS A BADGE OF HONOR

"A Roman Soldier's belt was also worn as a badge of rank by soldiers and officials and it designated who was who. A sash or strap decorated with emblems would go over the soldier's shoulder and come down and connect with the belt and then connect in the back. The emblems on this strap were insignias of previous victories. Just like modern day military decorations.

A soldier received them and placed them all over this area from the battles he'd fought and the things he'd done and his accomplishments. All of the medals and the awards of his accomplishment were placed there. Thus, the belt also became known as an emblem of accomplishment in battle.

A fitting combination. Only those ready, girded up, only those with the Sword of the Spirit hanging on the side were the ones who won the medals and went into battle as having been victorious."[9]

And that's the problem we have today. All we have is leftover memories of long ago spiritual accomplishments because nobody's getting the armor on and everybody's getting beat up and there are no more victories to hang! All we have is either no victories on our belt or nothing but old stories of the past victories when we actually did something years ago, typically when we first got saved, but nothing new and it's been that way for many years! Why? Because you never get the armor on, you can't even get the belt of truth on anymore, which holds all of it together. And all you have now is a daily log of spiritual defeats one after another instead of a daily spiritual string of victories, and it's your fault, I can't do it for you, you can't do it for me. Only those with the belt of truth on, Paul says, only those who put on God's Word every single day are equipped to not only fight and stand their ground but have the privilege to adorn testimonies of victories to the glory of God. As well as to encourage the other soldiers fighting in the battle as they too struggle in this war. Bottom line is, don't be like this soldier.

GET YOUR ARMOR ON

The alarm goes off, the guy jumps out of bed, takes his shower, drinks his coffee and brushes his teeth. He fixes his tie, picks up his briefcase and proceeds out the door. "That's as foolish as doing this" …

There are some soldiers in the woods sitting around talking. One soldier picks up his amo and the other soldier asks him, "What do you need amo for? It's not like you can aim. He's sitting there with his helmet laying on the ground with all his equipment. "I can't aim? I'll show you how I can aim." He jokingly replies. Suddenly there is an explosion next to them. Sounds of gun fire right next to them. He grabs his equipment and starts to put everything on. Buttoning his shirt, putting on his belt and helmet and off he runs to get into the fight. He was not prepared.

The second scene is the alarm goes off, the guy jumps out of bed, he reads his Bible, takes his shower, drinks his coffee and brushes his teeth. He fixes his tie, picks up his briefcase and proceeds out the door. "Put on the full Armor of God, so that you will be able to Stand Firm against the Schemes of the devil."

You got it? This is what Paul is saying. You're tired of getting shot in the back spiritually as a Christian? Get the armor on. Starting with the Belt of Truth. It holds it all together! That's what Paul's saying we need to do if we're going to experience the victory that God's already given to us in the daily spiritual battle we're in. I can't do it for you. You can't do it for me. But we can encourage each other with this…. Hold up your Bible, turn to somebody and say this, "Get your belt on! You're looking like a fool with your pants on the ground!" Amen?

Chapter Twenty-Five

Protection from Satan
and Demons Part 5

"It started out just like any other routine test in this nuclear facility. The turbines began to spin, the pumps began to circulate, the power supply seemed to be just fine, but by the time the operator moved to shut down the procedure, the facility was already in an extreme unstable condition.

Soon steam rapidly began to be produced, which then increased the pressure inside the unit, which then detached a cover plate, that then ruptured the fuel channels and jammed the control rods, producing a series of explosions, instantly killing two people, spewing forth nuclear waste high into the atmosphere.

But that was just the beginning. Soon, the deadly gas killed six firemen, then another 22 people, as it ascended 3 miles up into the air in a plume of smoke laden with deadly contaminants, creating a cloud that traveled northwest over Poland, then into Scandinavia, south to Greece, spreading poison throughout eastern Europe. Then it blew eastward over the length of the Soviet Union, and even a small amount of it reached California.

And even though some 220,000 people were evacuated from nearly 2,700 square miles, the damage was done. 800,000 children needed medical treatment, upwards to 200,000 people died, land was destroyed for miles around, it still causes birth defects in animals today and massive spikes in thyroid disease, anemia, and cancer in people as well.

It was the largest uncontrolled radioactive release into the environment ever recorded, it produced $358 billion dollars' worth of damage, and became the worst nuclear plant accident in all of modern history.

The year was 1986. The disaster is of course, Chernobyl."[1]

How many of you have heard of the Chernobyl Disaster? Okay, I think we all have. But how many of you would say it was one of the greatest disasters of all time, right? But with all due respect to those who lost their lives in Chernobyl, what if I were to tell you I know of a disaster that makes the Chernobyl Meltdown look like a tiny hang nail? And what if I were to tell you that this disaster didn't occur in just one place and one country at one time, but it's going on right now today all over the world and it's been leaving a trail of death and destruction for centuries. Folks, I'm talking once again about *the satanic War on the Christian.* We Christians don't battle here and there once in a while. We go to war, every single day. Whether you see it, feel it, believe it or not, the moment you got saved you entered a spiritual war against a demonic host whose sole purpose is to destroy you and extinguish your testimony for Jesus Christ. And what's wild is that most wars go on for a few years or even longer. But *the satanic War on the Christian* has been going on for the last 2,000 years non-stop and it's sending people straight into hell! And what's wild is most people will readily talk about all the other wars throughout history and all their atrocities, and rightly so, we have the History Channel, we need to talk about them! Yet how many people, even Christians, will openly discuss the longest war in mankind's history…*the satanic War on the Christian* that has destroyed more lives than all the wars put together? Therefore, in order to stop getting duped and beat up all over the place, we're going to continue in our study, *the satanic War on the Christian.*

Now so far, we've seen if you're ever going to win a war, then the **1ˢᵗ thing** you must do is **Know Who Your Enemy Is.**

Then we saw the **2ⁿᵈ thing** you need to know is **What Your Enemy is Like**, their character, amen? It's common sense, right?

Then we saw the **3ʳᵈ thing** you need to know is **The Tactic of Your Enemy,** what they're up to, what's their goal, why are they here.

Then we saw the **4ᵗʰ thing** you need to know is **The Destruction of Your Enemy,** what price you pay when you don't take this seriously.

Then we saw the **5ᵗʰ thing** you need to know is **The Temptation of Your Enemy,** how he's out there trying to get us to sin against God.

And the **last four times** we saw the **6ᵗʰ thing** you need to know is **The Protection FROM Your Enemy**.

And there we saw God has not left us hanging high and dry in this Great Cosmic War dealing with satan and demons. Are you kidding me? He's actually given us His full-blown protection and amazing weaponry to stand our ground and be victorious in all situations every single time! It's called The Armor of God!

So far, we've seen the **1ˢᵗ thing** about the Armor of God that **It's Designed for War**.

The **2ⁿᵈ thing, It's Designed for Victory.**

And the last time the **3ʳᵈ thing, It's Designed for Wear.**

This armor is simply the supernatural equipment that God has given to us for our protection, not our fashion! It's not something to look at, it's not meant just to stare at, or stick on a shelf and collect dust. It's designed for wear. You wear it daily, you continually wear it. You put it on! And again, the Greek says to put it on now and leave it on! Quick! Chop, chop! Don't delay! This is serious stuff! In fact, it also says, "to put on the full armor of God," literally "the complete armor of God" meaning you put on every single piece of it and leave it on and you better do it now! Not one piece, not half the armor, not a piece here and there, when you get around to it, no, no, no! You need every single piece, all of it right now, the complete package, the full uniform, Why? Because just like the army, when they give you a uniform and battle gear, they expect you to wear it. Why? Just because they're being legalistic! NO! It's for your protection! So, it is with this full armor of God. You need all of it if you're going to be able to come out on top, hold your ground, stand firm against the devil's schemes.

The **1ˢᵗ piece** we saw is what we are to hurry up and put on for God's Victory, **The Belt of Truth**.

It's not a literal belt that we put on, but it speaks of a literal belt worn by the Roman Soldiers, to teach us a literal spiritual truth. We need to wear The Word of God every day! We need to be in the Bible. Why? Because as we saw, just as the Roman Soldier's belt held all things together, kept things from falling apart, could only be put on by the individual, indicated seriousness & support as well as readiness, and was a place to hang their victories. So, it is with the Word of God and the Christian! If we're going to experience the victory that God's already given to us and stop looking like fools with our pants on the ground, spiritually, then we need to "Get the belt of truth on!" We need to be in the Bible every single day! This is what Paul is saying. But that's not all.

The **2ⁿᵈ piece** of armor we need to hurry up and put on, for God's Victory, that He's already given to us, is **The Breastplate of Righteousness**. But don't take my word for it.

Ephesians 6:10-14: "Finally, be strong in the Lord and in his mighty power, put on the full armor of God so that you can take your stand against the devil's schemes. For our struggle is not against flesh and blood, but against the rulers, against the authorities, against the powers of this dark world and against the spiritual forces of evil in the heavenly realms. Therefore, put on the full armor of God, so that when the day of evil comes, you may be able to stand your ground, and after you have done everything to stand, stand firm then, with the belt of truth buckled around your waist, with the breastplate of righteousness in place."

So here again we see the second piece of supernatural military equipment that God gives us, with the ability to effectively struggle and come out on top in our war against the evil ones, when they come at us every single day, not if. This is the second piece that gives us the ability to stand our ground and not buckle or break under pressure when the dust clears from the battle that we're in. It was called the breastplate of righteousness. And so the obvious big question is, "What in the world is this Breastplate of Righteousness?" right? Now, we saw last time, the Roman soldier's uniform and his weaponry speaks of a real reality, a real spiritual truth, that we need to know today. It was symbolic of something. But the question is, "What is it symbolic of?"

Well, the **1st thing** we're going to see about The Breastplate of Righteousness is that **It Protects Us from All Different Angles**.

Once again, let's take a look at what this piece of armor was like for the Roman Soldier and find out what it literally means for us today.

ROMAN SOLDIER'S BREASTPLATE

"A Roman soldier's breastplate was also known as the "lorica segmentata" which comes from the Latin phrase, "armor in pieces." It referred to a type of the ancient Roman military equipment that acted as a type of body armor that was put together in segments or plates, hence "segmentata."

It covered the chest and shoulders and was made up of four sections, two for shoulders and two for the torso, front and back, attached by means of brass hooks which were joined by leather laces. The broad iron or steel strips were fastened to internal leather straps and the strips were then arranged horizontally on the body, overlapping downwards. This design allowed the armor to be stored very compactly, since it was possible to separate it into four sections each of which would collapse on itself into a compact mass.

Also, since the "lorica segmentata" covered the shoulders and chest in the front and back, it afforded good protection from spears, missiles, swords, and knife piercings. In fact, the testing of modern replicas of this armor has demonstrated that it was impenetrable to most direct hits and missile strikes." [2]

That's why you wanted to make sure you had this on. But as you can see there's a lot going on with this breastplate. It was basically the central piece to the Roman's soldier's armor. It protected the whole mid-section, the torso, the whole central part of the body. Why? Because without this in place in battle, you're toast! This is where all your vital organs are! Your heart, your lungs, and so on! You could take a hit in the arm or legs, but without this armor, you were asking for death! You were easy prey, easy pickings! But with it, the enemy's blows to this vital area would just glance right off it. You just keep marching forward as they unsuccessfully tried to bring you down! The breastplate did all this important protection for you. But notice it wasn't just in the front that it protected you. This is where a lot of people get it wrong. It contained shoulder protection on the top, and on either side of the torso, front and back! Why? Because the enemy isn't going to just stab you in the front! They're going to come at you at all angles! And so, it is with satan. He's looking for a chink in our armor from any angle he can get! He's not always going to come at you head on! It's not always going to be that obvious. He's sneaky. He's cunning! Sometimes, he'll look down at you from on top, sometimes he'll sneak up and go around your back. He's evil and he'll look anywhere he can for a crack, just so he can stab us with his unrighteousness! And listen, the breastplate of righteousness counteracted this attack. One guy put it this way.

SATAN LOOKS FOR A CRACK

"No Roman soldier would have thought of going into battle without his vital organs protected. You can take a shot in the thigh, you can take a shot in the arm, you can take a shot in the shoulder, but you get one here and that's serious. And so, it is in our spiritual battle.

If there's a weakness in your armor, a chink in your armor, sins, acts of disobedience, wrong attitudes, if there are unconfessed sins, unrepented of sins, you're vulnerable.

And if you're courting sins in your life and you get aggressive and you go into the spiritual fray and you go on the offense to rescue souls from the kingdom of darkness and you've got some issues in your life that are undealt with, believe me, you are going out there without the breastplate of righteousness on, and you're going to fail.

That's what happened to one of my friends. I had a friend in high school, he was the youth leader in his Church. And his first year at college, he collapsed morally because there were issues that I could see in his life as a high school student but were not being dealt with.

You see, when satan sees sin, he moves into that crack. You become vulnerable as the world system appeals to that crack in your armor. And the smallest crack can be exploited in a very fatal way. That's why the Bible says to make no provision for the flesh in regard to its lusts.

Oh, you may have the commitment, you may have the eagerness, you may even say, 'Yeah, I want to go to seminary, I want to train, I want to serve the Lord,' but the breastplate has to be on.

It falls off so easily, and we go through life picking up the breastplate and trying to get it on before the next attack. But we have to keep it hooked on every day if there's going to be any real victory for Christ. It simply demands a life of righteousness."[3]

And that's the key word there. It wasn't the breastplate of "coolness" or "shininess" "fashion statement" to impress your Christian friends, it was the breastplate of righteousness. It's the Greek word, "dikaiosune" and it simply means, "Righteousness or right-living as defined by God, not man, not somebody else. It meant integrity, virtue, purity of life, right-living, correctness of thinking, feeling, and acting as defined by God's holy character." That's righteousness and that's what God says we need to put on and leave on every single day. Now, this makes total sense because satan is the total antithesis of this weapon. He's all about unrighteousness, sin, unholy living, wrong living. In fact, he's where it all began.

Ezekiel 28:15 "You were blameless in your ways from the day you were created till wickedness was found in you."

The word "wickedness" in the Hebrew (avval) actually means, "unrighteousness." So satan is where all unrighteousness comes from.
And again, that's why God gives us this particular piece of armor, the breastplate of righteousness. It's to counteract "unrighteous attacks" of satan the "unrighteous one." This is at the core of who satan is and what he does, and God hasn't left us hanging high and dry. He's made provision with the breastplate, the breastplate of righteousness. And again, notice the breastplate covers all angles, because that's what satan does. Again, he comes at us from all different kinds of angles. And this is emphasized by God. Some translations say we are to "put on" the breastplate or as we read in our translation "have it in place." But the Greek actually says, "immerse yourself into it." It's the Greek word "enduo" and it literally means, "to sink into (as in clothing), to put it on, to clothe one's self with." The idea is that you are totally wrapped with this breastplate from the front and back and the top, you are immersed in it." Why? Because you didn't want to have any area exposed to the enemy's weapons. And so it is with satan. He's going to come at you from all angles, and he is looking for a sinful crack, any tiny area of compromise where he can sneak in and jam us with unrighteousness. So, God says to totally immerse yourself into this breastplate. You better take this seriously, this breastplate of righteousness. Get it on quick, it's for your own protection. One guy puts it this way.

WHY DO WE CLOTHE WITH RIGHTEOUSNESS?

"Polybius, a Greek Historian, tells us that the breastplate was known as a heart-protector. And so, it is with the breastplate of righteousness.

It protects our hearts from the arrows and the spears and the swords and the crushing blows from satan in our spiritual battle.

It stands for uprightness and integrity of character and it protects this vital area.

Proverbs 11:4 says, "Riches do not profit in the day of wrath, but righteousness delivers from death.

Without righteousness, we leave ourselves open to almost certain death. With righteousness – just as with a breastplate – the otherwise fatal attacks of our enemy are thwarted."[4]

In other words, we are protected, keep moving forward, have a nice day, God hasn't left us hanging high and dry, in our battle with the evil one, the unrighteous one.

The **2nd thing** we see about The Breastplate of Righteousness is that **It Has to Be Put On By Me**.

Just like the Belt of Truth, as we saw last time, so it is with the Breastplate of Righteousness. I am the only one who has to do this for me. The Greek actually says, "having clothed yourself with the breastplate of righteousness." Nobody does this for me. I don't hire a servant to put it on for me because I'm too lazy. I don't hire an assistant to remind me about the importance of it. NO! I do it! I alone take the initiative and put on the breastplate of righteousness. I am the only one who can totally immerse myself with it. And so the question is, "Who's righteousness are we putting on and being immersed with?" Right? Well, when you look at the Bible, you only have three options.

The **first option** is **Self-Righteousness** which I don't believe we're talking about for obvious reasons.

Self-righteousness is a sin. You're basically trying to "prove your self-righteous to God" in order to get into heaven, as the Bible says.

Isaiah 64:6 "All of us have become like one who is unclean, and all our righteous acts are like filthy rags."

As we saw before, "filthy rags" is literally a "menstrual rag" in the Hebrew and it speaks of someone basically saying to God, "I don't need the blood of your Son Jesus to get into heaven, I'll produce my own blood," and throw a tampon at the feet of God. Not good! As one guy said,

Self-righteousness is when people put their trust in doing good works to be saved. This is not the breastplate of righteousness. You will be a victim of the forces of hell for sure if you're trying to cover yourself in this kind of righteousness."

So obviously, that's not the kind of righteousness Paul is talking about here that we need to "clothe ourselves with.' It doesn't make sense.

The **second option** is what is called, "**Positional Righteousness**."

Now, this is referring the "righteousness" that was given to us in Christ, or "imputed to us" by His death on the cross.

2 Corinthians 5:21 "God made Him (Jesus) who had no sin to be sin for us, so that in Him (Jesus) we might become the righteousness of God."

In other words, we are "made righteous with God" through the righteousness of Jesus Christ. It's imputed to me which is an accounting term. It speaks of God's Divine Ledger. Basically, God took all my unrighteousness, my sin, and placed it on the cross with Christ, then He put that on His side of the ledger. Then He took the perfect righteousness of Christ, and He put it on my side of the ledger. Pretty cool deal, huh? Yeah! You ain't a joking! That's why I'm eternally secure in my salvation because it's not based on my righteousness, no way, it's based on the righteousness of Christ! My righteousness is as filthy rags! His righteousness is perfect, it's complete, it cannot fail. That's why God calls me a "hagios" a "saint" a "holy one" not because of me, are you kidding me, but because of the righteousness of Christ that's "imputed to me." He only sees me as He sees Jesus. Try telling that one to your spouse! It's usually a hard concept to get through to them Biblically, especially if you're arguing, but hey, it's true, deal with it. So, is that kind of righteousness Paul is talking about, that we are to clothe ourselves with, get completely immersed with in our daily battle with satan and demons? Well...I still don't think so. I say that because the righteousness of Christ is something given to me and the breastplate of righteousness, as we read, is something I put on. One is a gift, the other I do. However, I will say this. I do believe that positional righteousness is something that does come in handy in our daily struggles, when we fail to put on the breastplate of righteousness, like we should. One guy says this.

BENEFITS OF POSITIONAL RIGHTEOUSNESS

"I stand righteous before God because of Christ's righteousness being imputed to my account. His righteousness will never fail. Regardless of the duration or intensity of the battle, the righteousness of Christ will prevail.

Our positional righteousness is not a piece of armor we put on. The saved are clothed in the righteousness of Christ from the moment of salvation, and that never changes. However, we do enter battle bearing the righteousness of Christ. It never leaves us.

That brings peace to my heart. I am often weak in the flesh and the enemy is strong. In the heat of battle, while we are prone to stumble and fall, Satan is never able to penetrate the righteousness of Christ. I have been adopted into the family of God. I am counted righteous because of Christ my Savior. I may lose the battle now and again, but His righteousness always prevails.

This "imputed righteousness" is the very foundation of the Christian life. This righteousness allows us access to God. It opens the door of Heaven to us. It protects us against the eternal fires of Hell. But, it does not protect us from the attacks of the enemy.

On the contrary, since the devil knows that he can't have us because we belong to Christ, he doubles his efforts to defeat us in an attempt to discredit the Savior, the Church, and the God of glory.

Satan comes at us and says, "Look at how you just exploded in anger! Look at how you lied to cover your tracks! Look at how you lusted after that girl! Some Christian you are!"

How do you answer him if his charges are true? You answer by applying Christ's imputed righteousness: "You are right, Satan, I did just sin. But my eternal life does not depend on my sinless behavior or perfect track record. I am trusting in the blood of Jesus Christ and His righteousness credited to my account. Take it up with Him!"

The imputed righteousness of Jesus Christ is our only hope for eternal life and our defense against Satan's accusations when we fail to put on the breastplate of righteousness."[5]

So, praise God for the imputed righteousness of Christ, amen? But I don't think that's what Paul is talking about here.

The **third option**, and this is the option I think he's talking about, is called **Practical Righteousness** and it's not the same a self-righteousness, that's a sin, we're not talking about trying to make ourselves righteous to get to heaven because we can't.

Rather it's talking about the daily process of Christian maturity in our behavior. The growing up process as we learn to walk in holiness, emulating Christ's holy character, as He says, "Be ye holy as He is holy." Not to get to heaven, but because we love Him and we want to be conformed to His image and be a positive righteous witness for Jesus to those around us. This is the daily choice Paul talks about in Romans Chapter 6.

Romans 6:12-13 "Therefore do not let sin reign in your mortal body so that you obey its evil desires. Do not offer the parts of your body to sin, as instruments of wickedness, but rather offer yourselves to God, as those who have been brought from death to life; and offer the parts of your body to Him as instruments of righteousness."

Now, there's something cool going on here in the Greek I need to point out. When Paul is saying here to "offer up the members of your body as instruments of righteousness" each and every day. The word he uses for "instruments" in Greek is, "hoplon." Hoplon was used as an implement of war, either offensive or defensive. Now listen, that means what Paul is saying here in Romans 6 is that he's picturing a spiritual war going on here, every day, between two armies, satan's and God's, and the believer is right in the middle of it. And what Paul is saying in essence is that when the Christian lays down his armor by sin and disobedience, he in essence is choosing to present his members as weapons at the service of the sinful nature [flesh]. At which point, listen, he is guilty of "high treason" for he is then fighting against his own Captain, the Lord Jesus. This is the daily choice Paul is asking us to make when we get out of bed every single day. Am I going to offer up this body today as an instrument or weapon of wickedness and commit treason or am I going to offer it up as an instrument or weapon of righteousness. This is why he says later in Ephesians 6, "put on the breastplate of righteousness." It's basically saying the same thing. It's the same daily choice. The same battle he is speaking of. And in both cases, he says choose righteousness, put on righteousness! Why? Because this is what keeps you from committing treason as well as makes you impregnable to the enemy's daily attacks! You choose to put on the practical righteousness, so the enemy won't have any crack to insert his unrighteousness. One guy puts it this way.

BENEFITS OF PRACTICAL RIGHTEOUSNESS 1

"I stand righteous before God because of Christ's righteousness being imputed to my account. His righteousness will never fail. Regardless of the duration or intensity of the battle, the righteousness of Christ will prevail.

Our positional righteousness is not a piece of armor we put on. The saved are clothed in the righteousness of Christ from the moment of salvation, and that never changes. However, we do enter battle bearing the righteousness of Christ. It never leaves us.

That brings peace to my heart. I am often weak in the flesh and the enemy is strong. In the heat of battle, while we are prone to stumble and fall, Satan is never able to penetrate the righteousness of Christ. I have been adopted into the family of God. I am counted righteous because of Christ my Savior. I may lose the battle now and again, but His righteousness always prevails.

This "imputed righteousness" is the very foundation of the Christian life. This righteousness allows us access to God. It opens the door of Heaven to us. It protects us against the eternal fires of Hell. But, it does not protect us from the attacks of the enemy.

On the contrary, since the devil knows that he can't have us because we belong to Christ, he redoubles his efforts to defeat us in an attempt to discredit the Savior, the Church, and the God of glory.

Satan comes at us and says, "Look at how you just exploded in anger! Look at how you lied to cover your tracks! Look at how you lusted after that girl! Some Christian you are!"

How do you answer him if his charges are true? You answer by applying Christ's imputed righteousness: "You are right, Satan, I did just sin. But my eternal life does not depend on my sinless behavior or perfect track record. I am trusting in the blood of Jesus Christ and His righteousness credited to my account. Take it up with Him!"[6]

The imputed righteousness of Jesus Christ is our only hope for eternal life and our defense against Satan's accusations when we fail to put on the breastplate of righteousness."

This is the choice you make when you get out of bed every single day. Am I going to offer up this body today as an instrument or weapon of wickedness, or am I going to offer it up as an instrument or weapon of righteousness. Whose master do I belong to. Who am I going to fight for today with this life. satan or Jesus. And if it's not Jesus, you're in horrible trouble! It's basically Paul's way of calling us to a holy pure life, each and every day, making that deliberate choice, in order to stand firm and stand strong against the enemy's attacks. And again, this should be common sense to us to choose righteousness, to choose the right living, because we all know that purity matters when it comes to water, like these folks admit.

PURITY MATTERS

In a video we see this guy stopping people that are walking down the street. He asks the first couple, "Excuse me, we are asking people about their preference of water. Would you rather drink from this bottle of water or this bottle of water?" He holds up two bottles but just then a van pulls up and about 5 different people jump out and run over to him and take one of the bottles from his hand and they each take a drink from that bottle. As the first couple watch this happen one of the bystanders makes the comment that 'there are about 6 mouths on it right now'. So now the bottle is passed back to the commentator and he again asks, "Which one would you want to drink from?"

One guy points to the full bottle and says, "That one." The commentator asks, "Why?" In response to the question he is told that, "I don't know where their mouths have been." The commentator says, I don't know, this one looks pretty good and everyone seems to like it." As he holds up the half full bottle. Then the guy replies, "I'm sure they do, but I don't know."

The commentator then tells him, "I have it under good authority that only one of those guys was sick. Would you drink out of this bottle if I gave you $5.00?" He shakes his head and says, "No." "What if I gave you $10.00 to drink from this bottle?" Another passerby says, "No." "For $10.00 you won't drink out of this bottle?" "No, I will only drink out of the pure bottle of water." "Purity Matters!"

Yeah, no kidding! Purity matters! Now how many of you would agree with those folks, ain't no way I'm drinking from that water bottle after somebody else's mouth has been on it They might be sick or have disease or something. In fact, I don't know if you've reached that stage as a parent yet, but early on when you first have kids, you share everything, drinks and all. And sometimes to your own detriment. They look up at you and say, "Can I have a drink, Poppa?" And they have slime on their face, snot coming out of their nose, saliva dripping from their chin, and what do you say as a parent? "Okay, have a drink." And sure enough three days later you're in the hospital with pneumonia. And why do you do that as a parent? Because you sacrifice, you share everything with your kids. You love them, but not when they become teenagers! Oh no, the double straw request comes out and breaks your heart. I'll never forget that day. And they look at you like you got some sort of disease and 14 scabs on your face and demand you drink out of another straw! My little heart broke! But I'm not bitter about it! And you're sitting there thinking, "Wait a second, are you kidding me? First of all, we share the same DNA sample...hello...I'm not going to kill you! And second of all, how many times did I get sick from your mucus lips!" But I'm not bitter about it! No! No! No!

But why do they act like this? Because the older they get, the more purity matters at least for drinks. In fact, speaking of which, I did that, one time at a conference in Colorado. We were eating at a restaurant after one session where I was speaking with one of the interns and his wife, Robert and Carlie, and Jess's mom Katy was there helping too. Katy and Carlie didn't want their own full desert after the meal, so they decided to share one together. And it was this big giant chocolate gooey mess of stuff. So, I waited until they were about halfway done and both of them are dipping their spoons in the same bowl and I just casually said to Katy, "So Katy, did that scab ever go away on your lip?" Man! You should have seen the look on Carlie's face! I thought she was going to vomit the whole thing back up! But why did Carlie react that way? Because purity matters! Who wants to eat with somebody that's got a scab on their lip! EEEWWW! GROSS!!! And how much more so with water! In fact, have you noticed we're all so wigged out about purified water? "I've got to have a filter,

I've got to have that device! I can't drink from the tap, that'll kill you, who knows what's in there!" And we spend tons of money on purified water and water equipment without batting an eye! In fact, we spend $16 billion dollars a year on bottled water, making it our favorite packaged beverage! And yet that costs 2,000 times more than tap water!!! And that's not even counting all the purifying equipment we buy! So, what's the real number? And why do we do this? Because we've got to have purified water, or we'll die! It's common sense!

That's in essence, what Paul is saying here. We need a purified life every single day or we're going to die! We need to put on the breastplate of righteousness, holy pure living, and, it's as common sense as the need for purified water! Why? Because unhealthy water leads to sickness or disease. Paul is saying in essence the same thing, spiritually. An unholy life leads to sinfulness and defeat! But let's take it a step further. What if a person purposely polluted their water and still went ahead and drank it? Now how foolish would that, be right? Well, that's right, to help understand the foolishness of that kind of behavior, I need my trusty volunteer…aka Intern????

PURE WATER ANALOGY

Now as you can see on the table there are two glasses filled with of crystal clear, clean pristine, refreshing cold water, and they represent a pure holy life in Christ, i.e. our practical righteousness. How many of you would like to drink out of either one? In fact, go ahead and drink out of that first one. However, what if he (Intern ??) started to purposely put in some unholy things into one of those glasses, for instance he starts to put in "relish of rotten actions," or "TV Tabasco sauce," (guaranteed to set your lusts on fire) or "mustard of dirty mouth," or even "mayonnaise of mean behavior," now watch the Intern drink out of that second glass! Sorry dude just wanted to see the look on your face like Carlie! It's cheap entertainment!

So, in all seriousness, this is the choice that Paul is asking us to make every day. When it comes to what you're putting into your life, would the Lord find it pleasing to drink? Is your behavior healthy for you? Will it make you sick? What kind of vessel are you? An instrument of righteousness or wickedness? And why would you purposely do that to yourself? Righteousness should be common sense as a normal desire for clean water. Why? Because we all know that purity matters. And so, it is in our relationship with God! This is what Paul is basically saying. What an insane choice. Who in their right mind would drink, on purpose, unholy living, filling their lives full of pollution! In fact, it's the same thing James says.

James 1:27 "Religion that God our Father accepts as pure and faultless is this: to look after orphans and widows in their distress and to keep oneself from being polluted by the world."

Why would you choose to be polluted by the world, to put inside your vessel unholiness, to surrender your body as an instrument of wickedness, instead of putting on the breastplate of righteousness? We all know pollution can make you sick or kill you! We all know germs are not good for you! And yet, you really wonder why you're getting sick spiritually? You wonder why your walk with God makes Him want to vomit? You wonder why satan is having a heyday with you and you feel like you're going to die! You need to hurry up and get back to common sense! Purity matters! You wig out about it when it comes to water, how much more to the living water that refreshes your soul! You need to get back to choosing to live a holy, pure, clean life with Jesus or you're going to get sick and sink!

THE BENEFITS OF PRACTICAL RIGHTEOUSNESS 2

"Having put on the breastplate of righteousness represents putting on the practical integrity, holiness, and purity in the life of the believer. The breastplates covered an area from the neck to the thighs. It served to protect the vital areas of the body, specifically the heart. We know the heart is essential to life. The same is true for our spiritual existence as well.

Just as a Roman soldier could not defend himself against a foe without such a coat of armor, so a lack of integrity will leave a man exposed to the assaults of the enemy.

As Dwight Moody once said, 'We Christians should live in the world, but not be filled with it. As a ship lives in the water; but if the water gets into the ship, she goes to the bottom. So, Christians may live in this world; but if the world gets into them, they sink.'

In other words, if there is a defect in our character with some want of integrity because we have been polluted by the world; that person is sinking, they are unguarded, and this will surely be the point of attack by our foe.

Just as David was tempted to commit the enormous crimes that stained his memory, and just as Peter denied his Lord, so it is many a minister of the gospel today that have been assailed and have fallen all because they were lacking this armor of righteousness.

Having the breastplate of righteousness is our only hope. The more righteous we become in character, the harder it becomes for satan to tempt us successfully and wound our spirits. The more righteousness becomes a part of our being, the easier it becomes for us to resist sin and satan.

It was the incorruptible integrity of Job, and, in a higher sense, of Jesus Himself, that saved them from the temptations of the devil. And it is as true now, today, that no one can successfully meet the power of temptation unless he is righteous in his character.

You must put on the breastplate of righteousness if you are going to successfully face the enemy. What a mighty protection you have if you are a righteous man or a righteous woman. Just say no to sin and stand your ground."[7]

In other words, put on the breastplate of righteousness, so you can stand against the wiles of the devil, amen?

The **3rd thing** we see about The Breastplate of Righteousness is that **It Requires Commitment**.

Now, when a soldier put this piece of equipment on, he was committed to fight. He was committed to the battle and going into battle with the mindset of victory. He knew this armor gave him a serious edge. He wasn't going in thinking he was going to lose, especially the Roman soldier because they were one of the most well-equipped soldiers in history. Rather he was going in expecting victory, he was committed to it. Putting on the breastplate was a part of that process, and it's the same process God calls us to.

THE BREASTPLATE MEANS I'M COMMITTED

"If you don't have righteousness in your life, you don't have commitment. Because righteousness is just a way of saying "a right relationship to God." And if you are to keep a right relationship with God, you have to be daily committed to making sure that is taking place.

Now, I'm not saying you never sin. What I mean is there is a decreasing frequency of it, and when you do, you confess it, you repent of it, and you turn from it. You deal with it before God. That takes commitment.

You are honest enough to evaluate your life. You're committed to "abstaining from fleshly lusts." You're committed to living a righteous life, a life above reproach.

Listen, the absolute end of stupidity is for a Christian to become engulfed in this wicked world system, to stop being committed to God, and allowing satan to move into your life and fill your mind with lies.

To purposely allow him to fill it with perversion, to fill it with garbage, to fill it with immorality, to fill it with a theology that isn't God's, to fill it with half-truths and untruths about sin, and say, "Oh, it's not that bad," And he literally drowns you in a sea of it so you become tolerant of it, and then entertains you with it, so that you don't think it's as evil as it really is.

Then he has you laughing at sin on your television or in the movies, then he has you hearing it put to so-called beautiful tunes and music, so that it clouds your mind and confuses your thinking.

From there he moves to destroy your conscience, to get you to do things that you shouldn't do, to sear a conscience that once warned you. Soon it will not warn you any longer.

He wants to debilitate your will, break down your will. He wants to confuse your emotions, corrupt your desires. He wants to draw your affections to the wrong things. And all this attack comes by Satan in that vital area, in the heart. And Paul simply says to counteract this battle, you need to be committed to putting on the breastplate of righteousness, every day. That's the antidote. That's the way out of this mess. And it all starts with commitment.

Listen, you can't be in the Lord's army and a civilian of the world. You can't be both, and if you've come to fight for the Heavenly Commander and to serve the Lord, then get out of the system.

Put on the breastplate of righteousness and get committed! Present our bodies as living sacrifices, holy and acceptable under God. Put on the breastplate of righteousness and do what Paul says to do in 1 Corinthians 15:34. "Awake to righteousness and stop sinning."

Why? Because a man of integrity, with a clear conscience, can face the enemy without fear. But for over a year, King David lied about his sin with Bathsheba, and nothing went right."[8]

And nothing will go right in your walk with Jesus, until you too get committed, like the Roman Soldier, ready for battle, expecting victory, by putting on the breastplate, and in our case, the breastplate of righteousness. It's a daily decision that I'm committed to, I choose to get up and offer this life as an instrument of righteousness, a weapon in the hands of Almighty God, by putting on the breastplate, and I get ready for war!

2 Timothy 2:3-4 "Endure hardship with us like a good soldier of Christ Jesus. No one serving as a soldier gets involved in civilian affairs – he wants to please his commanding officer."

Choosing to live a life of holiness as a soldier of Christ is hard work, it requires commitment, it's a deliberate act. You have to make that daily choice, there are no shortcuts, there's no gimmicks, as these folks found out.

PURITY RING 3000

A commercial shows two college students sitting on a park bench in a park. They are holding hands across the table. He says, "Since we are going to separate colleges, and we aren't ready to be engaged, I wanted to ask you if you would be engaged to be engaged in purity with me?" He brings out a ring to give her and she starts to weep. She says, "I would be honored to be engaged to engaged in purity with you." He tells her, "While we are apart these purity rings will be a semi-binding reminder of our limited commitment to each other."

Suddenly in the background there is a sound of laughter. A man comes to the table and says, "That's confusing! Cute, but also really dumb. When temptation hits, what are those rings going to do?" She jumps in with, "They are a symbol of our…" Suddenly you hear the sound of symbols ringing in her ears. The man tells her, "This is a symbol, honey. Those are finger decorations." He takes the rings and throws them in the grass. "What you need is an iron clad chastity safe guard. What we like to call a 'Purity Ring 3000'.

Symbols and promises are great if you are a cartoon monkey living in a coloring book in the 1600's but today in the real world what you need is something with a little more ump. The 'Purity Ring 3000' isn't just a ring, it's a fully automated personal chastity defense system. It comes embedded with a GPS tracker that lets someone keep tabs on you at all times. Example: Dad says, 'She's on the move', Mom says, 'It's nine AM, she's probably on her way to class.' As the dad runs to pick up his keys to track down his daughter.

"It is also pre-loaded with Abstin-incense, that is a laboratory scientifically formulated scent that is automatically emitted if too many pheromones of the opposite sex are detected in the air." Example: The daughter is sitting in class and a boy next to her starts to flirt with her. 'It's not me, it's the Purity Ring 3000.' As all the students in the class jump and run out of the room because of the smell that the ring emits. "When the ring detects an increase in heart rate due to inappropriate desire it triggers an ear-piercing alarm and a blinding strobe light.

If you are lecherous enough to make physical contact the 'Purity Ring 3000' immediately kills a fuzzy animal." Example: The man picks up the dead squirrel and asks the couple on the bench, "Is this what you wanted?" They slowly stop holding hands. Example: Another couple walks into an apartment. She sits on the bed waiting for her boyfriend. "If things get really bad, the 'Purity Ring 3000' kicks into full chastity lockdown mod. You get a pre-recorded video on the wall of your mother staring at you in disappointment. Try compromising your virtue with dear old mom looking back at you. Didn't think so."

So now we are back to the original couple that are now down on their knees looking for the rings that were thrown in the grass. "Why leave your honor and chastity to chance. Don't trust your virtue to a silly old-fashioned piece of scrap metal, trust it to the 'Purity Ring 3000'. Promises are nice, boundaries are great but if you really want to remain virtuous you need a ring that shoots lasers." Purity Ring 3000, Fully-automated personal chastity defense system.

Now how many of you wish it would be that easy to stay pure and live a righteous life? Just buy a ring and let it do the work for you! Not so! And this is what Paul is saying. Only you can do it. Only you make that deliberate choice, nobody's going to remind you about it, it's not going to be easy, there are no shortcuts, no gimmicks, it's a battle! I have to choose mentally, spiritually, every single day, to put on righteousness, not some fake ring reminder, and choose to be committed to Christ, like this girl.

COMMITTED TO CHRIST

"During the terrible Boxer Rebellion in China the insurgents captured a mission station, blocked all the gates but one, and before this placed a cross flat on the ground.

Then the word was passed to those inside that any who trampled the cross underfoot would be permitted their freedom and life, but that any refusing would be shot to death.

Terribly frightened, the first seven students trampled the cross under their feet and were allowed to go free.

But the eighth student, a young girl, refused to commit the sacrilegious act. (She was committed to God) So she knelt beside the cross in prayer for strength, then she arose, and moved carefully around the cross and went out to face the firing squad.

Strengthened by her example, every one of the remaining ninety-two students followed her to death."[9]

Now, that's commitment. And that's the commitment we need if we're going to experience the victory God's already given us over any and all attacks the enemy throws our way. The key is commitment to righteousness like that girl. There are no shortcuts, no gimmicks, it's a deliberate choice! We refuse to compromise with the world. We refuse to give in to their threats. We will not go along with their ungodly agenda. Rather we choose to uphold the cross of Christ, turn from this wicked world, and put on righteousness! That's the daily battle decision Paul is calling us to get committed to in order to stand against the wiles of the devil. This is serious! It's a battle not a game. And could it be this is the missing piece of the much-needed warfare, a commitment to righteousness and right-living, that we've all been searching for, but have been looking in all the wrong places, as this guy shares.

VICTORIES FROM RIGHTEOUSNESS

"Being committed to living a Holy life is simply the breastplate beloved, and I believe that somewhere along the line this is a forgotten commodity in the Church. You see, if you don't live a holy life, you lose.

You say, 'Well, what do you lose?' Number one, you're going to lose your joy. I'll promise you that. If you do not live a righteousness life, God withholds from you His blessing. First John says, "These things are written that your joy may be full." But the idea is they're written so that in obeying them your joy will be full. No obedience, no joy.

In fact, I'll tell you the reason why Christians are sad so often, and the reason they have sorrow in their lives is not because they need psychological counseling because they've got some kind of relational problem, it's just a lack of personal holiness. This is the bottom line.

And the Church today has pretty well ignored this, and we've substituted it with programs, seminars, and counseling. Listen, if you've got problems in your life, then the first place you need to look is at your own holiness. If you've got problems in your marriage, that's the first place to look. And I'll guarantee you right now if you're not living a holy life, you'll have problems, because God is withholding His blessing.

David knew it. When David was in sin and he said to the Lord, "Restore unto me the joy of thy salvation." I've got my salvation I just lost the joy. And it is a matter of a righteous life.

Christianity today is running around trying to tie on paper armor. It's like when you go to the restaurant with your little kids, and they put that little paper thing around their neck? I see that as the typical modern Christian breastplate. Absolutely useless.

It's made up of a system, or a program, a method. People come to us and say, 'You know, I'm having problems in my life, our family is having problems,' and we say, 'Well, what you need are about 10 or 12 sessions with a counselor.' And so, they put on the paper breastplate.

Now listen people! That is NOT what you need. You want to get rid of your problems? Then what you need is about 10 or 12 hours in the presence of God until you sort out the unholy characteristics in your life and get right with Him. That's what you need.

We don't need any more programs. We don't need any more methods. What we need is personal holiness in our lives. Put on the breastplate of righteousness. That's the bottom line."[10]

So, look at your own life. You've got problems in your family? Check your own holiness. Are you faithful in reading God's Word? Is your prayer life what it ought to be? Are you loving your family the way you should? Are you speaking for Jesus Christ unashamed in your society and your culture, wherever you are? Are you giving to the Lord what you ought to give sacrificially and taking care of the stewardship He's entrusted you? Are you living a righteous life in the manner God has outlined in His Word? Because if you're not, why would you expect your life to go well? If it did, then God would defeat his own purposes, right? He doesn't bless unrighteousness, He blesses righteousness, obedience to His Word. That's where we need to go. We need to get our armor on, folks. This is war, and we need to be committed like that girl in China and go down breathing our last breath saying, "Lord, I want to win this last battle. I don't want to lose." I'm committed! How do I know? Because I got the breastplate of righteousness on! Amen?

Its high time we the Church stop being ignorant of the devil's schemes. There's a war going on and it's not just abroad but its right here in our own country. It's a cosmic battle for the souls of men and women all around us. The stakes are high, and millions of lives are at risk. And if we're ever going to win this war then the American Church needs to once again shine for Jesus Christ. People, this is no time to be an Unprotected Christian! Wake up! The alarm has sounded. We are under attack, *the satanic War on the Christian.* Don't let the enemy get you! Amen?

Chapter Twenty-Six

Protection from Satan and Demons Part 6

"It started out just like any other sunny day in this tropical island paradise. The birds were singing, the trees were swaying, and the soothing sound of ocean waves blanketed the whole area. I mean, what could go wrong in such a beautiful location, right? Well, the answer came in a blink of an eye!

At precisely 12:53 p.m., on a Sunday, the mountain on this island erupted sending a cloud of gas and debris ultimately 50 miles into the air. And then soon after 4 more tremendous explosions were heard as far away as 3,000 miles and that was just the beginning.

The explosions not only plunged both nearby mountains straight into the sea, but it is estimated that this eruption was 10 times more powerful than Mount St. Helens and 13,000 times more explosive than the bomb that was dropped on Hiroshima. In fact, the sound from this eruption was so loud it was reported that if anyone was within 10 miles, they would have gone deaf.

And as you might expect, the damage was unbelievable! Thousands were killed by the hot volcanic gases, a wave it created went around the globe 3½ times, thousands more were killed by a devastating tsunami with a wall of water nearly 120 feet tall, nearby islands were completely overwhelmed, ships were destroyed, 165 coastal villages and towns were absolutely decimated, and people fought their neighbors just for a toehold on the cliffs.

And when all was said and done, the explosions hurled an estimated 11 cubic miles of debris into the air, it darkened skies up to 275 miles away, the immediate area didn't see the dawn for 3 days, ash fell as far away as nearly 4,000 miles, shock waves circled the planet 7 times, 120,000 people died with reports of groups of human skeletons found floating across the ocean washing up on other continents even a year after this eruption.

In fact, this eruption was so big that it actually caused temperatures to drop all over the world for the next 5 years.

The year was 1883. The disaster is of course, Krakatoa."[1]

How many of you have heard of the Eruption of Krakatoa before? Okay, I think most of us have. But how many of you guys would agree it was one of the greatest disasters of all time, right? But with all due respect to those who lost their lives in the Eruption of Krakatoa, what if I were to tell you I know of a disaster that makes Krakatoa look like a child's cough? And what if I were to tell you that this disaster didn't occur in just one place and one country at one time, but it's going on right now, today, all over the world and it's been leaving a trail of death and destruction for centuries. Folks, I'm talking once again about *the satanic War on the Christian.* We Christians don't battle here and there once in a while. We go to war, every single day. Whether you see it, feel it, believe it or not, the moment you got saved you entered a spiritual war against a demonic host whose sole purpose is to destroy you and extinguish your testimony for Jesus Christ.

What's wild is that most wars go on for a few years or even longer. But *the satanic War on the Christian* has been going on for the last 2,000 years non-stop and it's sending people straight into hell! And what's wild is most people will readily talk about all the other wars throughout history and all their atrocities, and rightly so, we have the History Channel, we need to talk about them! YET how many people, even Christians, will openly discuss the longest war in mankind's history, *the satanic War on the Christian* that has destroyed more lives than all the wars put together? Therefore, in order to stop getting duped and beat up all over the place, we're going to continue in our study, *The satanic War on the Christian.*

So far, we've seen if you're ever going to win a war, then the **1ˢᵗ thing** you must do is **Know Who Your Enemy Is**…

Then we saw the **2ⁿᵈ thing** you need to know is **What Your Enemy is Like**, their character, amen? It's common sense, right?

Then we saw the **3ʳᵈ thing** you need to know is **The Tactic of Your Enemy,** what they're up to, what's their goal, why are they here…

Then we saw the **4ᵗʰ thing** you need to know is **The Destruction of Your Enemy,** what price you pay when you DON'T take this seriously.

Then we saw the **5ᵗʰ thing** you need to know is **The Temptation of Your Enemy,** how he's out there trying to get us to sin against God….

And the **last five times** we saw the **6ᵗʰ thing** you need to know is **The Protection FROM Your Enemy**.

There we saw God has not left us hanging high and dry in this Great Cosmic War dealing with satan and demons. Are you kidding me? He's actually given us His full-blown protection and amazing weaponry to stand our ground and be victorious in all situations **every** single time! It's called The Armor of God!

We've seen the **1ˢᵗ thing** about the Armor of God that **It's Designed for War**.

The **2ⁿᵈ thing, It's Designed for Victory.**

And last time, the **3ʳᵈ thing, It's Designed for Wear**.

This armor is simply the supernatural equipment that God's given to us for our protection, not our fashion! It's not something to look at, it's not meant to just stare at, or stick on a shelf and collect dust. It's designed for wear. You wear it daily, you continually wear it. You put it on! And again, the Greek says to put it on now and leave it on! Quick! Chop, chop! Don't delay! This is serious stuff! Why? Because that's the second part of experiencing God's Victory that He's already given to us!

So far, we saw the **1ˢᵗ piece** we are to hurry up and put on for God's Victory is **The Belt of Truth**.

And last time the **2ⁿᵈ piece** was **The Breastplate of Righteousness**.

Just like the belt of the Roman soldier, so it is with the breastplate of the Roman soldier. It's not a literal belt or a literal breastplate that we put on, but it speaks of a literal breastplate worn by the Roman Soldiers to teach us a literal spiritual truth. It's called the breastplate of righteousness and it was Paul's way of telling us we need to put on practical righteousness or pure holy living every single day. Why? Because as we saw with the Roman Soldier's breastplate, practical righteousness also protects us from all angles from the enemy's attack of unrighteousness, that's how we counter him. And it can only be put on by me, nobody can make me decide to live a daily holy pure life as a Christian! I alone must make that daily commitment to be an instrument of righteousness or a holy weapon for God. Every day when I get out of bed I say, 'No I'm not going to be an instrument of wickedness or weapon for satan'. That's what I need to do if I'm going to experience the victory that God's already given to me and refrain from committing spiritual high treason against the Lord who bought me. That's what Paul is saying. But that's not all.

The **3rd piece** of Armor we need to hurry up and put on for God's Victory that He's already given to us is **The Shoes of Peace**. But don't take my word for it. Let's listen to God's.

Ephesians 6:10-15 "Finally, be strong in the Lord and in His mighty power. Put on the full armor of God so that you can take your stand against the devil's schemes. For our struggle is not against flesh and blood, but against the rulers, against the authorities, against the powers of this dark world and against the spiritual forces of evil in the heavenly realms. Therefore, put on the full armor of God, so that when the day of evil comes, you may be able to stand your ground, and after you have done everything, to stand. Stand firm then, with the belt of truth buckled around your waist, with the breastplate of righteousness in place, and with your feet fitted with the readiness that comes from the gospel of peace."

So here we see the third piece of supernatural military equipment that God gives us the ability to effectively struggle and come out on top in our war against the evil ones, when they come at us every single day, not if. This is the third piece that gives us the ability to stand our ground and not buckle or break under pressure when the dust clears from the battle that we're in. It was called the shoes of peace. So, the obvious big question is, "What in the world are these shoes of peace?" right? Well again as we saw before the Roman soldier's uniform & his weaponry speaks of a real reality, a real spiritual truth that we need to know today. It was symbolic of something, but the question is, "What is it symbolic of?"

Well, the **1st thing** we're going to see about The Shoes of Peace is that **It Keeps You from Stumbling**.

Once again, let's take a look at what this piece of armor was like for the Roman Soldier and find out what it literally means for us today.

ROMAN SOLDIER'S SHOES

"A Roman soldier's feet were fitted with a type of shoe that was known as the "Caligae" which in Latin means, "boots." Thus, Caligae were the heavy soled military boots worn by all ranks throughout the Roman Empire. No other shoes in history were as symbolic of the expansion of the Roman Empire as the famed Caligae.

Today they sort of resemble our modern-day sandals, but the Latin term referred to them as marching boots. Normal sandals were not worn outside by the Romans, but rather they were regarded as indoor footwear. Rather, these open-designed military boots were created in this way to allow for the free passage of air to the feet for comfort. If you were a soldier and walked with full gear up to 25 miles a day, you'd appreciate the sturdiness and coolness of the Caligae.

And unlike modern military boots, these Caligae were specifically designed to reduce the likelihood of blisters forming during these forced marches, as well as other disabling foot conditions like trench foot. Socks were not normally worn with Caligae, although in colder climates such as Britain, woolen socks were used.

Caligae were constructed from three layers of leather: an outsole, the middle layer which formed the boot's upper part, and an insole. They were laced up the center of the foot and onto the top of the ankle.

Another major difference between the Roman Caligae and our modern sandal is that the Caligae came fitted with iron hobnails that were hammered into the sole for added strength, similar to today's cleat. Thus, they provided great reinforcement and traction as well as an effective weapon against a fallen enemy."[2]

You see those spikes on there? They not only gave you great traction, but if your enemy fell on the ground you could stomp them with it! So even your shoes became a weapon! But as you can see, these Caligae, or Roman shoes, were the military boots of the day. And they not only provided comfort…but without these shoes you were toast! One guy puts it this way.

IMPORTANCE OF THE CALIGAE

"The soldier's life could depend on his shoes. Soldiers are required to march long distances, fight battles in all types of environments, walk through jungles,

over rocks, cross stream beds filled with sharp, jagged rocks, slog through the snow, and cross burning deserts.

If a soldier's feet become swollen, tender, cut, or blistered, that soldier would be greatly hindered in the day of battle. That soldier might not be able to stand and fight. He might not be able to march. He might not be able to properly handle his weapons. He certainly could not advance on the enemy.

Sore feet would undermine the soldier's ability to stand firm. The Roman soldier, the image Paul is using to illustrate 'the whole armor of God,' wore leather boots that protected the feet and ankles. These boots, called the 'caligae,' were a half boot that allowed the soldier to advance toward the enemy undistracted about what they might step on. This piece of the armor was essential to the Roman soldier's "preparation" for battle.

These boots usually had hobnailed soles, which means they had bits of metal, or nails, driven through them. These hobnailed soles gave the Roman soldier great traction as he climbed hills and fought on uneven terrain. The boots worn by the Roman soldier gave him great stability as he engaged the enemy.

If we are going to stand against 'the wiles of the devil,' we must have on the proper spiritual footwear. We can be 'girt about with the truth,' and we can have on 'the breastplate of righteousness,' but if we neglect to have our "feet shod with the preparation of the Gospel of peace," we are destined to stumble and fall."[3]

And that's the problem! We're focused on all the wrong footwear! We love shoes! We talk about shoes! We spend tons of money on shoes! In fact, as parents we'll freak out when our kids ask not just for shoes, but the $150 pair of shoes, right? Yet, adults, male and female alike will spend upwards to $200 on dress shoes or $400 on high heels. And some of you are saying that's nothing! In fact, men in the U.S. spent $26.2 billion on footwear in 2016, while women spent around $30 billion. We all love our shoes and will sacrifice and spend oodles of cash to get them. But we never get around to putting on our spiritual shoes that keeps us from stumbling, let alone finding out what they are for victory in our daily battle with satan and demons. The world has got us so focused on trying to be cool or fashionable with our natural shoes instead of focused on the most important shoes of all, our spiritual shoes.

And we wonder why we're stumbling, bumbling, falling all over the place as Christians! We're not taking it seriously! This is all part of our battle gear! We need to get these on our feet now! That's what the phrase implies, "And your feet shod with the preparation of the gospel of peace" Other translations say, "With your feet fitted with the readiness that comes from the gospel of peace." In other words, you're not pondering this over a cup of coffee considering whether or not you'll put this footwear on. You're not seeing if this will work on your schedule. There is no delay here! You're prepared! You're ready! Why? Just as this footwear, the Caligae, gave the Roman soldier great traction and protection and kept him from stumbling on the battlefield, so our shoes of peace do the same thing for us spiritually. Hurry up get them on as this guy tells us.

SHOES KEEP YOU FROM STUMBLING

"We all take shoes for granted, but they are a very important part of our apparel. We have different shoes for nearly every kind of activity. I have dress shoes, casual shoes, work shoes, and shoes that I wear when I go walking. I have lots of shoes. My wife has lots more shoes than I do. What I plan to do on a given day determines the type of shoes I put on.

I don't often think about my shoes, but I am grateful for them. They protect my feet from the dangers of walking around barefooted. They keep my feet warm, dry, and safe. I can't imagine going anywhere without them. Shoes are an important component of our wardrobe.

Now think about how important shoes are to certain professions. Construction workers would be crazy to try and do their job without proper footwear. Could you imagine a football player walking onto the field without his cleats? Could you see a baseball player doing that? What about a tennis player? No, it doesn't happen because athletes understand just how important the right shoes are to do what they do.

And just as important as shoes are to an athlete, a construction worker, a business man, a housewife, or even a toddler, they are even more important to a soldier, especially in war.

A Roman soldier wouldn't get in a battle with just a normal leather shoe with a slick bottom. He'd be slipping and sliding all over everyplace. He'd be trying to climb a rock to fight a guy, and he'd be slipping down the rock. And so, they had to have a special shoe, and it was very important, because in battle this shoe could very possibly save his life. Many wars have been lost because soldiers didn't have adequate shoes.

You've even read about times in the American Revolutionary War when you see the soldiers under General Washington with their feet being wrapped, because they could no longer have shoes, they were so worn out. There have been other points in human history where battles have been lost because they couldn't protect the feet of the soldiers from being frozen, or injured, or wounded.

And in the Roman wars, there was a common custom. Today we have mine fields to trap approaching armies. In those days, they would plant in the ground, sticks sharpened to a razor point, facing toward the army, hoping to pierce the feet of the advancing soldiers.

And so, in order to protect themselves, the Roman soldiers would wear a boot that had a heavy sole so that it couldn't be pierced, because if their feet were pierced they couldn't walk, and that could debilitate the entire soldier. He could be the best soldier there was, but if his feet were hurt, he's finished.

You can hurt your arm, your hands, your elbows, your shoulders, and still you can keep moving and function, but you hurt your feet, and you're done. You may be the strongest man alive, you may have the greatest sword there is, but if you can't stand up you're in real trouble.

And this is what Paul sees. He sees this Roman soldier standing there, and his feet are firm, and he's able to hold his ground, and make quick moves, and keep his feet. He doesn't slip, and he doesn't slide, and he doesn't fall.

Now he says to the Christian, 'You can get out there and you can have your waist all cinched up – boy, you're committed. And you can have your breastplate on, and you're living a godly righteous life as the Lord desires, but unless you can stand on your feet, you're going to fall over Christian, time and time again.'"[4]

In other words, there's urgency here. Your spiritual life depends on this. Get prepared, get fitted, don't delay, get the shoes of peace on now Christian soldier, because without them you're going to fail in the battle!

The **2ⁿᵈ thing** we see about The Shoes of Peace is that **It Can Only Be Put on By Me**.

Just as we saw with the Belt of Truth and last time with the Breastplate of Righteousness, so it is with the Shoes of Peace. I am the only one who can do this for me. The Greek says, "having sandaled your feet" other translations say "shod your feet" or "fit your feet" notice it's your feet! Nobody can put my shoes on for me. I alone need to do this. The word there "shod" or "fitted" is the Greek word "hupodeo" and it means, "to underbind, to bind under one's self." It's in the aorist middle participle which means "do it on your own accord." I can't hire a servant to put them on for me. I can't wait for my Mom and Dad to do it for me! The Pastor ain't going to do it for me! I have to do it! I don't need to have someone else make me feel guilty for not doing it. I do it because God says to and I see the utter importance of these shoes as with the rests of my armor and I know without all the armor including these shoes I'm toast in the day of battle! And notice it wasn't just any shoes, it was, "the shoes of the gospel of peace." And so the question is, "What is the Gospel of Peace and how do I put that on my feet?" Well, you have two options.

The **first option** is called the, **"Peace We Proclaim for Christ."**

In other words, this is referring to the "gospel" or the "good news" which is what the Greek word there, "Euaggelion" means. The "good news" that we are to proclaim to the lost that they can be saved and be at peace with God. And some draw that conclusion from other passages spoken of by Paul using a similar phrase.

Romans 10:13-15 "For everyone who calls on the name of the Lord will be saved. How, then, can they call on the one they have not believed in? And how can they believe in the one of whom they have not heard? And how can they hear without someone preaching to them? And how can they preach unless they are sent? As it is written, 'How beautiful are the feet of those who bring good news!'"

Well, there you have it! "the feet" that bring the "good news." This must be what Paul is talking about in Ephesians 6 with our "feet fitted" with the "gospel of peace." We share the Gospel with other people. We evangelize! Well, it sounds good, but personally I don't think that's the kind of "good news of peace" Paul is talking about. I say that because when it comes to sharing the

Gospel, we are commanded to go, and to go to the ends of the earth. However, the whole context of the passage here in Ephesians 6 with the armor is, with it we are to stand.

Ephesians 6:11 "Put on the full armor of God so that you can take your *stand* against the devil's schemes."

Ephesians 6:13 "Therefore put on the full armor of God, so that when the day of evil comes, you may be able to *stand* your ground, and after you have done everything, to *stand*."

Ephesians 6:14-15 "*Stand firm* then, with the belt of truth buckled around your waist, with the breastplate of righteousness in place, and with your feet fitted with the readiness that comes from the gospel of peace."

The whole context with the Armor of God is standing, not going. So, I don't think he's talking about sharing the Gospel with others here. However, I will say sharing the Gospel is a good thing to do and we are all called to do it, not only out of obedience to the Great Commission, not the Grand Suggestion. But in a sacrificial way which is precisely why it makes the feet, who do so, so beautiful in the first place, like this father did.

THE FATHER'S CHOICE

"After a few of the usual Sunday Church hymns, a Pastor stood up and walked over to the pulpit and gave a brief introduction of his friend. With that, an elderly man stepped up to the pulpit to speak.

He said, 'A father, his son and a friend of his son were sailing off the Pacific Coast, when a fast-approaching storm blocked any attempt to get back to the shore. The waves were so high, that even though the father was an experienced sailor he could not keep the boat upright, and the three were swept into the ocean.'

The old man hesitated for a moment, making eye contact with two teenagers who were, for the first time since the service began, looking somewhat interested in his story.

Copyright Trevor David Betts

He continued with his story, 'The father fought the wave and grabbed a rescue line. He had to make the most excruciating decision of his life: to which boy he would throw the other end of the life line. He only had seconds to make his decision. The father knew that his son was a Christian and he also knew that his son's friend was not. The agony of his decision could not be matched by the torrent of waves.

Again, the old man hesitated, bent his head while continuing his story. As the father yelled out, 'I LOVE YOU, SON', he threw out the life line to his son's friend. By the time the father had pulled his son's friend back to the capsized boat, his son had disappeared beneath the raging storm. His body was never recovered.

By this time, the two teenagers were sitting up straight in the pew, anxiously waiting for the next words to come out of the old man's mouth.

'The father', the old man continued with an emotion-clad voice, 'knew his son would step into eternity with Jesus and he could not bear the thought of his son's friend stepping into an eternity without Jesus. Therefore, he sacrificed his only son to save his son's friend.'

With that, the old man turned and sat back down in his chair as silence filled the Church.

As the Pastor again walked slowly to the pulpit to deliver his sermon, the two teenagers disrupted him and one of them said to the old man, 'That was a nice story, BUT I don't think it was very realistic for a father to give up his only son's life in hopes that the other boy would become a Christian.'

The old man got up from his seat, smiled and said softly to the teenagers, 'Well, you've got a point there; it sure isn't very true, is it? But I'm standing here today to tell you that the story gives me a glimpse of what it must have been like for GOD to give up His only Son for me.

You see, I was that father in the sea and your Pastor is my son's friend'

The two teenagers and the whole Church burst out in tears. "[5]

Why? Because, "How beautiful are the feet of those who bring good news!" Especially in such a sacrificial way!

Stuart Holden was in Egypt and met a sergeant in a Highland regiment. "How were you brought to Christ?" he asked this bright Christian.

"There was a private in the same company as myself who had been converted in Malta, and I gave him a terrible time. I remember one night in particular when it was very rainy, and he came in wet and weary from sentry duty. Yet, as usual, he still got down on his knees before going to bed. My boots were covered in mud and I threw them both at him and hit him twice on the head. He kept kneeling and praying.

The next morning when I woke up I found my boots beautifully cleaned and polished at my bedside. This was his reply to me and it broke my heart. That day I was brought to repentance."

And this is the problem. We love to talk about sharing the Gospel, we love hearing sacrificial stories like those two of sharing the Gospel, we even commend others when they actually share the Gospel... It's just that we ourselves, we don't share the Gospel and we end up like these people!

THE FISHLESS FISHERMEN

"I will make you fishers of men if you follow me.' This song is playing while we watch three men fish on the bank of the lake. A group of men are gathered together discussing fishing. "And it came to pass that there was a group of men who called themselves fishermen. Although the waters around them were full of fish, in fact the whole area where they lived were surrounded by streams and lakes full of fish.

Week after week, month after month and year after year, these who called themselves fishermen, met to talk about the abundance of fish everywhere. They

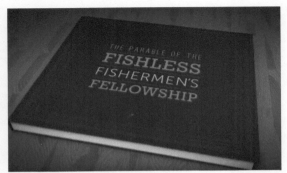

met to talk about their call to fish and how they might go about catching fish. Year after year in special meetings they carefully explained what fishing means and they outlined fishing as an occupation.

They declared that fishing is always the primary task of a fisherman! They were constantly looking for new and better ways to fish. They declared that the fishing industry exists only by fishing. They planned special get togethers called Fishermen's Retreat, and even established a month for their fishermen to fish.

They sponsored special fishermen's rallies and eventually included fishermen from all over the world in international seminars on fishing. Here they promoted fishing and discussed fishing, they heard about all the new fishing equipment and baits and the most attractive ways to display new lures to the hungry fish. These fishermen soon joined forces with others interested in promoting fishing.

They built large buildings where they could meet and teach new fishermen to fish and to improve their own skill by listening to what others had to say. The plea was that everyone should be a fisherman and that every fisherman should fish. One thing that they didn't do, however, was that they didn't fish.

All the fishermen seemed to agree that what was needed was a board that could challenge a fisherman to be faithful in fishing and to send out other fishermen to other places where there were many fish. This board was made up of those with great vision who could talk about fishing and promote fishing in faraway streams and lakes where many other fish of different colors lived.

The board hired staff members, appointed committees, and held many meetings to define fishing, to promote fishing, and to decide which new stream should be thought about but the staff and committee members did not fish. Over the years courses were offered on the needs of fish, the nature of fish, where to find fish, the psychological reaction of fish, how to approach and feed fish, and how to catch fish.

One guy says, "You just pop that thing in the water for a brief period of time and give it some quick jerks." Those who taught these courses had degrees in fishology. But the teachers did not fish. They only taught fishing. Some teachers and students alike spent much time in study and travel to learn the history of fishing.

They visited far off places where the founding fathers did great fishing in the early days of fishing and praised those who had handed down the idea of fishing. Presses were kept busy day and night making materials fully devoted to fishing methods equipment and programs to help meetings to talk about fishing.

Many responded who felt the call to be fishermen. They were commissioned and sent to fish but like the fishermen back home they never fished. Like the fishermen back home they engaged in all kinds of other occupations. They built power plants to pump water for the fish and brought in tractors to plow new waterways for the fish.

They established new centers to care for hurt and sick fish. Some said they wanted to be part of the fishing team, but they felt called to make and furnish fishing equipment. Others felt their job was to relate to the fish in a good way so that the fish would know the difference between good and bad fishermen.

Still others felt simply that letting the fish know that they were nice, land loving neighbors was enough. One man says, 'one day we really have to tell these people to go out and spread the word, but why don't we do it? Is it because we are afraid of failure, is it because we are afraid of being intimidated? Is it because we are afraid of rejection? I don't know why.

Why do we just look at this lake and not go fishing? Why? You are a prime example, you live on this lake. You are a fisherman and you don't fish. So, tell me why.' The answer back to him was, 'I guess I'm afraid of failure.' The first man says, 'Is that a fact? If you go with me, you won't fail. I've offered to take you fishing.'

After one stirring meeting on the necessity of fishing one young fellow left the meeting and went fishing. The next day he reported a very successful catch. He was honored for his success and was quickly scheduled to visit all the big meetings possible to tell how he did it. He was also placed on the board as the person who had considerable experience.

So, he quit his fishing in order to have time to tell his experience to other fishermen. Now it's true that many of the fishermen sacrificed and put up with all kinds of difficulties. Some lived near the water and bore the smell of dead fish each day. They received ridicule from those around them, beside them, going to fishermen's meetings and claiming to be fishermen yet never fishing.

Some of the fishermen wondered about their fellow fishermen that never attended the weekly meetings to talk about fishing. After all were they not following the One who said, 'Follow me and I will make you fishermen?' Imagine how hurt they were when one day it was suggested that those that didn't fish weren't really fishermen, no matter how much they claimed to be. Somehow it sounds great, is a person really a fisherman if he never really fishes? Is he following if he isn't fishing?"[6]

In other words, can he be a Christian if he never shares Christ? Which makes sense because how can you call yourself a follower of Christ if you don't follow in His footsteps and go fishing for men like He did? Sharing the Gospel with others so they can have peace with God through Jesus is not an option, it's a command. It's an order to be obeyed. It's the Great Commission not the Grand Suggestion. It's something for all of us to do, not think about, ponder, take a class and sit around. What makes the feet so beautiful is when we bring the good news of the Gospel, not elect a board to discover the economic viability of it! BUT, I still don't think that's the "good news of peace" that Paul is talking about here that we need to "fit our feet with" so we don't stumble.

The **second option**, and this is what I think he's talking about, is called the **Peace We Have with Christ**.

Now, the peace there in the Greek is, "eirene" and it means a couple things. First, it spoke of "the exemption from the rage and havoc of war," meaning that I am no longer at war with God, I am not His enemy, I'm His child, His beloved, and He will never cast me away. Why? Because I'm at peace with Him!

Romans 5:1,6,8-10 "Therefore, since we have been justified through faith, we have peace with God through our Lord Jesus Christ. You see, at just the right time, when we were still powerless, Christ died for the ungodly. But God demonstrates His own love for us in this: While we were still sinners, Christ died for us. Since we have now been justified by His blood, how much more shall we be saved from God's wrath through Him! For if, when we were God's enemies, we were reconciled to Him through the death of His Son, how much more, having been reconciled, shall we be saved through His life!"

Saved from what? From God's wrath! I was at war with Him but now I am at peace. "Eirene," Christ saved me from and gave me "the exemption from the rage and havoc of war," with God! The blood of Jesus saved me from being God's enemy and has now, made me a member of His family! Isn't that cool? That's the peace I believe he's talking about and that's precisely the kind of peace we need to walk around in life wearing on our feet wherever we go. Why? Because this is precisely where the enemy will strike! There will be times when you do fall on the battlefield. There will be times when you do blow it, when you do act like an enemy of God and you don't put on the breastplate of righteousness, you sin, you make a mistake and the enemy of our souls, the devil, will be right there trying to get you to think that God's mad at you, He doesn't love you, you don't have peace with Him, you lost it, He hates your guts for what you just did. When the whole time, it's a lie! God does loves you, you are His child, you're not His enemy, you're His Beloved and He's got your back! And when you fit your feet with this good news, with this peace with God, and realize He's got your back, you finally start to stand against your foe, with an incredible stature, like this kid did.

ROGER'S FIGHT

When I was in junior high in the 7th grade I had a little friend named Roger. Roger was a little guy. He looked like a 4th grader. He just hadn't really developed much. He was kind of pudgy. He looked like the Pillsbury man that you poke, you know? He was just puffy and cherubic.

Well, Roger was my little friend because I was the pastor's son, and he was in the Church too, and we were Sunday School buddies, and so, you know, we walked around this very rough junior high. I mean this was a really rough junior high. We had knife fights all the time, drugs, etc.

And me and Roger, we'd be walking along, and these bullies would come up, and hit the back of us, and knock all our books out, which we'd carry under our arms, and then they'd kick them. There'd be about six of them, and they'd just keep kicking them all down the walk, and into the bushes, and neither one of us could defend ourselves against that kind of stuff.

And so, this went on all the time, and this one kid named Johnny was the leader. Well, one day we were in the locker room, and we were just preparing to leave after gym class, and the gang came by. They thought they would be real cute. They elbowed us, and we went over the bench, and into the lockers, and hit the back of our heads.

So, there we were, laying on the floor, and Roger finally says, "That's enough." You can only take so much, right? Well, I said, "What are you going to do about it, Roger?" And he said, he was going to tell his brother. And I said, "Well, that's good."

His brother's name was Steve. I'll never forget him. Steve played middle linebacker for Long Beach State. Steve was 6'4", about 245 lbs, and had a 30-inch waist. And I'll never forget Steve because I remember the first time I heard him give his testimony. He was driving a bread truck, and he hit a concrete wall going 40, and walked away. That's the kind of guy he was; tremendous physical specimen.

Anyway, Roger said he's going to tell his brother, so I said, "Good, Roger." So, he came back the next day and he said, "Steve's coming to school tomorrow, and he's going to do something."

So, these guys all had an area by the gym where they'd come early every morning, and smoke, and sneak in pot, and everything. And they'd stand there, and wear out the grass, and just carry on their conversation; about six or so of them. They were always there.

So, this one day, Steve was there, only he stayed behind a building where they couldn't see. And it was about fifteen minutes before school, and Roger and I were just sort of hanging around, waiting to see what would happen.

Roger yelled, and he says, "Hey you," to this Johnny, "come here." And oh, they were laughing; they were really going to lay it on. So, this Johnny kid comes swaggering out. He had a police record. In fact, later on – it's kind of sad, you know – later on he actually wound up being killed in some kind of robbery or something.

But anyway, he came swaggering out, and he was laughing and mocking Roger. Just at that point, Steve walked around the corner of the building. And he walks up to Roger and he says, "Which one?" Roger says, "That one."

At which point, Steve walked over to this guy – I'll never forget it – this is exactly what happened. He just picked the guy up by the shirt, lifted him up, took his fist and knocked out four teeth with one shot. Just crushed his nose down, his two top teeth, and I don't know what all. And then he picked him up – and of course, the guy was out – he picked him up, and there was a big hedge in front of the wall of the gym. And he threw him over the hedge, against the wall, and down behind the bush. And then he said to the rest of the guys, "Don't you ever mess with Roger again," and he walked away.

You want to know what happened at our junior high? Roger ruled. No question about it. Roger ruled Junior High. You know why? Because Roger had resources.

You know, it's tremendous to know that Jesus Christ said, "I am not ashamed to call you my brothers." It's a great thing to know that He's on our side, amen?

The gospel of peace is the marvelous truth that in Christ we are now at peace with God and are one with Him. Therefore, when our feet are shod with the preparation of the gospel of peace, we stand in the confidence of God's love for us, His union with us, and His commitment to fight for us.

The believer who stands in the Lord's power need not fear any enemy, even satan himself. When he comes to attack us, our feet are rooted firmly on the solid ground of the gospel of peace, through which God changed from our enemy to our defender.

We, who were once His enemies are now His children, and our heavenly Father offers us His full resources to "be strong in the Lord, and in the strength of His might."

That's the confidence of having your feet shod with the preparation of the Gospel of peace."[7]

Well, that's just the first part. The **second thing** the word there is **peace**, in the Greek is, "eirene" and it means, "a state of tranquility, peace between individuals, security, harmony." It spoke of, "the tranquil state of a soul assured of its salvation through Christ, you're no longer afraid of death, you know where you're going." In other words, I'm forgiven, and my walk with Jesus is secure for all eternity. Therefore, no matter what happens I can keep on standing. I'm at peace with God! And this is another area satan will attack. When we fall or stumble on the battlefield he not only tries to get us to buy into the lie that we're enemies of God and He's turned His back on us, when He's right there fighting for us. But he then tries to demoralize us into thinking that we might as well just give up, lay down our weapons, quit, retreat, go AWOL, because we're nothing but a useless unqualified soldier who does nothing but make mistakes! But this is another reason for these "shoes of peace" that we are to "fit ourselves with." This is the "good news" we need to appropriate These shoes not only keep us from stumbling, but they keep us from going backwards.

SHOES KEEP YOU FROM GOING BACKWARD

"Josephus tells us of a Roman soldier, who, on one occasion, tried to run, and fell over on his back onto the stone ground, and he was dispatched from the Roman army. Why? Because you can't run in Roman soldier's shoes, they're not meant for running, they're meant for standing.

And there is also this thought: they're not for running away. When a Roman soldier saw that there was an enemy that was very large, he had to fight to the death because the shoes he was wearing couldn't take him away!

Now, we don't have to fight to the death and be worried about whether we'll win or not, the shoes of the gospel of peace can't run away because the Lord Jesus Christ who bought them with His blood can't be defeated!

In order to defend ourselves against the "flaming arrows of the evil one" (Ephesians 6:16), we must have confidence of our position in Christ. We must stand firm in the truth of God's Word, regardless of how terrifying the circumstances may be (1 John 5:14). We must understand grace without abusing it (Romans 6:1-6), remember that our position in Christ is not based on our own abilities or worthiness (Titus 3:5), and keep our belt of truth and breastplate of righteousness securely fastened (2 Timothy 1:12).

When satan stabs you from behind with "Remember what you did?" we dig in more deeply with our peace shoes in the turf of God's Word and reply, "It is written. 1 John 1:9 'If we confess our sins He is faithful and just to forgive our sins and to cleanse us from all unrighteousness.' I am at peace with God!

We have to appropriate that victory! We have to take the devil on, face-to-face, upon the victory of the Lord Jesus Christ at the cross - and that is the beginning of walking and standing in these shoes of the gospel of peace."[8]

In fact, speaking of 1 John 1:9, do you have any idea what it means when it says we ask God to forgive us? Let's break it down.

1 John 1:9 "If we confess our sins, He is faithful and just and will forgive us our sins and purify us from all unrighteousness."

The Greek word there for "forgive" is "aphiemi" and it means "to send away, to disregard, to abandon, to give up, leave behind, let go, to no longer discuss." This is in essence what we're asking God to do when we ask Him to "forgive" our sins. Not just forego the penalty for them, but in reality, "to no longer bring them up, don't ever discuss it, abandon it, let it go." And here's the "euanggelion" the "good news." Here's the "peace" factor. He will, and He does! "He will forgive us our sins and purify us from all unrighteousness." It's gone!

Micah 7:18,19 "Who is a God like you, who pardons sin and forgives the transgression. You will again have compassion on us; You will tread our sins underfoot and hurl all our iniquities into the depths of the sea."

Hebrews 8:12 "For I will forgive their wickedness and will remember their sins no more."

God's not going to bring it up again, it's abandoned, I'm not going to discuss it! What sin? In fact, God not only abandons our sins He obliterates them!

Isaiah 43:25 "I, even I, am He Who blots out your transgressions, for My own sake, and remembers your sins no more."

The Hebrew word there for "blot" as in "blot out our sins or transgressions" is the Hebrew word "machah" and it means, "to utterly wipe out, to destroy, to eliminate, to blot out, become invisible, disappear, obliterate and exterminates, it's gone! And this is why Paul says he obliterates his past!

Philippians 3:13 "But one thing I do: Forgetting what is behind and straining toward what is ahead."

The Greek word there for "forgetting" is "epilanthanomai" and it means "to forget, to no longer care for, to give over to oblivion." Paul says he too forgets the former things, his past, he obliterates it, he puts it into a state of oblivion, because of course, it's been obliterated by God! There's nothing there! It's gone! So, if God forgets it, SO AM I!!! But that's still not all. God not only abandons my sin, refusing to bring it up and then obliterates the whole thing till nothing's left, He then goes on and treats me as if I've never sinned! This is the other reason why I have peace with God through Jesus, because it's His blood that's made me blameless!

Ephesians 1:4 "For He chose us in Him before the creation of the world to be holy and blameless in His sight."

Ephesians 5:27 "And to present her to Himself as a radiant church, without stain or wrinkle or any other blemish, but holy and blameless."

Colossians 1:22 "But now He has reconciled you by Christ's physical body through death to present you holy in His sight, without blemish and free from accusation."

Jude 1:24 "To Him who is able to keep you from falling and to present you before His glorious presence without fault and with great joy."

The word there "blameless" in the Greek is the Greek word "amomos" it means a = without + momos = spot, literally without blemish morally, no fault, no flaw, no shame or disgrace (as a moral disgrace) I'm holy and pure. That's how God sees me because of the blood of Christ! That's why I'm at peace with Him! Isn't that good news! Doesn't that give you peace?

As one guys said, "Think of it, when the omniscient eye looks upon us, He will not find anything that to His immaculate holiness can be so much as a pimple or a mole on us. How incredible!"

People this is the incredible news. This is what Paul is trying to get through to us! Every single Christian is given the armor of God for one reason and one reason alone, to do battle against the enemy of our souls. The devil knows this. So, here's what he does. Since he can't take away the armor of God, he simply gets us to compromise and not use the armor of God, by getting us to doubt this wonderful Biblical truth that we have with God! all this peace! Yes, we're going to stumble, yes, we are going to make mistakes, here and there, as we learn to be a powerful soldier for Christ. But those mistakes or sins are abandoned, forgotten, obliterated by God, remembered no more! All God sees in us now is a blameless, faultless, beautiful, child that belongs to Him so get up and fight! These are the shoes we need to put on every day! Don't listen to the accuser who's trying to put you back under a false bondage, like this little boy learned.

REMEMBER THE DUCK

"There was a little boy visiting his grandparents and he was given his very first slingshot. Well, soon he was practicing in the woods, but he could never hit his target. And then he came back to Grandma's backyard, and he spied her pet duck. So, on an impulse he took aim and let it fly. The stone hit, and the duck fell dead.

So, the little boy panicked, and he desperately hid the dead duck in the woodpile, only to look up and see his sister watching. Sally, his sister, had seen it all, but she said nothing.

Then after lunch that day, Grandma said, 'Sally, let's wash the dishes.' But Sally said, 'Oh, Johnny told me he wanted to help in the kitchen today. Didn't you, Johnny?' And she whispered to him, 'Remember the duck!'
So, Johnny did the dishes.

Later Grandpa asked if the children wanted to go fishing, but Grandma said, 'I'm sorry, I need Sally to help make supper.' So, Sally smiled and said, 'That's all taken care of Grandma. Johnny wants to do it.' And again, she whispered, 'Remember the duck.'

So, Johnny stayed while Sally went fishing.

Then after several days of Johnny doing both his chores and Sally's chores, finally he couldn't stand it any longer. So, he confessed to his Grandma that he'd killed the duck.

And she said, "I know, Johnny," and gave him a hug, "I was standing at the
window and saw the whole thing. But because I love you, I forgave you. I
wondered how long you would let Sally make a slave of you."⁹

Folks, isn't that true? How many times do we listen to the accuser of sin,
feeling guilty and horrible, when Jesus has long since forgiven us of sin? This is
what His blood being spilled has done for us! Turn to somebody and say, "The
duck is dead and so is my accuser!" I am no longer a slave to sin! I don't have to
listen to you! I've been forgiven!!! Now folks, **is** that an amazing kind of love, or
what? I mean, stop and think about it. Put it in its context. Who in their right
mind would not only forgive those who sinned against you and hated your guts,
but get this, forgive you so completely that you will be presented to God the
Father as if you never sinned in the first place! When the accuser comes walking
around, you can tell him to shut up, I'm no longer a slave! I'm a son, I'm a
mighty soldier for Jesus! Isn't that awesome! People of God, whatever you do,
don't compromise by going window-shopping at the enemy's stores. Don't give
an ear to his lies about not being forgiven by God. Why? Because if you do,
you'll be tricked into thinking that God can't use you anymore. That you're not a
warrior, you're a failure. And the next thing you know, you'll stop fighting on
the battlefield of life when the whole time you are still a warrior for God.
So, people here me and here me loud and clear! If you're a Christian, you are a
mighty warrior for God so get up and fight! Don't give into the devils' lies!
Stand up you mighty warrior! Get back on the front lines! The Church of Jesus
Christ needs you!

Don't listen to the devil. Listen to your Savior! You have peace with
God! Put it on! All your sins have been forgiven, past, present, and future and
cast into the deepest sea to be remembered no more! So, get up and fight! It's
going to happen Christian. Not condoning it, just dealing with reality. You're
going to blow it. You're going to make a mistake. Nobody becomes a mighty
warrior in a day. It takes time. It takes time to learn how to wield your weapons.
But when you stumble, when you fall, when you get tricked into allowing a crack
in your breastplate of righteousness, or even flat out taking the whole thing off,
leaving yourself exposed to sin and unrighteousness, the enemy's there laughing
over you, mocking you and you feel like you're a total failure. You should just
give up, go back in a hole, retreat, stop serving Christ, run, hide, go AWOL,
listen to what Paul is saying! Put your shoes on! When the enemy comes
accusing, you don't have to go running. Just stand in the gospel of peace and
have a great day! Your sins are forgiven, forgotten, buried in the deepest sea,
obliterated, remembered no more. Get back up as a blameless, faultless, spotless,

one and stand for Jesus Christ! I wield my sword in the day of battle and when the enemy tries to point out my sin I just point Him to the Father who says, What Sin?

WHAT SIN?

It happened so long ago, I cried out for mercy back then, I pleaded the blood of Jesus and begged him to forgive my sin. But I still can't forget it. It just won't go away. So, I wept again. Lord wash my sin. But this is all He'd say, "What sin? What sin?" Well that's as far away as the East is from the West. "What sin? What sin?" It was gone the very minute you confessed. Buried in the sea of forgetfulness! The heaviest thing you'll carry is the load of guilt and shame. You were never meant to bear them, so let them go.

In Jesus name. Our God is slow to anger, quick to forgive our sins. So, let Him put them under the blood. Don't bring them up again! Cause He'll just say, "What sin? What sin?" That's as far away as the East is from the West. "What sin? What sin?" It was gone the very minute you confessed! Buried in the sea of forgetfulness! Oh Lord please deliver me from my accusing memory, nothing makes me weak this way, but when I hear you say, "What sin? What sin?" That's as far away as the East is from the West. "What sin? What sin?" It was gone the very minute you confessed! Buried in the sea of forgetfulness!

So, let's encourage each other with these words. Hold up your Bible and say, "Get your belt on…in other words…read your Bible! You're looking like a fool with your pants on the ground!" And two…stop drinking polluted water. Get the breastplate of righteousness on. You're grossing me out and getting puke on the floor… And three…get your shoes on…. you're limping around looking like a goober!" Amen?

Chapter Twenty-Seven

Protection from Satan and Demons Part 7

"It seemed like just an average ordinary existence in this agricultural country. Farmers planted their crops, people wove their wears, and herdsmen took care of their flocks. Everything seemed just fine in this agrarian society, but all that changed when the Communists moved in.

Over the next three years, due to their poor mishandling of natural disasters, failed government policies, and human mismanagement, millions of people wasted away like piles of dried twigs.

First, it began with food shortages, then came the rations, then came the full-blown starvation. People actually began to seek alternative food sources like grass, sawdust, leather, even seeds sifted from animal manure. In fact, thousands of peoples were forced to eat dirt, dogs, cats, rats, mice and even insects, dead or alive, until there were no more. Even the bark was stripped and eaten from the trees.

But that's when the malnutrition set in, which led to their bodies swelling, their birth rates plummeted, mental illness and hysteria skyrocketed, and suicide became commonplace. Millions of people killed themselves rather than having to face another day in this horrible wasteland.

And just when you thought it couldn't get any worse, many people even resorted to cannibalism. Nobody knows how often or how widely it occurred, but there were thousands of accounts of people eating human flesh and even exhuming the corpses of their neighbors and eating them just "to survive." The Zombie apocalypse became their reality.

And when all was said and done, some 47 million people died a horrible gruesome death and it became the worst manmade disaster of its kind.

The year was 1958-1961. The disaster is of course, The Great Chinese Famine."[1]

Now folks, how many of you have heard of the Great Chinese Famine before? Okay, some of us have. But how many of you guys would agree that it was one of the greatest disasters of all time? But with all due respect to those who lost their lives in the Great Chinese Famine, what if I were to tell you I know of a disaster that makes that Chinese Famine look like a child's stomachache? And what if I were to tell you that this disaster didn't occur in just one place and one country at one time, but it's going on right now, today, all over the world and it's been leaving a trail of death and destruction for centuries. Once again, I'm talking about the *satanic War on the Christian.* We Christians don't battle here and there once in a while. We go to war, every single day. Whether you see it, feel it, believe it or not, the moment you got saved you entered a spiritual war against a demonic host whose sole purpose is to destroy you and extinguish your testimony for Jesus Christ. And what's wild is that most wars go on for a few years or even longer. But *the satanic War on the Christian* has been going on for the last 2,000 years non-stop and it's sending people straight into hell! Yet how many people, even Christians, will openly discuss the longest war in mankind's history…*the satanic War on the Christian* that has destroyed more lives than all the wars put together? Therefore, in order to stop getting duped and beat up all over the place, we're going to continue in our study, *the satanic War on the Christian.*

Now, so far, we've seen, if you're ever going to win a war, then the **1st thing** you must do is **Know Who Your Enemy Is**…

Then we saw the **2ⁿᵈ thing** you need to know is **What Your Enemy is Like**, their character, amen? It's common sense, right?

Then we saw the **3ʳᵈ thing** you need to know is **The Tactic of Your Enemy**…what they're up to…what's their goal…. why are they here…

Then we saw the **4ᵗʰ thing** you need to know is **The Destruction of Your Enemy**…what price you pay when you DON'T take this seriously…

Then we saw the **5ᵗʰ thing** you need to know is **The Temptation of Your Enemy**…how he's out there trying to get us to sin against God….

And the **last six times** we saw the **6ᵗʰ thing** you need to know is **The Protection from Your Enemy**.

And there we saw God has not left us hanging high and dry in this Great Cosmic War dealing with satan and demons. Are you kidding me? He's actually given us His full-blown protection and amazing weaponry to stand our ground and be victorious in all situations every single time! It's called The Armor of God!

So far, we've seen the **1ˢᵗ thing** about the Armor of God that **It's Designed for War**.

The **2ⁿᵈ thing, It's Designed for Victory.**

The last three times the **3ʳᵈ thing, It's Designed for Wear.**

This armor is not something to look at, it's not meant just to stare at, or stick on a shelf and collect dust. It's designed for wear. You wear it daily, you continually wear it. YOU PUT IT ON! And again, the Greek says to put it on now and leave it on! Quick! Chop, chop! Don't delay! This is serious stuff! Why? Because that's the second part of experiencing God's Victory He's already given to us!

We saw the **1ˢᵗ piece** to hurry and put on for God's Victory, is **The Belt of Truth**.

The **2ⁿᵈ piece** was **The Breastplate of Righteousness**.

And last time the **3rd piece** was **The Shoes of Peace**.

Just like the belt and breastplate of the Roman soldier, so it is with the shoes or the "caligae." They weren't literal shoes or military boots that we put on…that's not what Paul is saying. Rather they speak of the literal spiritual shoes we put on. The shoes of peace were Paul's way of saying we need to put on the Peace we have with God through Jesus Christ and His death on the cross, to acknowledge that our sins are totally forgiven, obliterated, remembered no more. Why? Because as we saw with the Roman Soldier's real shoes, these spiritual shoes, the knowledge of the peace we have with God keeps us from stumbling spiritually and can only be put on by Me. I alone can acknowledge and appropriate God's wonderful good news of the peace I have with Him, through the forgiveness of all my sins, even to the point where He now considers me blameless and faultless and perfect. Why? Because this is where the enemy will strike! When you stumble, when you fall, when you get tricked into allowing a crack in your breastplate of righteousness, or even flat out taking the whole thing off, and leaving yourself exposed with sin and unrighteousness. The enemy's there laughing over you and mocking you and you feel like you're a total failure, he's accusing you and saying you should just give up and hide, go back in a hole, retreat, stop serving Christ, run, hide, go AWOL. Listen to what Paul is saying! *"PUT YOUR SHOES ON YOU MIGHTY WARRIOR OF GOD!"* When the enemy comes accusing, you don't have to go running! Just stand in the Gospel of peace we have with Jesus and keep fighting for Him! Amen That's what Paul is saying we need to do if we're going to experience the victory that God's already given to us and stop going AWOL in our walk with Jesus. Amen?

But that's not all. The **4th piece** of Armor we need to put on for God's Victory, that He's already given to us, is **The Shield of Faith**. But don't take my word for it. Let's listen to God's.

Ephesians 6:10-16 "Finally, be strong in the Lord and in His mighty power. Put on the full armor of God so that you can take your stand against the devil's schemes. For our struggle is not against flesh and blood, but against the rulers, against the authorities, against the powers of this dark world and against the spiritual forces of evil in the heavenly realms. Therefore, put on the full armor of God, so that when the day of evil comes, you may be able to stand your ground, and after you have done everything, to stand. Stand firm then, with the belt of truth buckled around your waist, with the breastplate of righteousness in place, and with your feet fitted with the readiness that comes from the gospel of peace.

In addition to all this, take up the shield of faith, with which you can extinguish all the flaming arrows of the evil one."

So here we see the fourth piece of supernatural military equipment, that God gives us, is the ability to effectively struggle and come out on top in our war against the evil ones, when they come at us every single day, not if. This is the fourth piece that gives us the ability to stand our ground, and not buckle or break under pressure when the dust clears, from the battle that we're in, it was called the shield of faith.

So that's the obvious big question, "What in the world is the Shield of Faith?" right? Well, again, as we saw before the Roman soldier's uniform & his weaponry speaks of a real reality, a real spiritual truth, that we need to know today. It's symbolic of something, but the question is, "What is it symbolic of?"

Well, the **1ˢᵗ thing** we're going to see about The Shield of Faith is that **It Protects the Whole Body**.

Once again, let's take a look at what that piece of armor was like for the Roman Soldier and find out what it literally means for us today.

ROMAN SOLDIER'S SHIELD

"A Roman soldier's shield was also known as the "thureos" which is derived from the word "thura" which literally means "door." In fact, some variants of the shield looked just like a large rectangular door.

Equipped with this size of a shield, the Roman Soldier was well suited to the tactical needs of the day, including border defense, skirmishes, and aerial attack. With its large rectangular shape, about 2½ feet wide and 4 feet long, it provided literal full body protection for the soldier.

The shield was made of wood and had a central spine as well as a metal strip boss. It was carried using a central handgrip and it was then covered with leather to make it flame retardant.

In fact, before a battle, in which flaming arrows might be shot at them, the soldiers would wet the leather covering of the "thureos" with water to extinguish the arrows. These "flaming darts" were sometimes set ablaze in order to set fire to the enemy's camp, or even their clothing preventing them from fighting.

And historians tell us that these "fire-arrows" sometimes carried a bulb filled with burning matter; or sometimes the point was merely wrapped in burning material. And it was against these flaming missiles that the Roman shield was "put up" to make its defense. And this was not done in passivity. It was said that the shield must be "taken up."

In fact, the Roman soldiers would then close ranks with these shields, the first row holding theirs edge to edge in front, with the rows behind them holding their shields above their heads. In this formation they were practically invulnerable to arrows, rocks, and even spears."[2]

In other words, everybody would be protected, the whole group of you, if each of you put up your shield at the same time working together. What a concept! But as you can see, this "thura," this shield, literally the size of a door, protected the whole body! And Paul says if you "take up" this shield just like the Roman soldier, you can, not maybe, not might, but you can extinguish all, not some, not most, of the what? The flaming arrows of the evil one. Is that good news or what? That's how important this fourth piece of spiritual equipment is. But notice it wasn't just a shield the size of a door, but what kind of shield? The shield of faith. It's the Greek word "pistis" which simply means "a conviction of the truth, i.e. God's truth, a belief or confidence in God, trusting in what He says." That's what faith or "pistis" means. When we say we have faith in God, we are literally saying I trust in what He says about my situation, my salvation, my circumstances, my needs, my hopes, my dreams, or in this case, my daily attacks against spiritual warfare! And Paul says when you put that "shield of faith up" when the enemy comes your way, you can extinguish all the flaming arrows of the evil one! In other words, you're invincible! One guy puts it this way.

IMPORTANCE OF THE SHIELD OF FAITH

"The Christian soldier's shield is simply faith, a faith in God's trustworthy Word and in the One Who is named Faithful and True, the Lord Jesus Christ. Such a faith firmly grounded on the Rock provides a sure defense against the fiery missiles of the evil one and his evil minions that are daily designed to hurt and harm the Christian.

Faith is an essential protection against these flaming arrows of temptation, or of doubt, or of fear, etc. Our unwavering belief in God's Word protects us from these harms. Where there is faith, there is nothing to fear.

And what is faith? Hebrews 11:1 "faith is being sure of what you hope for and certain of what you don't see." You're simply trusting God's Word no matter what things look like.

It is believing what God has said, for no other reason than that He has said it. It is taking God at His word. It is accepting His teaching, obeying His commands, heeding His warnings and laying hold of His promises. Where there is faith, defeat is unknown. Why? Because the Christian soldier who has it is never floored by anything. Faith makes us invincible."[3]

And that's the problem! We're not prepared to face the enemy and we're defeated all the time because the enemy has got us focused on all the wrong kind of protection! We talk about fire insurance, we have home insurance, car insurance, life insurance, we have home protection plans, smoke alarms, fire alarms, escape plans, you name it, we got it when it comes to protecting our homes! In fact, in some areas of our country people spend close to 20% of their annual income on different forms of insurance![4]

But Paul is saying you have to protect your walk with Jesus Christ! No wonder you turned into a burnt crispy critter, Christian! You have no protection. You're focused in the wrong area! You've left yourself vulnerable! You're not prepared for spiritual battle, for emergencies! No wonder you're walking around spiritually on fire all the time! You need to put up the shield of faith now, why? Because it protects the whole body! It makes sure you're totally spiritually protected. And without it, Paul says, just like the Roman Soldier, you're spiritually toast! You don't have any spiritual insurance plan in place!

The **2ⁿᵈ thing** we see about The Shield of Faith is that **It Can Only Be Taken Up by Me**.

Just as we saw with the Belt of Truth, the Breastplate of Righteousness, and last time, with the Shoes of Peace, so it is with the Shield of Faith. The consistent truth is this. I am the only one who can do this for me. And that's what Paul says, "take up." Again, it's the same phrase directed and used by the Roman Soldier, but it's the Greek word "analambano" and it meant, "to take up, to lift up in order to use (not stare at or ponder about later), to carry, to cause to go up." And again, it's in the Greek active voice that means, "Each believer has to make the choice to do this." That's what the verb tensing means. It means I can't do this for you. You have to do it for yourself. You have to lift up this shield of faith in the midst of the battle. You can't have another soldier do it for you. You can't wait for the artillery to show up. You can't send out a radio distress call! YOU HAVE TO DO IT! You have to place your faith in God and His Word in the midst of the temptation and thrust it up, the shield of faith, to keep yourself from going down in flames! Each believer must choose to believe God's Word, His goodness, no matter what happens when the enemy comes with his flaming arrows every day! He throws 50 arrows at you in a day, you thrust up the shield 50 times a day. He hits you with them 50 times in an hour. You raise up the shield 50 times an hour. And you don't stop because the enemy never stops! But listen to this bit of history.

"Soldiers often fought side by side with a solid wall (testudo) of shields. But even a single-handed combatant found himself sufficiently protected. After one particular siege, a soldier counted no less than 220 darts sticking into his shield."

The moment you put the shield down, you're toast! And that's what he's waiting for you to do! Either don't put the shield up, or wear you out, or wait until you goof off just one time, and bang! You're on fire and everything falls apart! And so that's the question, "How do you know when your shield is down? What's the acid test?" Simple! It's when you're like this guy.

HOW TO KNOW WHEN SHIELD IS DOWN

"A man named Thomas decided to become a monk and joined a monastery and took a vow of silence. The only exception to the vow was that, once every 10

years, the monks were allowed to make one statement then the silence must resume for another decade.

Well, after his first 10 years in the monastery, Thomas was called into the study of his superior, who said, 'Brother Thomas, do you have anything to say?'

And Thomas replied. 'The food is bad.' Then he went back to his duties.

A decade passed and again Thomas was summoned to the study of his superior and he said, 'Brother Thomas, do you have anything to say?'

And Thomas replied, 'The bed is hard.' Then he returned to his chores.

Another decade passed and again Thomas was called in before his superior who said, 'Brother Thomas, do you have anything to say?'

And Thomas replied, 'I quit.'

To which the superior replied, 'I'm not surprised. You've done nothing but complain ever since you got here!'"⁵

Friend, there is nothing clearer to indicate that we have succumbed to the schemes of the devil than when we complain about our lot in life. Again, and again, the Word of God shows us that the mark of a Christian who has learned how to be a Christian, a mature Christian, is one that rejoices in everything and gives thanks in all things. Now, this does not mean that God expects us to *enjoy* every circumstance in our lives! Nor does it mean that we should merely *pretend* to rejoice in everything. No! There is nothing ghastlier than a forced fake smile that people put on, or the superficial attitude they assume, in the midst of difficulties because they think it's the Christian thing to do. Rather, the truth of Scripture is that it is genuinely possible to rejoice even through our tears and pain, and there is nothing more that indicates that we have failed to understand what it means to be a Christian, than a whining, complaining, self-pitying attitude toward what happens to us. This is where the devil attacks. This is his nature. He gets us to think something unusual is happening to us. No one has ever gone through what we are going through. No one has had to undergo the depression of spirit we feel. But Paul says, 'No temptation has seized you except what is common to man. And God is faithful; He will not let you be tempted beyond what you can bear.' (1 Corinthians 10:13). He's given you His armor!

So, stop whining and complaining about what happens. Whining and complaining is simply distrusting God and His Word in action. It's a sign you're spiritually on fire, that you have no faith, and your shield is down! Instead of a fretful, peevish, whiny attitude, let us do what the Word of God says to do when these things occur: "Put on the full armor of God so that you can take your stand against the devil's schemes." There is no other way to handle the devil's attacks. There is no other solution to these basic human problems. What we've really done is tossed the shield aside when we are whining and complaining and are holding up a shield of our own vain and foolish imagination.[6]

In other words, it's time to do what the Captain of Star Trek does when under attack, don't whine and complain about being under attack, don't cry like a baby when the bombs are going off. Simply give the command, like he does, "Raise the Shields." And that's our problem. Instead "raising our shield" to ward off these flaming arrows of the evil one, we not only whine and complain about it, but we'd rather just talk about it, endlessly, like this lady.

NAIL IN THE HEAD

The Video opens with a girl talking with a painful look on her face. She is telling a male friend the following: "It's just, there is all this pressure, you know, and sometimes it feels like it's right upon me. And I can just feel it. I can literally feel it in my head. It's relentless, and I don't know if it's going to stop.

I mean that is what scares me the most. I don't know if it is ever going to stop." As she turns her head you can see a nail that is stuck in the middle of her forehead. The guy looks at her with a very serious expression. He takes a deep breath and says, "You do have a nail stuck in your head." She replies, "It's not about the nail."

He asks, "Are you sure? Because I bet if we got that out of there…" She is irritated now. She says, "Stop trying to fix it!" He says, "I'm not trying to fix it. I'm just pointing out that the nail is causing…" She replies, "You always do this! You always try to fix things when I just really need for you to listen!"

He answers, "I don't think that is really what you need. What you need is to get the nail…" She says, "See you're not listening to me now." He says, "Ok fine, I will listen to you, fine." She proceeds, "Sometimes it's this achy, I don't know what it is." He starts rolling his eyes but doesn't say anything.

She says, "I'm not sleeping very well at all. My sweaters are snagged. All of them." She turns to him, but he rolls his eyes, shakes his head and then says, "That sounds really hard." She replies, "It is, thank you." They lean in for a kiss and the nail bumps his head. She cries, "Oh! He says, "If you will only…" and she says, "DON'T!"[7]

Now, every man reading this, just secretly and silently said to himself, "My life is now complete Pastor Billy with that video. I can die in peace!" It explains a lot doesn't it? And, I share that not only to show what we guys go through ladies, when all you want to do is talk about your problems, instead of letting us fix your problems, get the nail out of your head, and that's a whole other topic. But I share it because I wonder if that's how God feels about us down here when it comes to dealing with the enemy's daily attacks. He's given us everything we need for victory, but instead of putting up the shield of faith, we whine or complain, or just talk about it endlessly and we wonder why we've got, not nails, but flaming arrows sticking out of our head and our back and torso and all over the place. God must be sitting there looking at us and saying, "WOULD YOU PLEASE PUT UP THE SHIELD OF FAITH? That's why I gave it to you!"

And that's what Paul is saying! When you put up this shield of faith, in the midst of your battle, Christian, every single time, not maybe, not might, but "you will be able to extinguish all the flaming arrows of the evil one." In other words, there's no reason to whine or complain, you don't need to endlessly talk about it. Just put up the shield of faith. And if you're on fire it's your fault for not "raising your shields." But it's not just a matter of raising your shield, it's making sure you're raising the shield of faith. It's the shield of faith not just the shield that you raise up to extinguish all the flaming arrows of the evil one. If you'll recall back to the description of the Roman Soldier's "thura" he dipped this door-sized shield in water. The water is what was needed to extinguish the flaming arrows and missiles coming at him. The shield didn't stop the arrows from coming at him, the shield that was dipped in water extinguished the arrows when they did come! And so, this tells us it's not enough to just have a shield and raise it when the arrows come, stop talking about it, stop whining about it, the question is, 'Have you soaked your shield in water." And I say this because this is where our faith comes from. The water of God's Word.

Ephesians 5:25-26 "Husbands, love your wives, just as Christ loved the Church and gave Himself up for her to make her holy, cleansing her by the washing with water through the Word."

Romans 10:17 "So then faith cometh by hearing, and hearing by the word of God."

If our shield is going to be dipped in water to extinguish all the flaming arrows of the evil one, like the Roman soldier, it's got to be dipped in the water through the word. Why? Because it's a shield of faith and "faith comes by hearing and hearing by the Word of God!" That's how we keep our shield wet, dipped, ready to go to extinguish anything that comes in our way. We're daily dipping it in the Word of God! Do you get it? Once again, the Bible, the Belt of Truth, is what holds all the rest of the armor in place! It's what ties everything together including the shield of faith! And that's our problem. Instead of dipping our shield of faith in God's Word every day to increase our faith and extinguish any arrow coming our way, we not only whine and complain about it, and endlessly talk about it, but we never dip it in God's Word. Oh, we got a shield alright, but it's one step away from being a flaming inferno. I've said it before and I'll say it again. Some Christian's Bible are so dry and dusty you could write the word "damnation" on it. And if all the Christians around the world would blow off the dust from the Bibles at the same time, you'd have the biggest dust storm in history! No wonder why we're dry crackly, crusty, crispy critter Christians! No wonder why one tiny little hit from a teensy-weensy flaming arrow from the enemy and we go up in smoke! We not only don't raise our shield, but the shield we have is a fire hazard! We're not dipping it in the water of God's Word! And this daily dipping and daily raising is important! This is why Paul says, "In addition to all this…" The Greek doesn't mean that this shield is more important that the other pieces of armor, as some translations may allude to. But rather, it means, "besides all these" or "with all these" meaning don't forget this shield, it's as important as the rest of the armor.

Again, that's why Paul put on the full armor of God. You need every piece of it including this shield. Why? Because the enemy is not just evil, he is the "evil one." It's the Greek word, "poneros" and as we've seen before, there are two Greek words for "evil" in the New Testament. One is "kakos" which means "bad or of corrupt character." An example of "kakos" would be a man who robs a store. His behavior is bad or "kakos." However, the second word for evil is "poneros." It implies much more than just being bad. An example would be of a man who robs a store and then gets caught while he's doing it. The police have him surrounded and there is no way of escape, but he refuses to come out. He knows he's a "dead man." So, what does he do? He starts killing as many people in the store as he can just to see how many he can take down with him. This is "poneros." This is the word used of the devil, he is the evil or "poneros" one. Which means every single day he's not just out to harm you but kill you Christian wake up! He wants to destroy you, extinguish your effectiveness for Jesus Christ, and Paul says he does the daily flaming arrow attacks! And so that's the question. "What does a daily attack of flaming arrows look like from the evil one, hoping to destroy or kill us? Simple, it looks like this.

HOW THE ENEMY THROWS FIERY DARTS

"When Satan came to Eve, what did he say? 'Did God really say?' Basically, don't you see there's something wrong with God? I'm the good guy, satan says, I'm telling you this is beautiful to eat, it's a delight to eat, you ought to have a right to eat it. And the fact that God doesn't allow you to eat that, tells you there's a flaw in Him. He's withholding something beautiful and something good

from you."

That's what Satan was doing with Eve. Those are the fiery darts. And what extinguishes them is faith. Believing that what God says, and that God's will be what's best for you. That's faith. Which means, when you sin, who do you believe? You're believing satan. You placed your faith in satan, not in God, and this is the mistake Eve made.

But it's not just in the Garden of Eden, you can hear those same flaming arrows at work even today. The enemy assaults us with temptations to immorality, hatred, envy, anger, covetousness, fear, despair, distrust, doubt, pride, and every other form of conceivable sin.

He is constantly trying to lead us astray with wrong thinking. We can't turn on the television without these "fiery missiles" bombarding our living room. We can't walk into the world without these thoughts bombarding our mind.

We live in a world that is controlled by the devil and thus in many forms (television, billboards, internet, media, magazines, etc) he is capable of continually bombarding us with a wide variety of temptations ("I'm not as attractive as that actor", "I'm not as rich as that man", "I'm not satisfied with my marriage.", "I deserve _____.", etc, etc).

That's why we must take up the shield of faith and stop cavorting with the enemy!

And yet many professing believers do just that! They know that satan and the demons are gunning for them, and yet they often stroll into enemy territory as if they were taking a walk in the park. They watch movies and TV programs that pollute their minds with filth.

They go to Las Vegas to gamble and watch sensuous dancers and listen to filthy-mouthed comedians. They sneak in a little pornography when they think the coast is clear. But that's like inviting an armed enemy into your home! The evil one is shooting flaming arrows at you! Watch out!

He knows we all have lusts within us which are easy to ignite. All that is needed is the tiniest flame and we are a roaring fire. So, we are assaulted with flaming arrows of sensuality, foul, diseased shafts of degrading passions, smoking arrows of materialism. And we burn so easily!

And one of our biggest mistakes is that we don't extinguish that dart immediately, by faith, with the shield of faith...

And as the arrows fly toward us, we pause and start to rationalize, "If God didn't want me to have this, then why did he make me with such a desire for this thing, this person, this pleasure? My neighbor has it. He does it. And he is doing so well..."

Then we start to justify it! We marry a lost person and try to justify it by talking about how much we love the other person. We gossip, and we justify it by talking about how concerned we are about the person. We do ten thousand other things and try to justify them in countless ways.

And God says, "Don't do it and satan says, "Do it, do it, do it." Who did you believe? God or satan? That's the bottom line, people; it's so simple. When you sin, you believe satan; when you obey, you believe God.

And the act of saying no to sin and no to satan and his flaming arrows is putting up the shield of faith. It is the act of believing God's Word that the shield flies up and the arrows fall to ashes. The only way to quench the darts of the devil is to believe in God and His Word and what he says about life.

Don't make the same mistake Eve did."[8]

I want to make sure we don't make the same mistake Eve did. I want us to practically see how we raise the shield of faith every day, so we don't get set on fire and experience defeat, amen? Let's see how we extinguish all "the flaming arrows of the evil one" not living a life walking around, screaming, whining, complaining, being on fire all the time! As one guy says, "We cannot stop satan from throwing the darts, but we can keep them from starting a fire." And you do that with counteracting with God's Word. This is the shield of faith in action. It is putting our faith in God's Word and obeying what He says about life. That's what extinguishes all the flaming arrows of the evil one. It's not just in having faith in God's Word, it's obeying God's Word, "putting" your shield up." You're doing something with it. You're not just staring at it! But if you do this, Paul says you win every single time! For instance, maybe the enemy is trying to flood your mind with illicit sexual images. What do you do? Shields up! I put my faith in God's word and obey what it says.

Psalm 101:3 "I will set no wicked thing before mine eyes: I hate the work of them that turn aside; it shall not cleave to me."

It fizzles out and goes away! Or maybe you come across some immoral content on TV, what do you do? Shields up! Faith in God's Word obey what it says…

Matthew 6:22-23 "The eye is the lamp of the body. If your eyes are good, your whole body will be full of light. But if your eyes are bad, your whole body will be full of darkness. If then the light within you is darkness, how great is that darkness."

I shut it off and the flame goes away! Notice I knew what to do and how to put the flame out because I knew God's Word, I had previously dipped my shield in it! Or maybe you're just simply driving down the road and there's some filth on a billboard. What do you do? Shields up! Faith in God's Word. DO what it says.

1 Corinthians 6:18,20 "Flee from sexual immorality. All other sins a man commits are outside his body, but he who sins sexually sins against his own body. Honor God with your body."

Turn your head, flame goes out, have a nice day! I keep my faith dipped in God's Word. It shields me every single time, as I obey it the flames fizzle out, all of them! This is what extinguishes all the flaming arrows of the evil one! Your shield of faith is dipped in God's Word! You do what it says, and it puts out all the enemy's flaming temptations, every single time! Isn't that awesome! And so, if you're sick and tired of being on fire all the time, stop listening to satan and start listening to God. Dip your shield of faith in His Word, obey it and enjoy His victory. It's that simple!

"When satan fires his flaming arrows, you need an impregnable shield, one that isn't flammable, one that can put out fires. Faith is that shield and God promises that shield for every Christian. It "can extinguish all the flaming arrows of the evil one" not a possibility, but a certainty.

And why is this shield so strong? Because God is strong, and when your faith is in Him and His Word, He becomes your shield, and you never lose because God never loses!

So, raise that shield of faith Christian! Put your faith in God! Reject all the insidious lies that burst into flames into your mind and trust in Christ. Trust him wholly. Trust him always. Trust him more and more. Go to him today and enjoy His victory!"[9]

Chapter Twenty-Eight

The Protection from Satan and Demons Part 8

"The skies were blue, the mountain views were breathtaking, and the sound of ocean waves soothed your troubled soul on the island paradise. But all that was changed with a sudden jolt.

At precisely 4:53 PM a massive earthquake struck this once peaceful location and turned it into an island of doom. Due to a lack of building codes and regulations, the infrastructure actually began to collapse. Some 250,000 residences, 30,000 commercial buildings, 4,000 schools and 50 health care facilities were

totally destroyed. And many more such structures were disintegrated under the force of this jolt, instantly killing or trapping their occupants.

Then, because many hospitals had been rendered unusable, survivors were forced to wait days for treatment with the morgues quickly reaching their capacity, totally overwhelmed with tens of thousands of bodies flooded their facilities, so the corpses were stacked in the streets. But soon the streets became too full of dead bodies, so they simply resorted to disposing them into mass graves.

Then to make matters worse, the looting and violence began, not only from the local population, but from several thousand prisoners escaping from a damaged penitentiary. Orphans were then created by all these mass mortalities which left them walking around parentless which left them vulnerable to abuse and even human trafficking.

And just when you though it couldn't get worse, cholera broke out causing 770,000 people to get sick, thousands more to die, and even two years after this event, more than half a million people were still living in tents which had now totally been deteriorated over the last two years of use.

And when all was said and done, this once vibrant country was in ruins. It caused nearly 13.5 billion dollars in damage, nearly 1.5 million people were displaced and over one million people were left homeless, and 316,000 people dying from this single event.

The year was 2010. The disaster is of course, The Haiti Earthquake."[1]

How many of you have heard of the 2010 Haitian Earthquake? Okay, most of us have. But how many of you would agree it was one of the greatest disasters of all time, right? But with all due respect to those who lost their lives in the Haiti Earthquake, what if I were to tell you I know of a disaster that makes earthquake look like a minor toothache? And what if I were to tell you that this disaster didn't occur in just one place and one country at one time, but it's going on right now today all over the world and it's been leaving a trail of death and destruction for centuries. I'm talking once again about *the satanic War on the* Christian.

And these are the facts. We Christians don't battle here and there once in a while. We go to war, every single day. Whether you see it, feel it, believe it or not, the moment you got saved you entered a spiritual war against a demonic host whose sole purpose is to destroy you and extinguish your testimony for Jesus

Christ. And what's wild is that most wars go on for a few years or even longer. But *the satanic War on the Christian* has been going on for the last 2,000 years non-stop and it's sending people straight to hell! How many people, even Christians, will openly discuss the longest war in mankind's history…*the satanic War on the Christian* that has destroyed more lives than all the other wars put together? Therefore, in order to stop getting duped and beat up all over the place, we're going to continue in our study, *the satanic War on the Christian.*

Now so far, we've seen if you're ever going to win a war, then the **1st thing** you must do is **Know Who Your Enemy Is**…

Then we saw the **2nd thing** you need to know is **What Your Enemy is Like**, their character, amen? It's common sense, right?

Then we saw the **3rd thing** you need to know is **The Tactic of Your Enemy**…what they're up to…what's their goal….why are they here…

Then we saw the **4th thing** you need to know is **The Destruction of Your Enemy**…what price you pay when you DON'T take this seriously…

Then we saw the **5th thing** you need to know is **The Temptation of Your Enemy**…how he's out there trying to get us to sin against God….

And the **last seven times** we saw the **6th thing** you need to know is **The Protection FROM Your Enemy**.

There we saw God has not left us hanging high and dry in this Great Cosmic War dealing with satan and demons. Are you kidding me? He's actually given us His full-blown protection and amazing weaponry to stand our ground and be victorious in all situations every single time! It's called The Armor of God!

We've seen the **1st thing** about the Armor of God that **It's Designed for War**.

The **2nd thing, It's Designed for Victory**.

And the last three times the **3rd thing, It's Designed for Wear**.

This armor is not something to look at, it's not meant just to stare at, or stick on a shelf and collect dust. It's designed for wear. You daily wear it, you continually wear it. You put it on! And again, the Greek says to put it on now and leave it on! Quick! Chop, chop! Don't delay! This is serious stuff! Why? Because that's the second part of experiencing God's victory He's already given to us!

And so far, we saw the **1ˢᵗ piece** we are to hurry up and put on for God's Victory is **The Belt of Truth**.

The **2ⁿᵈ piece** was **The Breastplate of Righteousness**.

The **3ʳᵈ piece** was **The Shoes of Peace**.

And last time the **4ᵗʰ piece** was **The Shield of Faith**.

And there we saw, just like the belt and the breastplate and the shoes of the Roman soldier, so it is with the shield. It wasn't a literal shield that we carry around with us, that's not what Paul is saying. Rather he's speaking of a literal spiritual shield we take up to defend ourselves. The shield of faith was Paul's way of saying we need to take up faith in God's Word and obey what it says when the enemy comes at us with his flaming arrows of doubt or fear, or temptation, etc. Why?

As we saw with the Roman Soldier's shield, It Protects the Whole **Body** and it Can Only Be Taken Up by Me, nobody can raise the shield for me, I alone have to give the command like Star Trek, "Raise the Shields." WHY? Because when I do, the shield of faith is what extinguishes all the flaming arrows of the evil one. But the question is, "Are you dipping the shield into God's Word every day keeping it nice and wet to extinguish the arrows?" Are you walking around being a dry, crusty, crispy, critter Christian with a flammable cardboard shield being set on fire wherever you go? The good news Paul is saying is, it doesn't have to be that way if you would just "take up" the shield of faith. It works every time! But that's not all.

The **5ᵗʰ piece** of Armor we need to hurry up and put on for God's Victory that He's already given to us is **The Helmet of Salvation**. But don't take my word for it. Let's listen to God's.

Ephesians 6:10-17a "Finally, be strong in the Lord and in His mighty power. Put on the full armor of God so that you can take your stand against the devil's schemes. For our struggle is not against flesh and blood, but against the rulers, against the authorities, against the powers of this dark world and against the spiritual forces of evil in the heavenly realms. Therefore, put on the full armor of God, so that when the day of evil comes, you may be able to stand your ground, and after you have done everything, to stand. Stand firm then, with the belt of truth buckled around your waist, with the breastplate of righteousness in place, and with your feet fitted with the readiness that comes from the gospel of peace. In addition to all this, take up the shield of faith, with which you can extinguish all the flaming arrows of the evil one. Take the helmet of salvation." So here again we see the fifth piece of supernatural military equipment that God gives us, the ability to effectively struggle and come out on top in our war against the evil ones, when they come at us every single day, not if.

This is the **fifth piece** that gives us the ability to stand our ground and not buckle or break under pressure when the dust clears from the battle that we're in, it was called **the helmet of salvation**.

And that's the obvious big question, "What in the world is the Helmet of Salvation?" right? Well again as we saw before the Roman soldier's uniform & his weaponry speaks of a real reality, a real spiritual truth that we need to know today. It was symbolic of something, but the question is, "What is it symbolic of?"

The **1st thing** we're going to see about The Helmet of Salvation is that **It Protects Your Head from Serious Injury**.

Once again, let's take a look at what that this piece of armor was like for the Roman Soldier and find out what it literally means for us today.

ROMAN SOLDIER'S HELMET

"A Roman soldier's head was adorned with a specialized helmet called the "galea" or the "cassis." These helmets varied in form. Some gladiators sported a bronze version of the helmet with a face mask and a decoration and a fish on its crest. Other helmets used by the legionnaires had crests on them made of plumes of horse hair to increase their apparent size just to strike terror into the heart of the enemy. While these plumes are usually shown in red they probably also occurred in other colors as well, like yellow, purple and black, or a combination of these colors.

The exact form or design of the Roman helmet varied significantly over time, but they were typically made up of two types: the "galea" (made of leather) or the "cassis" (made of metal).

These helmets had a band to protect the forehead and plates for the cheeks that also extended down in back to protect the neck as well. They typically were furnished with a visor to protect the face and once the helmet was strapped into place, it exposed little besides the eyes, nose, and mouth.

These helmets were typically hot and uncomfortable and would only be put on by a soldier when he faced impending danger. This is why no soldier's uniform was complete without a proper helmet. A Roman soldier who lost his helmet was in danger of receiving severe head wounds which would at the very least, disorient him and render him ineffective and in danger of further injury.

In fact, a Roman soldier would be foolish to enter a battle without his helmet on. He knew that the helmet would protect his head from arrows as well as ward off blows from the enemy's broadsword that was three to four-feet long with a massive handle that was held with both hands like a baseball bat. They would lift it over their heads to bring down upon an opponent's head dealing a crushing blow to the skull. The helmet on one's head was the only way to deflect this crushing death blow. In fact, an archaeological dig discovered a skeleton with a cleavage right through the skull, indicating that this fatal wound was quite likely made by someone who attacked the person with a broadsword and who didn't have their helmet on.[2]

And as I said last week, he ended up with a split personality! But seriously, as you can see, the Roman helmet was a vital piece of armor. Without it, you were in some serious danger on the battlefield! Why? Because it's common sense! The head is a vital area of the body! You can take a hit in the arm, get whacked in the leg, get an arrow in your shoulder, and yeah it hurts, but you can generally keep on fighting? But the head? You get whacked in the head, especially with a sword, you're done!

IMPORTANCE OF THE HELMET

"A Roman soldier would be foolish to enter a battle without his helmet on. He knew the helmet alone was designed to protect his head from the many fatal blows headed his way in battle.

And so, it is with the Christian. Beloved, please do not leave home today without your helmet on. In fact, don't ever take it off. Not even when you go to sleep (even spiritually!) because the helmet of salvation is part of the full armor, not an accessory to be added on later. You need it now! Why? Because imagine going into a battle where the enemy is so numerous you can't even count them.

On top of that, they are totally invisible. You can't even see them. The deadly weapons they hurl at us are all packaged into something as innocent as a thought, and we've got to deal with this every moment of our life. Satan has influenced and infected this world. Darkness is all around us. As a result, he seeks to take our minds. The battlefield is the mind, and he seeks to lead us astray from the truth of God's Word.

So, God gives us the helmet to protect our head from the enemy's attacks. So why does the enemy go for the head? Because your head is a very important part of your body. It contains your brain, which controls everything. Your head determines how you think about all of life. How you think in large part determines how you feel and how you act. To put on the helmet of salvation requires that you learn to think biblically about the world and its views. You must develop a Christian mind, a saved mind.

Your head determines how you function in all of life. If your brain is not working properly, it affects how other parts of your body work. A brain injury can affect motor skills or the ability to speak or think clearly. If a soldier got knocked unconscious by a blow to the head, he was probably doomed. He had to guard his head by having his helmet securely in place.

So, when Paul tells us to take the helmet of salvation, he is saying, "Don't go into the world with your head unprotected. Mind thy head!" It determines how you think, how you function in all of life, and how you relate to people.

As someone said, "Watch your thoughts, they become words; watch your words, they become actions; watch your actions, they become habits; watch your habits, they become character; watch your character, for it becomes your destiny."

The helmet protects all this…Someone has said, "What you think means more than anything else in your life. More than what you earn, more than where you live, more than your social position, and more than what anyone else may think about you." Why? Because what you think determines your behavior.

And God commands us to receive the helmet of salvation to protect how we think about the many worldly ideas that bombard us daily. You thinking that is protected by the helmet of salvation will enable you to live rightly before God and the right relation to others. So, mind thy head! Amen? Don't go out into the battlefront of the world without your helmet on! Stand firm against the enemy by taking the helmet of salvation!"[3]

And that's the problem! We're not prepared to face the battlefield in our minds against the enemy because we're all focused on the wrong kind of headgear! We're more concerned about the helmet of man than the helmet of God! Think about it! We will have a conniption fit if we see our child out on the street without a helmet on while riding their bike! It's against the law! We'll have a premature heart attack if we see another kid with roller blades on but no helmet! Why, I'm going to call their Mom! What kind of parent would do that! Don't they realize the risk they're taking! In fact, we even have laws to force people to wear a helmet! Remember the days when you didn't need a helmet for anything, including riding a motorcycle? Some of you young whippersnappers, yes, life was good back then! In fact, the only protection I had growing up in the front seat of the car, yes, I rode in the front seat of the car, was my mom's forearm keeping me from flying through the windshield, we didn't need seatbelts! Remember that? But not anymore! You have to have a helmet on wherever you go, even in sports! What's the big deal going on right now in the NFL? Concussions! They even made a big movie about it with Will Smith. You can't just have a helmet on, you have to have one that will prevent any kind of injury at any time lest you get some serious brain trauma! In fact, the NFL recently spent 100 million dollars just on Concussion Research.[4]

And then, when it comes to bike equipment, we spend nearly $14 billion annually on bike equipment, which of course includes helmets. Apparently, we are convinced, that without these physical helmets we're all going to die![5]

But Paul is saying, "How much more should we be serious about our spiritual helmet that protects us from the daily trauma against the evil one? Come on! Mind your head, like this guy shares.

MIND THY HEAD

"I don't remember where it was, but I was about to go down a stairway that had a low entrance. Above it was a sign that read, "Mind Thy Head!" It meant, "Look out or you will hit your head!"

As I ride my bike around town and notice other bike riders, I'm amazed at how many people ride bicycles in city traffic, but they're not wearing helmets to protect their heads. I once read an article about a medical doctor who went for a short bike ride around her neighborhood, without a helmet on. I don't remember whether a car hit her, or she hit a curb or what, but she was thrown from her bike and suffered a serious head injury. She had to give up her medical practice because of that injury, which could have been prevented if she had been wearing a helmet. Mind thy head!

I'm also amazed at how many Christians do not mind their heads. They swim in the currents of worldly ideas and entertainment without developing a Christian mind. They're oblivious to the godless philosophic assumptions that underlie worldly thinking. They buy into the postmodern idea that there is no such thing as knowable, absolute truth in the spiritual or moral realms.

These careless Christians ignore, or sometimes even ridicule, the need for sound doctrine. They want experience, not doctrine. They want good feelings, not careful thinking. Because they do not mind their heads, they are not transformed by the renewing of their minds. Rather, they are conformed to this evil world. But God gives us the helmet of salvation so that we will mind our heads:

WHY? Because how you think determines how you feel and how you act. For example, if you're an angry person, it is (to put it bluntly) because you are thinking selfishly. You think, "I have my rights! I'm not going to let that person treat me that way! I want my way!" Angry people think that the world owes them something. How they think determines how they feel about life and how they act. In the worst cases, they injure or kill others to get what they want. But it all stems from their thinking

How you think determines your worldview. A person with a postmodern worldview does not believe in moral absolutes. They do not think anything is absolutely evil. They do not believe in judging the behavior of others as wrong. Maybe homosexuality is not their thing, but who are they to say that it is wrong? That would be intolerant and judgmental, which are the only absolutely wrong attitudes for a postmodernist! Many young people are even hesitant to say that the Holocaust was morally evil. They don't like it, but they won't come out and say that it was evil for Hitler to kill six million Jews!

The point is, your head determines how you think about all of life. To put on the helmet of salvation requires that you learn to think biblically about worldviews. You must develop a Christian mind, a saved mind. You must Mind thy head!"[6]

In other words, don't leave home without your helmet on! Pay attention to your thought life. Don't ever take that awareness off! But that's our problem. We spend billions of dollars every year on physical helmets, but we never get around to putting on our spiritual helmet given by God for free, to protect our heads from thinking wrong. Why? Because wrong thinking leads to wrong behavior! This is precisely where the enemy will strike every single day! He knows what he's doing! Mind your head Christian! Get your helmet on!

The **2nd thing** we see about The Helmet of Salvation is that **It Can Only Be Put on By Me**.

Again, we're seeing a consistent pattern here. Just as we saw with the Belt of Truth, the Breastplate of Righteousness, the Shoes of Peace and last time with the Shield of Faith, so it is with the Helmet of Salvation. I am the only one who can "take it," God's headgear, for protection for my mind and put it on! I can't wait for the NFL to get done with their concussion study. I can't have my mommy or daddy put it on for me! I can't rely on the crossing guard to give me the guilty evil eye for not having it on! I have to "take it" and do it. "Take" as in "take the helmet of salvation" is from the Greek word, "dechomai" which means, "to accept deliberately, to receive readily." It's also in the aorist imperative and it implies, listen, "an urgent command to do this now!" Don't delay! Receive or accept, take the helmet of salvation from God right now so your head can be protected! That's really what's going on here in this short verse! And notice it wasn't just any helmet, it was, "the helmet of salvation." And so that's the question is, "What is the Helmet of Salvation and how do I put that on my head right now?" Well, most people believe it refers to two parts of our salvation.

The **first part** is referred to the, "**Salvation We Have for All Eternity.**"

In other words, one we're saved, praise God, we're saved forever! Amen? We have an eternal salvation that's eternally secure! I didn't say that. God did! I'll just give you a couple verses just from John.

John 5:24 "I tell you the truth, whoever hears my word and believes Him who sent Me has eternal life and will not be condemned; he has crossed over from death to life."

John 6:37 "All that the Father gives me will come to Me, and whoever comes to Me I will never drive away."

John 10:28 "I give them eternal life, and they shall never perish; no one can snatch them out of My hand."

1 John 5:13 "I write these things to you who believe in the name of the Son of God so that you may know that you have eternal life."

No wonder, no doubt, no question about it, when we are "saved" we are saved forevermore! Amen! And "salvation" here from Paul is the Greek word "soterion" from the root word "soter" meaning "savior" and it means, "bringing deliverance, preservation, safety, or salvation." This is what our "Savior" Jesus brought for us. An eternal salvation. And "helmet" is the Greek word, "Perikephalaia" and it means not just "helmet" but it's made up of two words, "peri" which means "around or about" and "kephale" meaning "the head or hair area." So, this eternal salvation we are to "take" and "wear as a helmet" is literally something we better hurry up, right now, and wrap our heads around! You better get this about your head! Get it on through and through! It speaks of a total coverage! It is something we are to tightly fit around our head! It's deeply imbedded in our mind. Nothing is going to dislodge it! Get it on now!

And so that's the question, "Why is the knowledge of our salvation being "eternal" such a big deal? Why is it so important for me to securely wrap that around my head when it comes to daily spiritual warfare?" Because that's precisely where the enemy will strike! How many times does he try to get you to doubt your salvation and when you give into it even for a second, what happens? You get knocked for a loop! You can't even stand!

THE BENEFITS OF ETERNAL SECURITY

"Why did a Roman soldier need a helmet that was so tightly wrapped about his head as the Greek word implies? Because this kind of helmet was essential because the Roman soldier's opponent carried a broadsword or even short-handled ax called a battle-ax - and when they were used, heads rolled!

Therefore, if the Roman soldier didn't have a helmet on when he went out to fight, he could be absolutely sure that he would lose his head. Thus, the Roman helmet was designed to save a man's head. And that's exactly what the knowledge of our eternal salvation will do for you when you wear it like a helmet on your head!

The helmet of salvation protects our mind and thus protects against discouragement, doubt, despair and the desire to give up. But if you don't walk in the fullness of all that your salvation entails, the eternality of it, its security, then you will feel the brunt of your enemy's battle-ax slicing through your mind and he will attack and steal your victory.

He will hack away at your foundation, telling you your healing, deliverance, preservation, and salvation was not eternal, that there's no guarantee, maybe it will happen, maybe it won't, and your head begins to roll! Satan's double edged sword is discouragement and doubt and he wants to get you discouraged by getting you to doubt your salvation.

He's really good at that. He comes right after you've done something sinful and says, "You're not a Christian. You couldn't be a Christian. Look at you! Why would the Lord ever save you? You're not good enough. You don't deserve to be saved. How do you know you meant it when you did it? And on and on it goes!

Satan comes after people in that area and he even gets whole churches to teach his lie that you can lose your salvation. Now whole bodies of Christ are living in constant fear! Churches are immobilized! Christians can't even function properly! There's no peace. There's no security. There's no stability! All because they've taken a serious head wound from the evil one by not putting on the helmet of salvation.

Instead of eternal security, they have daily insecurity. They wobble, they stumble, they bend, they break, they fall down, and never stand victorious.

Can you imagine living, that way? All your life, wondering am I going to make it? Oh, it's getting close. Am I going to make it? What a horrible existence. That would be anything but "These things are written unto you that your joy may be full because you know you have eternal life." You'd have to rewrite the New Testament to say, "These things are written unto you that you might be miserable." You could never be happy knowing that salvation was a guessing game.

I'll never forget the guy on television, Channel 40, he was being asked questions. And somebody called up and said, "If you sin a sin and you're a Christian, and you forget to confess it before you die, or the rapture happens, what happens then?" He said, "You go to hell." Now, can you imagine living under that kind of fear?"

This is what satan wants. He wants us to be afraid that we don't have eternal salvation. He wants us to doubt our salvation. Why? Because he wants us to doubt the promises of God. He wants us to believe that God doesn't keep His promises, His Word. He wants us to think that salvation isn't forever. That God can't hold onto us. That He can't keep us secure. He wants us to deny God's power, His resources, His ability to hold on to us forever, and in essence deny the fact that God only speaks the truth. To in essence call God a liar. All of these things are simply part of that.

And so satan comes against us, making us doubt our salvation. How do we react to that? You take up the helmet of salvation! In other words, you acknowledge what the Bible says, that there is no other kind of salvation other than that which is eternal.

Why? Because God is eternal and our Eternal Savior Who brought us salvation said, that if you come to Him, He will in no wise cast you out. And no wise means under no circumstance whatsoever! There are no circumstances that, in existence anywhere in the whole universe, whereby Christ would cast out somebody who came to Him. That's what he's saying. There's no way to lose. We've got eternal victory!

There is no power in the universe stronger than God. And if God wants to hold on to us, that's the way it's going to be. Nobody can take us out of the Father's hand because He's greater than all. So, don't listen to satan's doubts. Just take the helmet of salvation and acknowledge you're going to win in the end…it's guaranteed!"[7]

That's what the helmet of salvation is all about. What you think, determines your behavior! And if you don't think your salvation is secure you're toast! That's why Paul says, "take the helmet of salvation," and have a great day! Amen? Just acknowledge your future has been reversed, like this guy.

CHANGE OF COMMA

"Alexander III was the Czar of Russia from 1881-1894. And his rule was marked by repression and persecuting the Jews.

His wife Maria though, provided a stark contrast, being known for her generosity to those in need. And on one occasion her husband had signed an order consigning a prisoner to life in exile.

It simply read, 'Pardon impossible, to be sent to Siberia.'

So, Maria changed that prisoner's life by moving the comma in her husband's order. She altered it to, 'Pardon, impossible to be sent to Siberia.'

One change…

And so, it is that in Christ God has changed the comma that stood against us from satan. From, 'Pardon impossible, send to Hell" to 'Pardon, impossible to send to Hell.'"[8]

The **second part** of our salvation referred to in the Helmet of Salvation is the, **"Salvation We Have from All Suffering."**

1 Thessalonians 5:6-8 "So then, let us not be like others, who are asleep, but let us be alert and self-controlled. For those who sleep, sleep at night, and those who get drunk, get drunk at night. But since we belong to the day, let us be self-controlled, putting on faith and love as a breastplate, and the *hope* of salvation as a helmet."

So here we see Paul using the exact same verbiage dealing with our daily battle with the darkness out there, except this time he adds a word. It's not just the "salvation as a helmet" it's what? The hope of salvation. And most people believe Paul's referring to not just the fact that our salvation is guaranteed and secure, that's true. But he then adds another element of our salvation that helps us in our daily battle against the evil ones, and that is one day, this battle is through! We're done! Finito! It's over! Praise God! That's why he uses the word "hope". It's the Greek word, "elpis" and it means, "the joyful and confident expectation of good, something hoped for." And "hope" by definition means it's something you haven't received yet, it's still in the future, otherwise why would you "hope" for it, right?

Romans 8:24 "For in this *hope* we were saved. But *hope* that is seen is no *hope* at all. Who *hopes* for what he already has?"

And the future hope that most people believe Paul's talking about here in connection with our salvation is our future inheritance in Christ.

Ephesians 1:18 "I pray also that the eyes of your heart may be enlightened in order that you may know the *hope* to which he has called you, the riches of His glorious *inheritance* in the saints."

And what is that inheritance? That one day this battle gets turned into a major mega blessing!

Revelation 21:3-5 "And I heard a loud voice from the throne saying, 'Now the dwelling of God is with men, and He will live with them. They will be His people, and God Himself will be with them and be their God. He will wipe every tear from their eyes. There will be no more death or mourning or crying or pain, for the old order of things has passed away. He who was seated on the throne said, 'I am making everything new!'"

Isn't that awesome! That's our future inheritance! That's our hope down here in the midst of this current, bloody, daily, dark battle against satan and the demons, that we need to put on our heads! One day, IT'S OVER! The battle becomes a blessing where satan will be bound. There will be no more fighting, no more struggling, no more sin, no more heartache, no more spiritual warfare, no more crying, or pain, or suffering, or even tears! It's gone! Forever! And that's great news as this couple found out.

85-YEAR-OLD COUPLE

"One day there was this 85-year-old couple who had been married for almost 60 years, and suddenly they both died in a car crash. They had been in good health for the last ten years mainly due to her interest in health food, and exercise. Well, when they reached the pearly gates, St. Peter took them to their mansion which was decked out with a beautiful kitchen and master bath suite and Jacuzzi.

They 'oohed and aahed' but the old man asked Peter how much all this was going to cost. 'It's free,' Peter replied, 'this is Heaven.'

So next they go out to survey the championship golf course that the home was backed up to. And they learned they would have golfing privileges every day, also, each week the course would change to a new one representing one of the great golf courses back on earth.

So, the old man asked, 'What are the green fees?' And Peter replied, 'This is heaven, you play for free.'

Next, they went to the clubhouse and saw the lavish buffet lunch with all the cuisines of the world laid right out before them.

The old man asked, 'Well, how much to eat?' And Peter by now is getting a little exasperated and he says, 'Don't you get it yet? This is heaven, it's free!' So, the old man asked timidly, 'Well, where are all the low fat and low cholesterol tables?'

And Peter exclaimed, 'Well, hello, that's the best part...you can eat as much as you like, of whatever you like, and you never get fat and you never get sick. This is Heaven.'

With that the old man went into a fit of anger, throwing down his hat and stomping on it, and shrieking wildly. Peter and his wife were both trying to calm him down and they asked him what was wrong.

The old man looked at his wife and said, 'This is all your fault. If it weren't for your stupid prunes and bran muffins, I could have been here ten years ago!'"[9]

Yes, our future inheritance is something to look forward to, not avoid, amen? What Paul is talking about, as the second part of our salvation. We need to put it on our heads as a helmet every day! It's more important than 'one day I don't have to eat prunes, bran muffins, or even rice cakes or chicken.' Contextually it's this; one day, here's our hope. We aren't ever, ever, ever going to have to deal with spiritual warfare ever again! One day it's over. This is precisely the other area the enemy will strike! He tries to get inside our head not just to discourage us, but to deflate us. To get us wiped out! To get us to think this will never end, we'll never win, just give up, give in, this will never stop, there's no end in sight! I quit! It's the same never-ending spiritual grinding pain and agony of wielding this, and parrying with that, blocking this, and shielding that, on and on and on it goes, I'm just so tired. I just might as well STOP! Have you ever been there? That's a sign your helmet's off. Your personality's split. Oh, you're glad you're saved, eternally so, the first part of the meaning of the helmet, but now you just want to give up...WHY? Because you've been tricked! You're so tired because you think there's no end in sight and that's a lie! It's penetrated your head! In fact, I knew of a Pastor like that once. He had a biblically split personality. I was driving with him in his truck and he pulled into his driveway beating on his steering wheel screaming, "I just wish it would stop!" I looked at him and said, "DUDE! STOP EATING CHICKEN!" No just kidding! Although I'm sure that would have helped. But seriously I looked at him and said, "Dude, buck up! It's never going to stop until we get to heaven!" In other words, there's hope in the future don't quit! But this is what the enemy wants you to do. Not only to get you to doubt your salvation but to get deflated by buying into the lie that there is no hope in the future. This is just an endless battle. You might as well just give in, give up, get discouraged, quit! But if you just do what God says to do, He hasn't left us hanging high and dry. Put on the hope of salvation as a helmet, acknowledge our future hope, then not even this can penetrate your brain.

THE BENFITS OF FUTURE SALVATION

"Do you know there's coming a day when there'll be no more sin? That's right. You know how I know? Because the Book of Revelation says there'll be no more death, and the wages of sin is death – so no death, no sin.

Also, in Romans Paul talks about the curse of sin and how it affected creation. Right now, the whole world knows it's out of whack. The whole world knows that something is desperately wrong. All of us know things aren't right, we know this isn't the way God intended it, we know this isn't the way God made life to be. But the Bible says we are, "Saved in hope!" What hope? That one day it won't be like this forever!

In other words, the world is going to get better! Did you know that? It isn't going to get perfect by man's efforts. Oh no! It will get better when Jesus comes back. In fact, it's not just going to get better; it's going to be perfect. And that hope is very important to the Christian experience.

You see, if someone told me, "Nothing is going to change, ever, it's always going to be this way," then I'd say, "You mean I've got to fight the flesh the rest of my life and throughout eternity? You mean I've got to fight the devil like this, and I've got to live with the human weakness? You mean I'm going to stay in Romans 7 forever crying out, 'Oh, oh wretched man!' This is it?"

If that were true, I'd say to you, "Salvation is not complete." It would be like running a race without a finish line – somebody saying, "Start running, and run the rest of your life." "What? Where? There's no finish." "That's right. And give everything you've got all the way."

Are you kidding? Can you imagine God saying that...to in essence fight forever? Oh, come on! But this is the good news of salvation. There is a future hope to it.

We are waiting in hope that someday the battle will be over, and someday we won't have to struggle with sin, and the flesh, and the devil, and the world, and demons. Someday we'll know the hope of heaven and receive the eternal inheritance that He's planned for us.

And because of that, we don't mind a little pain down here – because there is a finish line. We don't mind a little effort – because there is a goal to reach. What drives us is the sense of victory. That one day, the race will be done, the battle is over, we've won, you made it across the finish line, now it's time to rest and enjoy the victory!

So, when satan tries to get into your brain and get you discouraged or deflated, remember there's coming a great and glorious day for us, Christian, a victory celebration. When you get weary in well-doing, remember you reap if you faint not. Someday, there's going to be a reward. Someday we'll stand with Jesus as He says to us, "Well done, good and faithful servant. Enter the joy of your Master."

So, pace yourself Christian, put on the helmet of salvation and stand in God's victory."[10]

The helmet of salvation is not just salvation, it's everything that comes with our eternal salvation, including all the promises of an eternal life of bliss with God through Jesus Christ forever and ever. That is our hope. That's what protects our head! So, no matter what it looks like, don't listen to the evil one. Don't let his lies try to penetrate your head. Don't let his evil thoughts dictate your behavior and your attitude in life. There is no excuse! God has given you what you need! And even if you've been a little weary, and you've become battle scarred over time, as a Christian, and have fought long and hard, don't listen to the evil one thinking God has done you wrong. Rather, have you ever thought of this? Maybe the scars you have Christian, aren't from God leaving you in a lurch all alone, like the devil wants you to think. Don't let that penetrate your head. Maybe it's from God refusing to let you go, like He promised He would, like this Mom did for her son.

ALLIGATOR SCARS

"Some years ago, on a hot summer day in south Florida a little boy decided to go for a swim in the old swimming hole behind his house.

In a hurry to dive into the cool water, he ran out the back door, leaving behind shoes, socks, and shirt as he went. He flew into the water, not realizing that as he swam toward the middle of the lake, an alligator was swimming toward the shore.

His mother - in the house was looking out the window - saw the two as they got closer and closer together. In utter fear, she ran toward the water, yelling to her son as loudly as she could.

Hearing her voice, the little boy became alarmed and made a U-turn to swim to his mother. It was too late. Just as he reached her, the alligator reached him.

 *From the dock, the mother grabbed her little boy by the arms just as the alligator snatched his legs. That began an incredible tug-of-war between the two. The alligator was much stronger than the mother, but the mother was much too passionate to let go.*

A farmer happened to drive by, heard her screams, raced from his truck, took aim and shot the alligator.

Remarkably, after weeks and weeks in the hospital, the little boy survived. His legs were extremely scarred by the vicious attack of the animal and, on his arms, were deep scratches where his mother's fingernails dug into his flesh in her effort to hang on to the son she loved.

The newspaper reporter who interviewed the boy after the trauma, asked if he would show him his scars. The boy lifted his pant legs and showed him.

But then, with obvious pride, he said to the reporter, "But look at my arms. I have great scars on my arms, too. I have them because my momma wouldn't let me go."

Friend, you and I can identify with that little boy. We have scars, too. No, not from an alligator, or anything quite so dramatic. But, the scars of a painful past. Some of those scars are unsightly and have caused us deep, deep regret.

But, some wounds, my friend, are because God has refused to let go. In the midst of your struggle, He's been there holding on to you.

The Scripture teaches that God loves you. If you have Christ in your life, you have become a child of God. He wants to protect you and provide for you in every way.

But sometimes we foolishly wade into dangerous situations. The swimming hole of life is filled with peril - and we forget that the enemy is waiting to attack. That's when the tug-o-war begins.

And if you have the scars of His love on your arms be very, very grateful. He did not - and will not - let you go."[11]

That's the Helmet of Salvation! Put that baby on and have a great day! Amen?

Chapter Twenty-Nine

The Protection from Satan and Demons Part 9

"It started out just like any other day in this small rural community of Wisconsin. People went off to work, farmers took care of their crops, kids went to school. But all that was to change in a flash!

What started out as a deliberate fire to help clear some forest land for farming, soon turned into a flaming nightmare. The weather changed bringing with it strong winds that fanned the flames into a massive firestorm. And in just one hour, the town it started in, was gone! And it wasn't just destroyed, it was

 incinerated by a fire of biblical proportions.

In the words of two witnesses there, 'superheated flames of at least 2,000 degrees Fahrenheit advanced on winds of 110 miles per hour and blew into the surrounding area creating nature's nuclear explosion.'

That's because the fire generated a 'fire whirl' (it's like a tornado but made of fire) that threw railroad cars and even houses into the air. In fact, this fire was later studied by the American and British military during World War II to learn how to create their own firestorm conditions for bombing campaigns against Germany and Japan.

And for those who tried to escape they didn't fare too well. Many immersed themselves into a nearby river, or even wells, but many of them drowned while others succumbed to hypothermia in the frigid waters. And for those who couldn't make it to the water, they didn't just die, they died in a multitude of horrible ways.

Some spontaneously combusted because it was so hot, others were cremated by the heat, others died instantly from breathing in the poisoned superheated air, some died of smoke inhalation, still others were run over by panicked livestock, crushed in collapsing buildings, impaled by flying debris and even pulverized by all kinds of things dropping out of the sky on top of them. Some even committed suicide rather than having to face death by fire.

As one person stated, 'It was so horrific that some people thought it was the end of the world and even remarked…this must be what Hell looks like.'

And when all was said and done, some 3.8 million acres were scorched, 16 towns were damaged or totally destroyed, and upwards to 2,500 people died, but an accurate death toll has never been determined due to the fact that local records were destroyed in the fire, so many had died in the fire, that no one remained alive to identify all the bodies.

It became the single worst wild fire in all of U.S. history, both in size and fatalities, yet it has basically been forgotten because it occurred on the same day as the more famous Chicago Fire.

The year was 1871. The disaster is of course, The Great Peshtigo Fire."[1]

Now folks, how many of you have heard of the Great Peshtigo Fire? Okay,

hardly any of us have. But how many of you guys would agree it was one of the greatest disasters of all time, right? But with all due respect to those who lost their lives in the Peshtigo Fire, what if I were to tell you I know of a disaster that makes that fire look like a puff of smoke? And what if I were to tell you that this disaster didn't occur in just one place and one country at one time, but it's going on right now today all over the world and it's been leaving a trail of death and destruction for centuries. Folks, I'm talking once again about *The satanic War on the Christian.* And these are the facts. We Christians don't battle here and there once in a while. We go to war, every single day. Whether you see it, feel it, believe it or not, the moment you got saved you entered a spiritual war against a demonic host whose sole purpose is to destroy you and extinguish your testimony for Jesus Christ. And what's wild is that most wars go on for a few years or even longer. But *The satanic War on the Christian* has been going on for the last 2,000 years non-stop and it's sending people straight to hell! And what's wild is most people will readily talk about all the other wars throughout history and all their atrocities, and rightly so…we have the History Channel…. we need to talk about them! YET how many people, even Christians, will openly discuss the longest war in mankind's history…*The satanic War on the Christian* that has destroyed more lives than all the wars put together? Therefore, in order to stop getting duped and beat up all over the place, we're going to continue in our study, *The satanic War on the Christian.*

Now so far, we've seen if you're ever going to win a war, then the **1st thing** you must do is **Know Who Your Enemy Is**…

Then we saw the **2ⁿᵈ thing** you need to know is **What Your Enemy is Like**, their character, amen? It's common sense, right?

Then we saw the **3ʳᵈ thing** you need to know is **The Tactic of Your Enemy**…what they're up to…what's their goal…. why are they here…

Then we saw the **4ᵗʰ thing** you need to know is **The Destruction of Your Enemy**…what price you pay when you DON'T take this seriously…

Then we saw the **5ᵗʰ thing** you need to know is **The Temptation of Your Enemy**…how he's out there trying to get us to sin against God….

And the **last eight times** we saw the **6ᵗʰ thing** you need to know is **The Protection FROM Your Enemy**.

And there we saw God has not left us hanging high and dry in this Great Cosmic War dealing with satan and demons. Are you kidding me? He's given us His full-blown protection and amazing weaponry to stand our ground and be victorious in all situations every single time! It's called The Armor of God!

And so far, we've seen the **1ˢᵗ thing** about the Armor of God that **It's Designed for War**.

The **2ⁿᵈ thing, It's Designed for Victory.**

And the last three times the **3ʳᵈ thing It's Designed for Wear.**

This armor is not something to look at, it's not meant just to stare at, or stick on a shelf and collect dust. It's designed for wear. You Daily wear it, you continually wear it. YOU PUT IT ON! And again, the Greek says to put it on NOW and leave it on! Quick! Chop, chop! Don't delay! This is serious stuff! Why? Because that's the second part of experiencing God's Victory that He's already given to us!

And so far, we saw the **1ˢᵗ piece** was **The Belt of Truth**.

The **2ⁿᵈ piece** was **The Breastplate of Righteousness**.

The **3ʳᵈ piece** was **The Shoes of Peace**.

The **4th piece** was **The Shield of Faith**.

And last time the **5th piece** was **The Helmet of Salvation**.

      There we saw, just like the belt and the breastplate and the shoes and the shield of the Roman soldier, so it is with the helmet. It wasn't a literal helmet we put on our head…that's not what Paul is saying… Rather he's speak of a spiritual helmet we put on to defend ourselves with. The helmet of salvation was Paul's way of saying we need to wrap God's Word around our mind to deflect the enemy's assault on our thought life that gets us to sin, fear, doubt, not trust in God, etc. Why? Because as we saw with the Roman Soldier's helmet, It protects your head from serious injury and it can only be taken up by me…nobody can put this helmet on my head but me, I alone can do it. Why? Because when I do, it deflects 2 important areas the enemy will strike at my head concerning my salvation. Gods Word reminds me that I have salvation for all eternity and nobody can snatch me out of the Father's Hand…And two, the salvation we have from all this suffering so that one day we have no more of this baloney! All this current bloody, daily, dark battle against satan and the demons is over! ONE DAY satan will be bound, there will be no more fighting, no more struggling, no more sin, no more heartache, no more spiritual warfare, no more crying, or pain, or suffering, or even tears…FOREVER! And that's GREAT NEWS to wrap around your brain everyday…amen? But that's not all.

The **6th piece** of Armor we need to hurry up and put on for God's Victory that He's already given to us is **The Sword of the Spirit**. But don't take my word for it. Let's listen to God's.

Ephesians 6:10-17b "Finally, be strong in the Lord and in His mighty power. Put on the full armor of God so that you can take your stand against the devil's schemes. For our struggle is not against flesh and blood, but against the rulers, against the authorities, against the powers of this dark world and against the spiritual forces of evil in the heavenly realms. Therefore, put on the full armor of God, so that when the day of evil comes, you may be able to stand your ground, and after you have done everything, to stand. Stand firm, then, with the belt of truth buckled around your waist, with the breastplate of righteousness in place, and with your feet fitted with the readiness that comes from the gospel of peace. In addition to all this, take up the shield of faith, with which you can extinguish all the flaming arrows of the evil one. Take the helmet of salvation and the sword of the spirit, which is the word of God."

So here again we see the sixth piece of supernatural military equipment that God gives us the ability to effectively struggle and come out on top in our war against the evil ones, when they come at us every single day...not if. This is the sixth piece that gives us the ability to stand our ground and not buckle or break under pressure when the dust clears from the battle that we're in...it was called the sword of the spirit. And so that's the obvious big question is, "What in the world is the Sword of the Spirit?" right? Well, this time, the context defines it for us. You don't have to pray and fast for 15 years to figure this one out. You don't have to spend money on that Fasting Conference with meals included to get a Word from God... NO! Paul tells us. It is the WORD OF GOD!

Once again, the BIBLE is embedded in every single piece of armor. Now you know why the enemy wants to keep you way from it! And certainly, when it comes to using this Sword. However, with that said, I believe there's even more we can glean about this sword when we do what we did with the other pieces of armor and take a look at the Roman soldier's uniform and weaponry.

Well, the **1st thing** we're going to see about The Sword of the Spirit, the Word of God, is that **It Provides an Offensive Attack**.

Once again, let's take a look at what that this piece of armor was like for the Roman Soldier and find out what it literally means for us today.

ROMAN SOLDIER'S SWORD

"The Roman sword of Paul's day was called the "machaira" or the "short sword" and was about 1½ to 2 feet long typically made of iron and was double-edged so you could cut both ways with it. It was simply a precision instrument. In fact, the word "machaira" literally means, "a large knife used for cutting up flesh."

In training with this short sword, the soldier was taught to stab and thrust instead of slashing. The reason is because the slashing, even though delivered with force, it frequently didn't kill. It only wounded because of the protective armor and bone. But a stab with this "short sword" nearly always penetrated the body hitting vital organs killing their opponent.

This was not the only sword the Romans had. In fact, they had at least two different kinds of swords, one which was quite large and much longer. It was called the "rhomphaia." It was a type of broadsword that was 6 to 8 feet long and was used to hack off the limbs and heads of enemy soldiers. But because of its size and weight, it had to be used with two hands, which didn't allow the soldier to hold his shield. And since they didn't have the full metal suits like the knights had in the medieval times, a soldier without a shield left himself exposed to arrows and spears.

Furthermore, if all you had was just a "rhomphaia" and no shield, and you went up against a soldier who had a short sword and a shield, the one with the short sword would almost always win because here you have this eight foot long sword, and it takes everything you can to swing it in a great, slicing sweeps, and once you get it swinging, it takes even more energy to stop it. So, all the soldier with the short sword has to do is dodge one swing from your sword, and then step in with his short sword and stab you with it.

This is why most Roman soldiers used the "machaira" or the short sword. It was light and could be maneuvered quickly and with relative ease and it only took one hand to use it, allowing the soldier to carry a shield with the other. It also had a big metal knob at the base of the hilt that not only gave the soldier a better grip but could also be used to bash an enemy in the head or face with a back swing. The Roman soldier would have these swords hanging by their side attached via his belt."[2]

Oooh! Once again, the Word of God, which was represented by the belt, is where this Sword, which is also the Bible, hung on. The Bible holds all the armor together! But as you can see, this "machaira" or short sword, was not only a precision instrument, cutting up the opponent's flesh, but it was an offensive weapon. And that's an important distinction to make because up until now, all the armor has been basically defensive in nature! One guy puts it this way.

THE SWORD IS AN OFFENSIVE WEAPON

"The Roman short sword could be used to defend the soldier against the attacks of the enemy, but it could also be used for a quick offensive thrust or jab at an exposed or unprotected part of the enemy's body.

As such, the sword was a vital piece of the soldier's armor. Even if you had none of the other pieces, if you had your sword, there was still some hope. With the sword you could both ward off and deflect some of the attacks of the enemy, and with the sword you could also effectively wound your enemy.

Although you could defend yourself adequately with your shield and breastplate and helmet, without a sword, there is no hope of wounding your foe, and so the most you could do is run away from him.

Yes, you could stand there, and get wailed upon, but eventually, the enemy would wear you down too much, and you would end up getting injured or killed. So, the sword was a vital piece of the armor. "[3]

Why? Because you didn't need to just stand there and endlessly get whacked on! With the sword, you could fight back and take your enemy out. You could stop the attacks from happening! Isn't that awesome! But again, notice it wasn't just a sword that got used for offensive purposes, but what kind of sword? It got defined for us. The sword of the spirit which is the word of God...the Bible! This is important because some people wrongly assume that the "sword" is speaking of the "Spirit." Not so. You might think I'm getting hung up on semantics, but my concern is, if you don't get this "sword" right, how can you ever use it correctly, let alone effectively, right? But that's not what the Greek says. The "sword" is not the "Spirit." It literally says, "the sword supplied by the Spirit, which is the Word of God." And this is consistent with where the Bible says it came from. It's not some book whooped up by man! It came from the Spirit of God.

2 Peter 1:21 "For prophecy never had its origin in the will of man, but men spoke from God as they were carried along by the Holy Spirit."

2 Timothy 3:16-17 "All Scripture is God-breathed and is useful for teaching, rebuking, correcting and training in righteousness, so that the man of God may be thoroughly equipped for every good work."

So, the "sword" is not the "Spirit" but rather it was "supplied by" the Spirit which means this is not just a sword, it's a spiritual sword that the Bible also says is designed for precision cutting just like the "machaira."

Hebrews 4:12 "For the Word of God is living and active. Sharper than any double-edged sword, it penetrates even to dividing soul and spirit, joints and marrow; it judges the thoughts and attitudes of the heart."

So, God not only gave us a "sword" but a "spiritual sword" to offensively cut into our enemy with precision jabs, when he comes our way. The Bible knows exactly where to jab and cut into and to stop his evil attacks. It's precise! No matter what the enemy throws at us, there is a precise counter attack from God, in His Word, to defeat him. That's what the Bible is for us. This is our "spiritual sword" from God to offensively jab and take out our enemies in the midst of the battle, no matter what he throws our way, in a precise manner, just like the "machaira." Isn't that good news? In fact, it's also consistent with how the Bible says God takes out His enemies too! He uses a "sword."

Isaiah 27:1 "In that day, the LORD will punish with His *sword*, His fierce, great and powerful *sword*."

Amos 9:4 "Though they are driven into exile by their enemies, there I will command the *sword* to slay them."

Revelation 6:7,8 "When the Lamb opened the fourth seal, I heard the voice of the fourth living creature say, 'Come!' They were given power over a fourth of the earth to kill by *sword,* famine and plague, and by the wild beasts of the earth."

Revelation 19:11,13,15 "I saw heaven standing open and there before me was a white horse, whose rider is called Faithful and True. With justice He judges and makes war. He is dressed in a robe dipped in blood, and His Name is the Word of God. Out of His mouth comes a sharp *sword* with which to strike down the nations."

So, God uses a "sword" to take out His enemies, Old and New Testament, and we too His children are given a "sword" by God, "supplied by the Spirit" to take out our enemies. And it's the Word of God the Bible! It came from the Spirit, He "supplied it to us," and it's our offensive weapon given by our

Heavenly Commander to precisely cut up and destroy our enemy when he comes our way! That's awesome! Which tells us, we're not designed to just sit there and get pummeled day after day after day as Christians, endlessly so, not at all! God gives us a sword, the Bible, to fight back with, and STOP every single attack! That's amazing! And this is what we have here with the sixth piece of armor. Now, the bad news is, we're focused on all the wrong kind of weaponry! We talk about how to protect our homes offensively and the first step apparently, is to make sure you have a home security system in place to "jab" those bad guys if they come your way. That's our weapon! In fact, we spend on average $20.64 billion on home security systems every single year! That'll stop those bad guys! And I'm not against that! I got one on my house. That's not my point.[4]

But, just in case that alarm system doesn't "jab" the bad guy enough and keep him out, we have our own weaponry! We spend on average for personal weaponry $31.8 billion a year.[5]

And again, I'm not against that. I'm not against owning a gun...not at all! I grew up hunting, fishing, trapping, the whole nine yards. You need to offensively protect your family. I get that! In fact, I believe in the Second Amendment "the right to bear arms." And no, it's not talking about "wearing sleeveless shirts.... the right to bare arms." Wrong spelling! It's means to offensively protect yourself from a Government gone bad!" And I even believe in Gun Control...and you might be thinking...now wait a minute....but hear me out...what I mean by that is when you do go and buy a gun...learn how to control it properly. That's proper gun control. In fact, the 2018 Defense Budget was signed into law on December 12, 2017 by President Trump. The defense budget authorizes just under $700 billion in defense.[6]

And I'm not against Militaries either...not at all! You guys know me! I'm a big supporter of the Military. Just come here on Memorial Day or Veteran's Day and you'll find out! But in today's wicked world I personally think we need to have the biggest baddest military there ever was.... Because we need an offensive deterrent from the other countries seeking to take us out....they ain't laying down their weapons...so we need to be able to offensively protect ourselves! It's common sense! But here's my point. We get that, and we invest in those offensive weapons, and we see the desperate need and rationale for that. But what Paul is saying here, how much more then do you need to be focused on offensively protecting your walk with Jesus Christ with the Word of God...the Bible! It's our weapon from God! Its stops the enemy from attacking us! It keeps him at bay! It defeats him every single time! It takes him out! And because we're focused on the wring thing…no wonder your walk with Jesus is getting robbed! No wonder you're all tied up by the enemy as he's ransacking your life spiritually. No wonder you're defeated all the time! You're basically letting him slap you silly as you sit there doing anything in return, like this guy.

SPAGHETTI WESTERN SLAPPING SCENE

The scene opens with two cowboys standing at the bar facing each other. No words are spoken but the other men sitting at the tables know there is going to be a showdown. The guy in the back hat goes for his gun but before he can even touch it the other guy has pulled his gun out of his holster with one hand but with the other hand has slapped the one in the black hat right across the face. The guy is in shock. He didn't get a chance to even touch his gun. But now he is angry and ready to try again. The cowboy with no hat asks him, "Do you want to see that again? It's hard to catch the first time." They stare at each other waiting to see who will draw first, but before the cowboy with the black hat could draw, the other cowboy had already slapped him and pulled his gun. The black hat hadn't even touched his gun. The action was repeated three more time and the cowboy with the back hat still hadn't been able to draw his gun. The rest of the men in the bar are watching in amazement. As it keeps being repeated over and over again one of the guys that was playing cards at the table yells out, "Cut it out!"[7]

Yeah, he got it! Right in the head! How many Christians are like that! Getting slapped around, with a surprised look on their face, over and over again getting beat up by the enemy, just standing there! But this is what Paul is saying! You don't have to live that way! Wake Up! God gave you a weapon to slap back and not just slap back but shoot and take the enemy out. Stop all this nonsense! You don't need to just stand there and take it! Getting slapped around silly! Use what He gave you. It's called the Sword of the spirit which is the Word of God, the Bible, and it will defeat the enemy every single time!

THE IMPORTANCE OF THE SWORD OF THE SPIRIT

"The Word of God should be our constant companion. Like a sword – always at our side.

The only way to take up the Sword is to immerse ourselves in the Word of God. There are no short cuts or fast tracks. The only way to take up the Sword of the Spirit is to spend as much time as you possibly can in the Word of God.

Read it. Study it. Memorize it. Talk about it. Meditate upon it. Pray through it. Think about it. Attend a church—where the Word of God is faithfully and systematically taught—so that, over time, you receive the whole counsel of God.

But beyond this, you can listen to Christian sermons or the Bible on CD while you drive around. Or, if you don't want to get CDs, just tune your radio to a station with lots of biblical preaching on it. Get involved in a Bible study where you are encouraged to read the Word of God and then come and discuss it with other people.

In summary, if you want to have your sword with you in spiritual battle, you need to know the Word. And the only way to know the Word is to spend as much time in the Word as possible.

Roman soldiers knew that their skill with the sword was their lifeline in battle. The better you were with your sword, the greater your chances were of survival. And so that is why the best soldiers spent almost all of their free time practicing with the Sword.

The same is true for the Christian. We need to spend as much time in the Bible as we can. No matter what we do in life, we need to make sure that our sword is always nearby.[8]

But again, that's the problem. We're getting slapped around and defeated all the time because we not only don't have the Sword from God, the Bible, always nearby, we don't even have a clue what's in there! Oh, we may own a Bible, and maybe even several of them, but we never get "into" them and "study" them and now we've created a culture of Bible-less Christians who are losing the fight! We've simply been tricked into laying our weapon down, as this man shares.

QUOTE BIBLE-LESS CHRISTIANS

"Listen, beloved, the Bible in your life is a weapon. No question about it. It's a weapon. It's only a matter of whether you know how to use it. And learning how

to use it is dependent upon how diligently you get involved in studying the Word of God. That's why the apostle Paul spent three years in Ephesus, and said, "I have not failed to declare unto you the whole council of God". Why? He wanted to teach them how to use the sword. He wanted to give them the whole thing so that they would be able to use it effectively.

Just because you own a Bible doesn't mean you have a sword. You can own a Bible warehouse and not have a sword, if you don't know how to use it defensively and offensively.

H. P. Barker was a master of illustrations. One day he described himself looking out a window and watching a garden full of plants and flowers. And he said, "I saw three things" in the garden. "First, I saw a butterfly. The butterfly was beautiful, and it would alight on a flower and then it would flutter to another flower and then it would flutter to another flower.

Only for a second or two would it sit, and it would move on and it would touch as many lovely blossoms as it could but derived absolutely no benefit from it. Then" – he said – "I watched a little longer out my window and there came a botanist. And the botanist had a big notebook under his arm and a great big magnifying glass.

The botanist would lean over a certain flower and he would look for a long time and then he would write notes in his notebook. He was there for hours writing notes, closed them, stuck them under his arm, tucked his magnifying glass in his pocket, walked away."

And then he said, "The third thing I noticed was a bee, just a little bee. But the bee would light on a flower and it would sink down deep into the flower and it would extract all the pollen that it could carry. It went in empty every time and came out full.

And H. P. Barker said, "So it is with people who approach the Bible. There are those who just flutter from lovely sermon to lovely sermon, from class to class, fluttering here, fluttering there, bringing nothing, and gaining nothing. What a nice feeling.

Then there are the spiritual botanists who take copious notes who are trying to make sure that all the vowel pointing's are correct, but they don't have the capacity to draw anything out of the flowers; it's pure academics. Then there are the spiritual bees who draw out of every precious flower all that is there, to make the honey that makes them so blessed to those around them." Which are you? You can come to Church services and be a butterfly.

You can flit from class to class, Bible study to Bible study, seminar to seminar, book to book, flipping your little pretty wings, never changing. Or you can be a botanist. Some of you have enough notebooks to sink a small battleship. Or you can be a bee coming in empty and going out full and turning it into the honey that makes life sweet. Which are you? The sword is there, it's available. Are you using it?

Satan doesn't like a fully taught congregation. Satan doesn't want you to know everything you need to know about the Word of God, about what God expects. Satan doesn't want you to understand all that Scripture teaches because he doesn't want you to be able to defend yourself against his deceptions.

But when you do come to know what Scripture teaches, you're like a spiritual young man who has overcome the evil one because you're strong in the Word and you've overcome the evil one, John says. Believe me, if there are areas where you are ignorant, Satan will find those areas and you'll find yourself defenseless there.[9]

Why? Because you've laid your weapon down. And even though you might pick it up once in a while, you never learn how to yield it, let alone effectively, because you've become a spiritual butterfly or botanist instead of a busy bee studying, digesting, learning, memorizing "sword techniques" that will defeat the evil one every single time. If you're sick and tired of getting slapped around living a life of spiritual defeat, it's high time you start learning how to yield the Bible, Sword of the Spirit.

That leads us to the **2nd thing** we see about The Sword of the Spirit, is that **It Can Only Be Taken Up By Me**.

Just as we saw with the Belt of Truth, the Breastplate of Righteousness, the Shoes of Peace, the Shield of Faith, and last time with the Helmet of Salvation, so it is with the Sword of the Spirit. The consistent truth is this. I am the only one who can do this for me. And that's what Paul says there… "take the helmet of salvation and the sword of the Spirit." "Take" as we saw before is from the Greek word, "dechomai" which means, "to accept deliberately, to receive readily." It's also in the aorist imperative and it implies, listen, "an urgent command to do this now! Don't delay! Receive or accept, take the sword of the spirit from God right now so you can fight back! And again, He tells us that the "sword" is the Bible! So, in essence Paul is saying, get into the Bible right now, take your Bible with you wherever you go right now, read your Bible right now, study your Bible right now, understand what it says right now. Why? Because nobody else can do it for you! It's common sense! I can't defeat the enemy by staring at the Bible, just owning a Bible, looking at the Bible, or even hiring somebody else to read it for me. No! I have to do it…and I have to do it now! Why? Because the enemy is out there slapping you every single day! Are you tired of it yet? Then get into the Word of God now and fight back! The answer is right before you…stop just standing there! But that's what we do! We don't even study the word of God, let alone read the Word of God, so we have no sword from God to stab our enemies with and we're getting slapped around like that Spaghetti Western! And we have that same goofy look in our face…. WAA, WAA, WAA! And it's not that we don't have time…we just spend that time studying everything else but the Word of God! So, when the battle comes we either just stand there doing nothing or pull out what weapon we've been investing our time with and say… En garde!" I stab you with….

- Pop Psychology
- Freudian Thinking
- Sports Statistics
- Local News Report
- Latest Fashions
- Hollywood Icons
- Best Selling Novel

It's like going up to the enemy saying, "I come against you with a…

Sword of the Sack of Psychology…. take that…and that…
Sword of the Sock of Useless Facts…ha ha ha…victory is mine!
Sword of the Spaghetti Best Sellers…you're doomed now!

And God must be looking down on us fighting like His kids saying, "Oh yeah… (sarcastically pumping His chest) that's my kids…mighty…. warriors in the making…. NOT!" I mean, can you imagine how goofy this must be to Him? Especially when He's given us an effective weapon? NO! We don't attack with a sack, sock, or useless spaghetti! We take up the Sword of the spirit which is the WORD OF GOD! In fact, Paul adds further emphasis on our need to do this…not just own a Bible or stare at a Bible, but to know the Bible so you can use it precisely like the "machaira" …And he does that by his choice of words for the Word of God. The Greek word for "Word" is not "logos" like we commonly think of…. it's "rhema" and that takes on a whole different meaning!

THE IMPORTANCE OF RHEMA vs LOGOS

"You don't have the sword simply by having or owning a Bible. It's not— "Well, I've got my Bible, so I've got my sword." No! That's not what the Greek says. When Biblical authors wanted to refer to the whole Bible, all of its parts and all of its books and all of its chapters and verses—all the teachings written down and recorded in the Bible—they used the Greek word logos.

Logos means "word" but when used of Scripture, it refers to "all" of the written Word of God, all of the Bible, in its entirety, as it is written down with pen and ink on the pages of Scripture. That is the logos.

But logos is not the Greek word Paul uses here. Instead, he uses the word rhema. Rhema, does not refer to the entire Bible in its written form. Instead, it refers to speaking individual verses and passages from the Bible.

Maybe these are verses you have memorized so you can recite them when needed, or maybe the specific passages you know where they occur in the Bible, so you can find them when needed. That is rhema.

So, with that in mind, here's what it means. The Bible is not merely the sword of the Spirit, it is the armory. There are thousands of "rhema" swords in [the Bible] and every one of them is a powerful and two-edged sword.

If Paul meant that the Sword of the Spirit was the Bible—he would have used the word logos. But he didn't. He used the word rhema, which shows us that the Sword of the Spirit is the individual verses and phrases and passages of the Bible which we can wield quickly in battle—which we can thrust and stab with force into the enemy.

A lot of people seem to think that they don't have to study the Bible and don't have to listen to sermons and don't have to have daily devotions because the

Holy Spirit can just pop the verse into their minds when they need it. And while the Holy Spirit could do this, He most often doesn't.

John 16 tells us that He helps us to remember what we have learned. He can't have you remember something you've never learned. So, our responsibility is to learn the Word, and only then will He help us remember it and help us use the Word correctly in the right situations and in the right ways. And when we do this, the Word of God becomes powerful and effective. It can do many things for us.

So, every time you memorize a verse or learn where it can be found in the Bible, you have added another sword to your arsenal. Every time you learn something new about a verse, you have sharpened the blades on that sword. Every time you learn a new way to apply a verse, you have become quicker and deadlier in using that sword. That is why so much practice is needed in correctly handling the Word of Truth."[10]

In other words, that's why you need to be in the Bible...not all those other books. They do nothing for you when it comes for Spiritual Warfare! In fact, we see this "rhema" use of the Bible from Jesus. This is exactly what He did when he faced satan and battled with him at His temptation.

Matthew 4:1-11 "Then Jesus was led by the Spirit into the desert to be tempted by the devil. After fasting forty days and forty nights, He was hungry. The tempter came to Him and said, 'If you are the Son of God, tell these stones to become bread.' Jesus answered, 'It is written: Man does not live on bread alone, but on every word that comes from the mouth of God. Then the devil took Him to the holy city and had Him stand on the highest point of the temple. 'If you are the Son of God, he said, throw yourself down. For it is written: He will command His angels concerning You, and they will lift You up in their hands, so that you will not strike Your foot against a stone.' Jesus answered him, 'It is also written: Do not put the Lord your God to the test. Again, the devil took Him to a very high mountain and showed Him all the kingdoms of the world and their splendor. 'All this I will give You,' he said, 'if you will bow down and worship me.' Jesus said to him, 'Away from me, satan! For it is written: Worship the Lord your God and serve Him only.' Then the devil left Him, and angels came and attended Him."

In other words, Jesus won! Why? Because every time the devil came at Him, what did He do? He jabbed back with what? The Word of God! It is written! It's the same word used here in Ephesians. The phrase there in Matthew 4, "Man does not live on bread alone, but on every word that comes from the mouth of God." Word there is the Greek word "rhema." Jesus used the "rhema" not the "logos" to defeat the devil. He didn't just show a Bible as a whole to the devil, "logos," He quoted specific, precise passages of the Bible "rhema" to counter the devils lies. That's what we see here in our passage. Jesus used "rhema." We're to use "rhema" And after three jabs of it what happened with the devil? He left. The devil left Jesus! The attack stopped! Jesus didn't just stand there and get slapped! Are you kidding me? He countered with the "rhema!" And so, it is with us! This is the GOOD NEWS! God hasn't left us hanging high and dry in dealing with the devil and demons. He didn't do that with Jesus, and He doesn't do that with us! And He certainly doesn't want us to stand there and get slapped silly! NO! He's given us the Sword of the Spirit which is the Rhema or Word of God! And its high time we get back to doing "Christian Sword Drills" like we used to if we're ever going to experience the same victory Jesus did over the devil!

CHRISTIAN SWORD DRILLS

"Did any of you ever do sword drills when you were younger? I attended a Christian school and we did them all the time. And I remember up at a Bible camp I used to go to as a kid, every chapel was spent in doing some Sword drills. Were they teaching us innocent children how to use swords? No, not real swords made of steel. But a sword much more powerful and effective than that—the Sword of the Word of God.

A sword drill goes like this. The speaker—or drill sergeant, if you could call him that—would say "Bible's high." And we would all have to raise our Bibles, with the spines in our hand so that we couldn't cheat by sticking our fingers into the pages.

Then the speaker would say a Scripture reference—like John 3:16. And we would all answer back, "John 3:16." Then...after a pause...he would say, "Charge!" and we would all pull our Bibles out of the air, and frantically look through our Bibles for John 3:16. The first person to find it would stand up and read it. And if they were right, they would get some points for their team or a prize or something.

Now those were the types of sword drills we did as children. But as we got older, we stopped doing them. But I think we should have kept on doing them and made them more challenging. As adults, we still need to do sword drills.

We need to be Bible experts. We need to know the Word of God backward and forward. We need to be able to recite the books of the Bible in order. We need to be able to know roughly what is in each book and what each book is about. We need to know key verses and key chapters in each book. We need to know key verses and key chapters in the Bible. We need to know key verses and key chapters to help us confront false teachings and false ideas.

So, I think that as adults, we should still have sword drills of sorts. We need to sit around and drill each other. We won't do this today, but what if we sat around and I said, "Bibles high...OK, a Jehovah's Witness has just knocked on your door, and he is telling you that Jesus Christ was just a god, He was not actually God himself. Where would you turn in Scripture? Charge!" Where would you go? (Answer: John 1; Mark 2; Luke 18)Or, "

A coworker has gone through some troubling times in her life, and she walks up to you some day, and says, 'You're a Christian right? What must I do to get to heaven?'" What would you tell her? What verses would you show her? Do you know? (Answer: John 3:16; 5:24; 6:47; 1 John 5:11-13)

What if you are talking to your neighbor some day and he says, "Hey, I'm a pretty good person. I haven't done too many bad things. God will let me into heaven." What would you tell him? Can you think of a few verses that would show him the truth? (Answer: Matt 5; Jas 2:10)

What if you sin—as we all still do, and—as we talked about previously—Satan comes in and starts to whisper in your ear that you aren't saved, or that God doesn't love you anymore? Do you remember some of the verses to go to? (Answer: Rom 8; John 5:24; 6:47; 10:27-29)

These are sword drills for the Christian. Do you know the Bible well enough so that you are ready for any challenge that comes your way? Are you prepared to give an answer to anyone who asks you to give a reason for the hope that you have in Jesus Christ (1 Pet. 3:15)."[11]

In other words, "How can you use the "rhema" of God if you never get into the WORD of God!" No wonder the enemy doesn't want us in there! He doesn't want us to access God's spiritual armory and the thousands upon thousands of swords designed to take him out every single time in precise ways just like Jesus did! Do you get it? Study what you want...But just don't let it be the Bible! Read whatever you want.... but just don't let it be the Bible! Learn whatever you want... Grab that sock, grab that sack, that spaghetti noodle...whatever. But just don't get into the Bible and learn the "rhema" weapons from God! Don't access the spiritual armory and slap him silly! And how silly is that...if that's how you're living! He's got us all twisted around! Therefore, to make sure none of us, live that way unnecessarily so...I wanted to close with a practical illustration to show us how to practically counteract the enemies lies just like Jesus did, with the "rhema" Word. You simply retranslate the enemy's lie with the truth, like this guy did.

THE MANSLATOR

The wife is sitting on the couch. Her husband walks behind the couch carrying his golf clubs and she looks up and asks, "Hey, are you golfing today?" He answers, "Yeah." She says, "It's the second time this week!" Then he replies, "But you said it was fine." Then she throws her magazine down and says, "It is fine! It's perfectly fine!" Then she gets up and walks into the other room. The Announcer: "Are you confused about female behavior?"

The husband is standing there looking totally lost as to what just happened. Announcer: "Would you like a translator to understand what she means?" He shakes his head yes. Announcer: Well you're in luck. Introducing the 'Manslator'. On the screen you see a monitor with numbers, symbols, and the word in big letters, Manslator. "A revolutionary device that translates woman language into simple man words. Finally, the way to know what she means."

The next scene is where the wife is sitting on the couch working on her computer. Her husband passes behind the couch while talking on the phone. He says to the person he is talking to, "Sure just let me check with my wife." Then he turns to his wife and says, "Hey babe, a t-time has opened up later, would you mind if I go?" She replies, "Fine, if that's what you want to do." He then looks at his Manslator and it says, "No go, stay home!"

He then turns to his wife and says, "On second thought, I think I will just stay home with you and watch The Notebook." She looks at him, closes her laptop and smiles at him and say, "Oh, how sweet!" Then he sits down beside her and puts his arm around her, making her very happy.

Announcer: "Now that's more like it. The Manslator uses an Emotion Deciphering Technology to help you out of the toughest jams. Another husband is sitting in his car talking on the phone to his wife. He asks, "Hey is everything ok, you sound upset?" She is at her desk and answers, "Why should I be upset?" and she slams down the phone. He smiles and but looks at his Manslator. It is telling him, Forgot Anniversary, Jerk! He realizes he blew it and says, "Oh, no way!"

Now when she gets home from work and walks through the door, her loving husband has dinner on the table, he is sitting there all dressed up and he says, "Happy Anniversary, babe." She is near tears saying, "You remembered." She runs over to hug him and he says, "of course I did." Announcer: "Thanks to the Manslator's Femlogic Processing Chip, any man can decode statements like 'Are you wearing that?'

The Manslator says, 'You change now!' She asks, 'Do you want to get some coffee?' The Manslator says, 'Me want coffee.' She asks, 'Do you think she is pretty?' The Manslator says, 'You think she is prettier than me'. Another gal says, 'You are such a good friend.'

The Manslator says, 'Me never date you.' She says, 'I'm fine.' The Manslator says, 'Me not fine.' She says, 'I'll be ready in five minutes.' The Manslator says, 'Me ready in 30 minutes.' She says, 'You do whatever you want!' The Manslator says, 'You no do what you want!' She says, 'Could you rub my shoulders a little bit?'

The Manslator says, 'No hanky panky, only massage! Me serious!' Announcer: 'The Manslator even works on men. Finally, women can learn the deeper meaning of his words.' He says, 'Oh.' The Manslator says, 'Your beauty is stunning.' He says, 'Mind if I catch a movie with the guys?' The Manslator says, 'You are a lovely wonderful woman who meets all of my needs and even though I will miss you, this night I wish to see Death Cop 9 with my bros.'

He says, 'I'm fine.' The Manslator says, 'I'm fine, really, stop looking at me.' Announcer: 'The Manslator can also be customized with voices of real celebrities being impersonated. Like Yoda, 'See how much trouble you are. To the doghouse go you.' Or Mr. T. 'I petty the fool who leaves the toilet seat up.'

Buy yours today. The Manslater, Start understanding women today for only 7 easy payments of $99.99. Manslater Labs, 1337 Impossible Avenue, Nomansland, AK 10110. Clarity is only a phone call today. Other celebrity voices include: Arnold Schwarzenegger, Louis Favreau, Robin Williams.[12]

Now men, how many of you are going to be dialing that number as soon as you get in your car? And for those of you who just raised your hands, you're going to wish you had one when you and your wife get to the car! You're going be driving home and you look at her and she's all mad and you ask her what's wrong and she says, "I'm fine!" NO! SHE NOT FINE! But seriously folks, here's the point. That translator device, believe it or not, is the exact same kind of device we need every day, if we're going to counter the lies of the evil one, like Jesus did. Only in **Matthew 4**, our device is not called the Manslater, it's called the Wordslator, it's the "rhema" Word of God! And here's what you do with this device. We simply retranslate all these lying temptations from the evil in the Word of God, a specific verse from the Bible… a "rhema" and defeat the enemy every single time. Let me show you how it works. This is awesome folks! You don't want to leave home without this device…the Wordslater! For instance, maybe you're getting low on finances, and things are getting a little tight, and you're wondering how you're going to pay your bills… And maybe you're starting to freak out and get a little afraid, because you've allowed the enemy to smack you with his lies that God can't provide, He won't provide, and you'll be out on the street…what do you do? Simple! You retranslate it with a "rhema" Word of God! Wordslator says…

Psalm 37:35 "I have never seen the righteous forsaken or their children begging for bread."

2 Corinthians 9:8 "God is able to make all grace abound to you, so that in all things at all times, having all that you need, you will abound in every good work."

Philippians 4:19 "And my God will supply all your needs according to His riches in glory in Christ Jesus."

Do you see how it works? You translate your attack with a specific piece of Scripture, a "rhema" that's designed to counter the attack and enjoy God's victory! That's how you STOP the attack! Don't stand there and get slapped silly in the head! And neither do you need to whine and complain about it! Just take the Sword of the Spirit which is the Word of God and take the enemy out! Or here's one. Maybe the enemy's laughing at you, tormenting you, scoffing at you because you blew it big time with sin this week... And maybe you're starting to freak out and get a little afraid, you know, doubt your salvation, because the enemy is smacking you with his lies! What do you do? Simple! You just translate it with a "rhema" Word of God! Wordslator says...

Romans 8:1 "Therefore, there is now no condemnation for those who are in Christ Jesus."

I John 1:9 "If we confess our sins, he is faithful and just and will forgive us our sins and purify us from all unrighteousness."

Psalms 103:12 "As far as the east is from the west, so far has He removed our transgressions from us."

Hebrews 8:12 "For God will forgive all our wickedness and will remember our sins no more."

Or maybe people are threatening you or persecuting you for being a Christian and maybe they're even saying they're going to take your life and so you're totally freaking out and getting afraid. What do you do? You take the Sword of the Spirit which is the Word of God and you throw a "rhema" at him and take him out! The Wordslator says...

Hebrews 13:6 "So we say with confidence, the Lord is my helper; I will not be afraid. What can man do to me?"

Psalm 18:2-3 "The LORD is my rock, my fortress and my deliverer; my rock, in whom I take refuge. He is my shield and the horn of my salvation, my stronghold. I call to the LORD, who is worthy of praise, and I am saved from my enemies."

Psalm 27:1,3 "The LORD is my light and my salvation – whom shall I fear? The LORD is the stronghold of my life – of whom shall I be afraid? Though an army besiege me, my heart will not fear; though war break out against me, even then will I be confident."

Psalm 91:1-7 "He who dwells in the shelter of the Most High will rest in the shadow of the Almighty. I will say of the LORD, He is my refuge and my fortress, my God, in whom I trust. Surely, he will save you from the fowler's snare and from the deadly pestilence. He will cover you with his feathers, and under his wings you will find refuge; his faithfulness will be your shield and rampart. You will not fear the terror of night, nor the arrow that flies by day, nor the pestilence that stalks in the darkness, nor the plague that destroys at midday. A thousand may fall at your side, ten thousand at your right hand, but it will not come near you."

Why? Because **1 John 4:4** "Greater is He who is in you than he who is in the world."

That's what the Wordslator can do for you! That's utilizing the Sword of the Spirit which is the Word of God, the "rhema" in action just like Jesus! That's what Paul is saying here. This is the GOOD NEWS! If you're sick and tired of being slapped around all the time, don't just stand there and take it, and go WAA, WAA, WAA, with a goofy look on your face! Stop listening to satan and start taking the Word of God and JAB THE ENEMY RIGHT OUT OF YOUR LIFE! Amen? That's how you use the sword of the spirit which is the Word of God. I close with this....

FINAL WORDS

"The Christian life is not a playground; It is a battleground. The Bible is an armory of heavenly weapons, a laboratory of infallible medicines, a mine of exhaustless wealth. It is a guidebook for every road, a chart for every sea, a medicine for every malady, and a balm for every wound. Rob us of our Bible and our sky has lost its sun.

The idea is that the Spirit provides a sword for you, and that sword is the word of God. To effectively use the Sword of the Spirit, we can't regard the Bible as book of magic charms or tie one around our neck the way that garlic is said to drive away vampires.

To effectively use the sword, we must regard it as the word of God...If we are not confident in the inspiration of Scripture, that the sword really came from the Spirit, then we will not use it effectively at all. But we must also take the sword of the Spirit in the sense of depending that He helps us to use it. Not only did the Spirit give us the Scriptures, but also, He makes them alive to us, and equips us with the right thrust of the sword at the right time.

The sword is the only offensive weapon in the panoply. But it is indispensable. For, while the Christian soldier is exhibited here mainly in the attitude of defense, as one who stands, in order to take his position and keep his ground, thrust and cut will be required. The Word of God is the weapon provided by the Spirit for meeting the lunge of the assailant and beating him back.

Just as a small dagger is applied with skill and precision to a vital area of the body, so we must use the Word carefully and expertly, applying specific principles from it to every situation we face. How's your skill with the spiritual sword? Do you have a thorough grasp of Scripture and know how to apply it with precision? If you learn how to use it properly, the Word can be an effective weapon for any challenge. If you waste time and energy with manmade, plastic weapons, however, you'll find yourself a defenseless victim in the spiritual battle.

The "sword of the Spirit" is the saying of God applied to a specific situation in your life. That is the great weapon placed in the hands of the believer. Perhaps you have had some experience with this. Sometimes, when you are reading a passage of Scripture, the words seem to suddenly come alive, take on flesh and bones, and leap off the page at you.

Sometimes they seem to grow eyes that follow you around everywhere you go or develop a voice that echoes in your ears until you cannot get away from it. Perhaps you have had that experience in some moment of temptation or doubt when you were assailed by what Paul calls here "the flaming arrows of the evil one." And immediately a passage of Scripture that supplies the answer comes flashing to mind. That passage of Scripture is God's rhema for you.

Or perhaps you have been asked a question that caught you off guard for a moment and you were about to say, "I don't know," when suddenly you had a moment of illumination and a word of Scripture came to mind that provided the answer. Perhaps this experience has happened while sitting in a meeting where some message has come home to your heart with an unusually powerful effect.

You were greatly moved, and in that moment, you made a significant and lasting decision.

That illuminating word of Scripture was God's <u>rhema</u> for you. The rhema-word of God in your life is called "the sword of the Spirit" because it not only originated by the Spirit as the author of the Word, but it is also recalled to your mind by the Spirit and made powerful by Him in your life. It is His specific, well-chosen answer to the attack of the devil. Like a swordsman with a trusty blade in his hand, the Spirit brings a flashing, sharp-edged, highly polished word to our mind to parry the sword-thrust of the devil.

Think of a soldier or a gladiator in training, practicing sword thrusts and moves and positions. Now, he must practice them ahead of time, and if he is a superior fighter, and has a great fighting instinct, at the time of battle he will instantly recall which thrust, which position suits the precise moment. He will never be able to use the thrust in the fight if he has not first practiced it, but he still needs to make the move at the moment.

Therefore, effectively using the sword takes practice. The great example of this was Jesus combating the temptation of satan in the wilderness. Proper use of Scripture in spiritual warfare enables the Christian to stand fast "against the wiles of the devil".

God's spoken word is powerful. As Hebrews 11:3 states, 'By faith we understand that the worlds were prepared by the word [rhema] of God, so that what is seen was not made out of things which are visible.' God spoke, and the entire universe came into existence out of nothing! The picture of the Word as a sword also implies its power. The sword wasn't used in battle to tap your enemy on the shoulder or to hold up to threaten him. It was used to kill him! While we cannot kill Satan, God's Word is powerful to defeat him and to put to death the temptations that he puts in front of us.

The instructive thing for us is that each time, Jesus responded with a specific, appropriate Scripture, which He knew verbatim from memory Jesus didn't say, "I know that there's a verse somewhere about that. Just a minute while I get my concordance!" He knew the Word and used it to ward off Satan's temptations. We should do the same.

One of the wonderful Vance Havner quotes that he gave to us was this: 'Show me a Christian whose Bible is falling apart, and I'll show you a Christian who isn't.' Isn't that beautiful? If your Bible is falling apart, if the word has been worked deep into your bones, into your being, you're not going to fall apart in the day of battle. Paul's saying that to you here: Put on the word of God, so that it's part of your armor. That's why we teach it every chance we get–Sunday morning, Sunday evening, Wednesday night, Sunday School, discipleship groups. Wherever we can, we want to be in that word...not just so you'll know more stuff, but so that you're armed for this battle."[13]

Chapter Thirty

The Protection from Satan and Demons Part 10

"It's not one of the most pleasant areas to live in the first place, being one of the most densely populated areas in the world and all. Its people are crammed into every single nook and cranny they could find nestled near the Himalayan Mountains and they are constantly surrounded by Islamic terrorists. But an even greater nightmare was headed their way as they lay fast asleep.

Just a few days prior, a tropical storm developed in the ocean that intensified rapidly. It started off with winds approaching 85-90 mph but the next day arose

to 140 mph. Then, to make matters worse, even though meteorologists knew about the approaching storm, there was no way to communicate it fast enough to those in its path, and the results were horrific!

As it reached land it pushed up a 20-30-foot storm surge (some reports say even higher) and since most of the area was just barely above sea level the damage was unbelievable. 13 islands were totally wiped out, crops were decimated, whole villages were gone, tens upon tens of thousands of people instantly drowned and some areas lost over half its population.

And in a matter of moments, when all was said and done, this tropical storm became the deadliest of its kind of all time. Just for perspective, Hurricane Katrina caused only 1,200 fatalities. But this storm caused well over a ½ a billion dollars damage, 9,000 fishing boats were destroyed, 65% of the fishing industry was totally annihilated, approximately 85% of homes in the area were demolished or damaged, and it is estimated that some 300,000-500,000 people were killed by this single storm.

The year was 1970. The disaster is of course, The Bhola Cyclone."[1]

Now folks, how many of you have heard of the The Bhola Cyclone? Okay, probably a few of us. But how many of you guys would agree it was one of the greatest disasters of all time, right? But with all due respect to those who lost their lives in The Bohla Cyclone, what if I were to tell you I know of a disaster that makes The Bohla Cyclone look like a baby ice cream cone? And what if I were to tell you that this disaster didn't occur in just one place and one country at one time, but it's going on right now today all over the world and it's been leaving a trail of death and destruction for centuries. Once again, I'm talking about *The satanic War on the Christian.* And these are the facts. We Christians don't battle here and there once in a while. We go to war, every single day. Whether you see it, feel it, believe it or not, the moment you got saved you entered a spiritual war against a demonic host whose sole purpose is to destroy you and extinguish your testimony for Jesus Christ. And what's wild is that most wars go on for a few years or even longer. But *The satanic War on the Christian* has been going on for the last 2,000 years non-stop, and it's sending people straight to hell! And what's wild is most people will readily talk about all the other wars throughout history and all their atrocities, and rightly so…we have the History Channel…. we need to talk about them! YET how many people, even Christians, will openly discuss the longest war in mankind's history…The satanic War on the Christian that has destroyed more lives than all the wars put together?

Therefore, in order to stop getting duped and beat up all over the place, we're going to conclude our study, *The satanic War on the Christian.*

Now so far, we've seen if you're ever going to win a war, then the **1st thing** you must do is **Know Who Your Enemy Is**...

Then we saw the **2nd thing** you need to know is **What Your Enemy is Like**, their character, amen? It's common sense, right?

Then we saw the **3rd thing** you need to know is **The Tactic of Your Enemy**...what they're up to...what's their goal.... why are they here...

Then we saw the **4th thing** you need to know is **The Destruction of Your Enemy**...what price you pay when you DON'T take this seriously...

Then we saw the **5th thing** you need to know is **The Temptation of Your Enemy**...how he's out there trying to get us to sin against God....

And the **last nine times** we saw the **6th thing** you need to know is **The Protection FROM Your Enemy**.

And there we saw God has not left us hanging high and dry in this Great Cosmic War dealing with satan and demons. Are you kidding me? He's actually given us His full-blown protection and amazing weaponry to stand our ground and be victorious in all situations every single time! It's called The Armor of God!

And so far, we've seen the **1st thing** about the Armor of God that **It's Designed for War**.

The **2nd thing It's Designed for Victory**.

And the last three times the **3rd thing It's Designed for Wear**.

This armor is not something to look at, it's not meant just to stare at, or stick on a shelf and collect dust. It's designed for wear. You Daily wear it, you continual wear it. YOU PUT IT ON! And again, the Greek says to put it on now and leave it on! Quick! Chop, chop! Don't delay! This is serious stuff! WHY?

Because that's the second part of experiencing God's Victory He's already given to us!

So far, we saw the 1st **piece** was **The Belt of Truth**.

The 2nd **piece** was **The Breastplate of Righteousness**.

The 3rd **piece** was **The Shoes of Peace**.

The 4th **piece** was **The Shield of Faith**.

The 5th **piece** was **Helmet of Salvation**.

And last time the 6th **piece** was **The Sword of the Spirit**.

And there we saw, just like the belt and the breastplate and the shoes and the shield and the helmet of the Roman soldier, so it is with the sword. It wasn't a literal sword we stab our opponents with, that's not what he's saying. Rather he's speaking of a spiritual sword, the Bible, the context defines it for us. You don't have to pray and fast for 15 years to figure this one out. It's clearly the Word of God. And the Sword of the Spirit, the Bible, is given by God as an offensive weapon to take out our enemy and stop getting slapped around unnecessarily so. Why? Because as we saw with the Roman Soldier's sword, It Provides an Offensive Attack and it Can Only Be Taken Up By Me…nobody can wield this Sword, the Bible, I alone can do it. Why? I alone have to get in there and memorize it, chew on it, read it, study it, take it to heart so I can have thousands and thousands of offensive swords to take out the thousands and thousands of attacks I experience from the enemy. God hasn't left me hanging high and dry. I use the Bible and throw a "rhema" word at the enemy and he's defeated every single time! Isn't that AWESOME NEWS! What a God…amen? But that's not all.

The 7th **piece** of Armor we need to hurry up and put on for God's Victory that He's already given to us is **The Power of Prayer**. But don't take my word for it. Let's listen to God's.

Ephesians 6:10-20 "Finally, be strong in the Lord and in His mighty power. Put on the full armor of God so that you can take your stand against the devil's schemes. For our struggle is not against flesh and blood, but against the rulers, against the authorities, against the powers of this dark world and against the spiritual forces of evil in the heavenly realms. Therefore, put on the full armor of God, so that when the day of evil comes, you may be able to stand your ground, and after you have done everything, to stand. Stand firm then, with the belt of truth buckled around your waist, with the breastplate of righteousness in place, and with your feet fitted with the readiness that comes from the gospel of peace. In addition to all this, take up the shield of faith, with which you can extinguish all the flaming arrows of the evil one. Take the helmet of salvation and the sword of the Spirit, which is the word of God. And pray in the Spirit on all occasions with all kinds of prayers and requests. With this in mind, be alert and always keep on praying for all the saints. Pray also for me, that whenever I open my mouth, words may be given me so that I will fearlessly make known the mystery of the gospel, for which I am an ambassador in chains. Pray that I may declare it fearlessly, as I should"

So now we see the seventh piece of supernatural military equipment that God gives us the ability to effectively struggle and come out on top in our war against the evil ones, when they come at us every single day…not if. This is the seventh piece that gives us the ability to stand our ground and not buckle or break under pressure when the dust clears from the battle that we're in…and it was simply called prayer.

It's mentioned 5 times in just three verses which obviously adds emphasis. I mean, think about the rest of the armor that Paul talked about. Paul didn't say, "Grab the Sword of the Spirit," five times. He didn't say, "Put on that Helmet," five times in a row. He didn't say, "You got your shoes? You got your shoes? You got your shoes? You got your shoes? You got your shoes?" But he did with prayer.

Why? Well, one again, I think we can glean more about what Paul is talking about with prayer when we take a look again at the Roman soldier's uniform and weaponry including his form of communication… Which is what prayer is, we're communicating to God.

And the 1st thing we're going to see about The Power of Prayer is that It Provides Constant Communication.

Once again, let's take a look at what that piece of armor was like for the Roman Soldier and find out what it literally means for us today.

ROMAN SOLDIER'S COMMUNICATION

"Good communications are of prime importance for the efficient conduct of military operations and so it was with the Roman Military. They used a form of communication called Military Signaling. For a short distance messages, the Roman officers overseeing a battle from an elevated position on a hillside would have a team of runners whose job it as to run at full tilt to the commander of a unit.

Upon arrival they would pass a message verbally or written on a wax tablet. But over longer distances, the utilization of runners was not an effective means of communication. So, the Romans developed a system of communication over longer distances where the legate (general) of the legions stayed behind in a spot where he could give orders and instructions several different ways to the troops. Sometimes they used messengers on horseback to transmit those orders to the front.

Other times they would use trumpets that were easily identifiable in a battle for the soldiers to follow. Still others, they would use fire signals where a series of bonfires were erected on hilltops from the scene of a battle where as one fire was lit, the team at the next hill in the chain would see it and light theirs, and so on until the last fire was lit. They also utilized what was called the "five flags method."

This was a communication system the Romans developed using two sets of five flags that could be raised or lowered. They were mounted on poles some 12ft high with a rigid triangular or square flag at the top. They were usually painted bright red for clarity and used a master list of letters from the Roman alphabet.

To send a message, each side, the sender and receiver, had a tablet with the alphabet laid out and a number of flags from each of the two groups would be raised to indicate the corresponding letter in the communication. This would continue until the message was sent. The messages were short and straight to the point as this method was naturally slow in use. Instead of sending "The enemy is in full retreat with our legions in hot pursuit" they would have sent a tabloid newspaper type of headline such as "Enemy retreat." And if flags were not available, sometimes they would utilize five torches in like manner."[2]

So, as you can see with the Roman soldier, one of the vital things they needed during a battle was an effective means to communicate, right? This is how they stayed in touch with the Commanders and Generals. They alone had a vantage point that could see the whole battle and could give the soldiers specific orders on what to do in order to insure success. And this is what Paul is saying prayer is for us! The words there for "prayers" and "requests" are the Greek words "proseuche" and "deesis." "Proseuche" means "communication addressed to God" and "Deesis" is simply "seeking, asking, or making a request to God." So, you put it all together and what you're seeing is that Paul is saying... Just as a secular soldier needs to stay in communication with Command Control Central Headquarters to give him directions and wisdom, provide aerial support if needed, or inform him of what lies ahead.... etc. So it is with the spiritual soldier, the Christian! We too need to stay in constant communication with our Heavenly Commander, Jesus Christ, Who alone has the ultimate perspective to see the battlefield all at once and not only tell us what we specifically need to do in a skirmish but to also support us so we can have success in dealing with the daily spiritual warfare we're in! Listen, in essence, what Paul is saying is that this last piece of equipment, prayer, is your Spiritual Walkie Talkie to God to be used in times of conflict! And without it, you're toast! As these men share.

CHRISTIAN WALKIE TALKIE

"The believer must keep in constant contact and communication with his Heavenly Commander in every season of conflict because it is the only way he is enabled to follow the leading of his Master closely.

Prayer is a war-time walkie-talkie, not a domestic intercom. It's for a mission in battle. It's for use on the front lines of war to call in for headquarters to help. One of the reasons for our prayers malfunction is that we try to treat it like a domestic intercom to call in a butler for another pillow when it's supposed to be a wartime walkie-talkie for calling down the power of the Holy Spirit in the battle for souls.

Prayer is vital in warfare because it represents communication with 'Command Central' so to speak and its absence is a sure means of cutting oneself off from God and making us vulnerable in warfare. Prayerlessness produces sterility of spiritual perception, you can't see what lies ahead.

No matter how complete the armor; no matter how skilled we may be in the science of war; no matter how courageous we may be, we may be certain that without prayer we shall be defeated. God alone can give the victory; and when the Christian soldier goes forth armed completely for the spiritual conflict, if he looks to God by prayer, he may be sure of a triumph.

I once borrowed a car and as a favor to the owner filled it with gas. It was a big Oldsmobile station wagon and it had an ornament on the hood that said 'diesel,' a sticker on the rear gate that said, 'Oldsmobile Diesel,' and a note on the fuel gauge reading, 'Diesel Fuel Only.' So naturally I put diesel fuel in the tank.

But it was a big mistake since the owner had recently converted it to gasoline. So, when it broke down on a main street in New York, I had to explain why I had put diesel fuel into a vehicle with a gasoline engine. I don't think I'll ever live that down.

But this is a perfect illustration for Christians. We are human beings, and we have 'Human Being' written all over us, but we've been converted into something else. We're 'spiritual' now. So, if you try to run your new spiritual self on the old kind of fuel, it won't work. And there are a lot of Christians who haven't figured that out yet.

The fuel for the Christian life is prayer. Prayer is the energy that makes it possible for the Christian warrior to wear the armor and wield the sword. You cannot fight the battle in your own power. No matter how talented you are, if you try to fight the spiritual battle in your own strength, you will be defeated.

F.B. Meyer said: 'With the perpetual use of the weapon of All-Prayer, there is no enemy born of hell that shall be able to withstand us.'

Which is why one guy said, 'If you have long-standing problems, try kneeling!'"[3]

So surely that's what we're doing right? We're kneeling, we're praying, we're in constant contact with our Heavenly Commander for protection and wisdom and strength. I mean we totally get it why Paul mentions prayer 5 times in just three verses here, it's obvious, because without it we're spiritually toast! Are you kidding me? If we're honest, for many of us, we not only don't pray, but we're so lazy about it, if we could, we'd hire somebody else to do it for us, like these guys!

PRE-BLESSED FOOD

The video begins with a man sitting down at the dinner table ready to eat. The Announcer says: "Hold it right there! Do you still say grace before you eat breakfast, lunch and dinner? If you answered yes, then I have a product that is going to revolutionize the way you do food. 'Pre-Blessed Food'. That's right, 'Pre-Blessed Food.'
We pray for it, so you don't have to. This is the 21st Century folks, we can sell anything. Around the clock we have thousands of employees buying brand named foods, praying over them and then putting them back on the shelves of your local grocery store, with our official sticker of approval. We've got breakfast cereal, lunch meat, TV Dinners and if you don't want a white guy praying over your food we've got that too. (Then we see different nationalities blessing the food.)

Just listen to how the Pre-Blessed foods have changed these peoples lives. The first guy tells us, "Since I have been eating the Pre-Blessed foods nothing has changed."

Another says, "We have always prayed religiously before eating. But we've been so busy with work and watching TV that Pre-Blessed food has not only saved us time, but it has saved our souls."

Announcer: "So visit your local grocery store today and look for our official sticker of approval. Then the next time someone asked you to bless the food, you say, "It's already been blessed."[4]

Yeah, if you know anything, praying over chicken is wrong! But the point is, that video would be funny if what? If it weren't so true! We're so lazy when it comes to prayer! And we wonder why our walk with Him isn't blessed? Or double pre-blessed or whatever... And we wonder why we aren't having a blessed time in our dealings with spiritual warfare? We wonder why we've lost the blessed connection with our Heavenly Commander! Are you kidding me? We're trying to do this on our own! A lack of prayer for the Christian is like fighting a one-man battle when the whole time we have all of Heaven at our disposal. It's ridiculous, let alone suicidal! Just bust out your spiritual walkie talkie, prayer, and call in for support! Why would you torture yourself like that? No wonder the enemy wants you to do anything and everything but pray! Watch TV...social media... And this is precisely why the Apostle Paul not only says to pray...but to pray continually! Notice how many times he uses the word there all. He not only says to pray 5 times in three verses, but he repeatedly says to pray all the time!

HOW OFTEN TO PRAY

- And pray in the Spirit on ALL occasions.
- With ALL kinds of prayers and requests.
- ALWAYS keep on praying.
- For ALL the saints.
- He says it 4 times in just verse 18 alone!
- Why? Because the enemy is ALWAYS attacking us therefore we ALWAYS need to be in connection with the Heavenly Commander for wisdom, direction, and support!
- It is to be prayer of all kinds – public and private, oral and mental, formal and spontaneous.
- It is to be spiritual prayer – "In the Spirit." (Not speaking in tongues but simply means, "to pray in concert with the Spirit, pray consistent with His will and nature.)
- It is to be persevering prayer. "At all times."
- It is to be watchful prayer.[5]

And that we get from the word there, "be alert." It's from the Greek word, "agrupneo" which means, "without sleep," or literally, "no sleep." And boy, isn't that the secondary problem. Even when we finally do get around to praying to God, we either literally do fall asleep, or we act like were sleeping in our brains when praying to Him. We get all repetitious or rote, perfunctory, saying the same thing over and over again, like this man shares.

FATHER, FATHER, FATHER

Tim Hawkins: *Some people, when they pray, get nervous and say 'just' too much. They say, 'and we just', 'if you just', 'can you just', just, just, just... and justification, etc. And you are like... "just finish the prayer! We just not ready for this. Go start stacking chairs. Come back next week and try again." My dad does this when he prays. He uses Father way too much when he prays. It's "Father, we come to you, Father. You are Father, Father just, just, Father, just, just, Father, Father." You don't talk to your friends like that. "Ed, come over Ed, Ed, Ed, Ed, Ed...he wouldn't be your friend any more if you did that. He keeps saying Ed and he says, 'my name is Joe.'*[6]

Can you imagine that in real life? A soldier on his walkie talkie calling in, in the midst of a battle saying, "Commander, Commander, Commander, Commander, or Hey Sarge, Sarge, Hey Sarge, Sarge, Sarge... You'd think they'd reply back..." I HEARD YOU THE FIRST TIME!!! WHAT DO YOU WANT?" And here's the point. What do you think we're doing when we do that to God! Praise God we're at least praying, but we're going to sleep at the wheel! We're not alert! We're just going through the motions! Slow down! Talk intelligently. Think of what you're saying. Mean what you say! WHY? Because you're really talking to God and He's really listening and He's really willing to help if you could just get past His Name! I heard you the first time! How can I help you? Don't just go through the motions. Let Him know what you need, and He'll help you! In fact, the word there "be alert" (agrupneo) is in the present tense which means, "to continually be on standby alert as you pray." It's speaking as a way of life as a Christian. In other words, this is to be our lifestyle. We are in constant communication with the Head, our Heavenly Commander, Jesus, and because of that He's constantly helping, aiding, empowering, protecting, and strengthening us during the battle.

THE IMPORTANCE OF CONTINUAL PRAYER

"Prayer is not our last resort, it should be our first resort. It's not a spare tire in the trunk to be used only in emergencies, it's our daily lifeline, our air supply, our oxygen support from God in a spiritually deflated atmosphere. It's the spiritual air that we Christian soldiers are to breathe.

That's why no period of life should be without it. Prayer to God is the all—pervasive strategy in which warfare is fought.... Ephesians begins by lifting us up to the heavenlies and ends by pulling us down to our knees. We are called to pray and keep our spiritual eyes open, for the enemy may assault us at any time! And the only way we can be continually be on "high spiritual alert" is to be continually in communication with the Spirit of God for God alone makes us adequate in spiritual matters!

We need to realize that a Holy War cannot be carried out in our own unholy strength but only by God's Holy Spirit! Don't fall into the trap of thinking you can stand against supernatural powers in your own natural strength! You are already defeated (or soon will feel that way) if that is the way you are thinking. You'll never be able to stand against your unseen foe!

Praying is simply showing our dependency upon God. We demonstrate that we need Him and His strength by praying at all times in every way. A lack of prayer is thus showing your independence from God. It's saying that you don't need Him or His strength in the spiritual battle you're in. And yet we wonder why we're getting chewed alive!

We pray all the time because we're being attacked all the time. The battle never stops, and we have to be constantly on the alert. No soldier can afford to close his eyes to the enemy. That would be suicide.

In fact, it is interesting to note that the prayer posture of closing the eyes, bowing the head, or folding the hands is not found in Scripture. The Jews prayed with their eyes open toward heaven and their hands lifted toward God. "Watch and pray" was our Lord's repeated admonition. We are to be constantly alert to what the devil is doing otherwise he'll even attack us while we're praying!

We are to persevere like the early cowboys guarding a herd at night. Sometimes they took drastic measures to keep alert and hold fast to their work. They rubbed tobacco juice in their eyes to keep at their vigil and to stay awake when weary. They did it in the interests of their boss and for the safety of the cattle. Can we as

Christians at least do the same in prayer for the sake of our Lord and for the benefit of others?

You see, what the Church needs today is not more machinery or better new organizations or better novel methods, but men whom the Spirit of God can use, men of prayer, men mighty in prayer. The Holy Spirit does not flow through methods, but through men. He does not come on machinery, but on men. He does not anoint plans, but men—men of prayer.

And that's why it's high time that we in the Church learn what Paul is saying here. Satanic wars cannot be won by human energy. But they can be won in prayer, which is why satan trembles even when he sees the weakest saint upon his knees."[7]

Which brings us to the **2ⁿᵈ thing** we see about The Power of Prayer is that **It's Not Only for Me**.

Notice how Paul says in these verses how this "Power of Prayer" is not only for my good and my support, but it's for the support of your fellow Christian soldier.

Ephesians 6:18b-20 "And always keep on praying for all the saints. Pray also for me, that whenever I open my mouth, words may be given me so that I will fearlessly make known the mystery of the gospel, for which I am an ambassador in chains. Pray that I may declare it fearlessly, as I should."

Here we see that Paul not only encourages us to use the Power of Prayer for ourselves, but for who? For our fellow soldiers, "all the saints" (every Christian) and for "Paul himself" (i.e. a Church leader an Apostle). Why? Because we're all in this battle together! And therefore, we need every able-bodied solder on the front lines in this battle if we're ever going to make any dent in the enemy's territory. It's common sense, right? And so is it any wonder the enemy not only gets us to NOT pray ourselves but we rarely ever pray for other believers! Rather, what's he got us doing? We don't pray for each other, we beat each other up over secondary issues like this guy.

DIE YOU HERETIC!

"One day a guy was walking across a bridge and he saw another fellow who looked like he was ready to jump off the bridge. So, he thought he'd try to stall him until the authorities showed up.

So, he yelled to the guy, 'Don't jump!' To which the guy replied, 'Why not? Nobody loves me.' 'Well, God loves you. You believe in God, don't you? 'Yes, I believe in God,' he said. 'Good. Are you Christian or Jewish? 'Christian,' he said. 'Me, too! What kind of Christian?' 'Baptist,' he said. 'Me, too! Independent Baptist or Southern Baptist?' 'Southern Baptist,' he said. 'Me, too!

New Evangelical/Moderate Southern Baptist or Conservative Southern Baptist?' 'Conservative Southern Baptist,' he said. 'Me, too! Once Saved Always Saved Conservative Southern Baptist or Lose-Your-Salvation Armenian Conservative Southern Baptist?' 'Once Saved Always Saved Conservative Southern Baptist,' he said. 'Me, too!

King James Only Once Saved Always Saved Conservative Southern Baptist OR Modern Versions Once Saved Always Saved Conservative Southern Baptist?' And the guy said, 'Modern Versions Once Saved Always Saved Conservative Southern Baptist,' he said.

And the other guy said, 'What??!! You heretic!' And he pushed him over the bridge."[8]

Yeah, that joke would be funny if what? If it weren't so true as well! Folks when are we going to wake up and realize that we're in this fight together as soldiers of Christ. Turn to somebody and say, "I need you man!" We don't need to be fighting among the ranks! We'll never win the war like that! Rather we should be doing what Paul says to do… "Always keep on praying for all the saints." Why? Because we need every soldier healthy and whole to fight in this battle! And when we pray for each other, people get healed and rejoin the battle.

PRAYING FOR OTHERS BRINGS HEALING

"In a recent missionary trip to Romania, I got so sick. I had the highest fever I have ever had. I was delirious at times. I was in a hotel and was so sick. I remember laying there thinking, 'God, I don't know what to do.' I was so sick. My fever was so high.

Well, it was 1:00 in the morning and I remember God impressed on my heart, 'Wayne, while you are praying now, remember it is 6:00 back at home. At 6:15 church services are going to start, and they are going to pray for you, Wayne. They are going to pray for you.'

Sure enough, between 6:15 and 6:18 that evening my fever broke. It broke. During the night I got better and better and better. When I got home I told that story to the congregation. And an Associate Pastor came to me and said, 'Wayne, that night in choir, we were trying to get ready to go upstairs. We were running late, and we couldn't leave because we felt so impressed to pray for your healing at exactly the same time your fever broke in Romania!'

And he says, 'Oh, folks. We haven't even begun to tap into prayer yet!'

And another guy says, 'What would happen if a Church called on its members to begin to intercede for each other, and their whole Church, for their spiritual well-being according to the pattern of the Pauline prayers? And what if they called upon them to intercede in this manner not just for a week or a month, but a year-round as the Spirit leads.

I think God's Spirit would move in families, in marriages, in teenagers, in individuals, in the pastoral staff, etc, in a way that can only be described as supernatural so that only God receives the glory?"[9]

But we beat each other up because we have a different Bible translation! Folks when are we going to wake up and realize that when we intercede for our fellow soldiers in Christ, be it their healing or wholeness or whatever, don't you realize what's going on? We're acting like a spiritual infirmary, a holy hospital, that's working together to get as many injured soldiers back on the battlefield, as they can, so they can fight again. No wonder the enemy doesn't want us to "always keep on praying for all the saints" as Paul says! He wants our supply of soldiers to be completely depleted so we will always be defeated! Do you get it? Turn to somebody and say, "I'm praying for you!" In fact, we're not only to pray for each other's wholeness, we're to also pray for each other's boldness specifically when it comes to sharing the Gospel. What'd Paul say?

Ephesians 6:19-20 "Pray also for me, that whenever I open my mouth, words may be given me so that I will fearlessly make known the mystery of the gospel, for which I am an ambassador in chains. Pray that I may declare it fearlessly, as I should."

The battle we are in as Christians is not a battle for you to get a bigger house, it's not a battle for you to have a better car, it's not a battle for you to obtain a bigger bank account, it's not a battle to be a better you! That's a lie from the pit of hell! That's what the Apostate Church is teaching! Paul says it's a battle for souls! God gives us His armor for protection yes…but it's to also to win souls!

PRAYING FOR OTHERS BRINGS SALVATION

"We hear of the D. L. Moodys and the Billy Grahams. But we seldom hear of common, ordinary people that have prayed for the great evangelists. In prayer, those ordinary people have believed God to do extraordinary things.

In September 1985, Billy Graham visited Romania on an 11-day preaching tour. The Chicago Tribune reported, 'His crowds of more than thirty thousand were the largest for religious gatherings in that country since World War II.'

The Crusade Information Service for the Billy Graham Team was even more descriptive: Well over 150,000 turned out to see and hear evangelist Billy Graham on a whirlwind 11-day, seven-stop preaching mission in Romania, described by local officials and religious leaders alike as 'extraordinary' and 'unprecedented.'

Huge throngs-applauding, singing, and chanting, 'Billy Graham, Billy Graham'- greeted the American evangelist in the streets of almost every city where he preached....

The crowds were the largest Mr. Graham has attracted in a special ministry that has taken him to six countries in Eastern Europe, including the Soviet Union.

There was one aspect of Dr. Graham's crusade that will never be in the newspapers. God moved mightily through Dr. Graham in the large Second Baptist Church of Oradea, where Josif Ton formerly pastured.

Three months prior to Dr. Graham's visit to Oradea, I preached in that church on the principles of spiritual awakening. A layman asked in English if he could speak with me.

He said, "Friday, I was prompted by the Holy Spirit to cut my vacation short and return immediately to Oradea. I felt I needed to be in my own church on Sunday morning. And you were here preaching on the necessity and principles of spiritual awakening.

'I have been praying for revival in Romania for 11 years. I would like to travel with you throughout Romania and learn more of these principles of spiritual awakenings.'

When he told me his name, I realized who he was. An evangelist friend had been to Romania a year earlier and said he had never before met such a man of prayer.

We discussed with the pastors of the church the idea of his traveling with our team. They agreed. He could also serve as interpreter.

It didn't take long for me to realize he would not be learning from me; I would be learning from him. I asked him what he thought of the preaching of my evangelist friend.

'I have never heard him preach.'

'I thought he preached a week of evangelistic meetings at your Church.'

He nodded. 'When an evangelist comes to preach, I go to pray. When your friend came to our Church, I gathered a group of men. We met prior to the worship service and prayed all through the service. As a result, we saw your friend reap a great harvest each evening.'

As we drove from city to city together, he often said, 'Let's pray for this city and this country.' Or, 'Let's pray and fast today.' He continually challenged me, 'We must pray! We must pray!'

I never saw as many conversions to Christ in my ministry in Eastern Europe as I saw in those two weeks. The last four nights I spent in a major university city. Nearly 1,000 commitments to Christ were made in those four days.

The last night was one I'll never forget. Every inch of the Church was packed. Every available room was full, and people were gathered all the way out to the street. I preached, and my friend interpreted. We were both exhausted.

MY MESSAGE...NO POWER

My message seemed to have no power. The people were there and hungry, but I seemed unable to feed them. Then something happened. My friend began to pray silently for me while I was preaching, and I prayed for him as he interpreted.

After about 10 minutes of ministering in this manner, I felt impressed of God to cease preaching and just quote Scripture. For about 15 minutes I quoted Scripture while he interpreted. And the glory of God came down.

As we quoted Scripture, people inside and outside the building began to weep. Hearts were broken by the Holy Spirit. More people were converted to Christ that one night than any other night of my ministry in Eastern Europe.

I didn't think we would ever be able to get back to the West. Hundreds of people gathered around our van weeping and praying and singing.

We left our new friend at a train station. He would return to Oradea. He said, 'You have your ministry of preaching in the West. I must return to Oradea and pray. Billy Graham is coming, and I must organize the brothers to pray for the mightiest outpouring of God's Spirit that we have ever seen.'

I drove all night through Hungary to Austria. I knew my life would never be the same. I had been with a man of prayer. Romania would never be the same again either; not just because Billy Graham was going there, but also because a man of prayer was already there. It was no surprise to hear of the wonderful results of Dr. Graham's ministry. He went to a country where the roots of evangelism were deep in the soil of prayer.

When the winds of revival begin to blow, there's always a wedding between the ministry of the evangelist and the ministry of the intercessor. They can't operate without each other.

Leonard Ravenhill, in his book 'Why Revival Tarries' says this: 'We have many organizers, but few agonizers; many players and payers, but few pray-ers; many singers, but few clingers; lots of pastors, but few wrestlers; many fears, but few tears; much fashion, little passion; many interferers, and few intercessors; many writers, but few fighters' - and I've added one of my own: a few less preachers on prophecy, and a few more prophets of prayer! We need to be in the battle now!' "[10]

And when we pray for others they speak the Gospel with boldness, they do! And then the next thing you know, lost people get saved and join God's Army too, including those we think would never get saved, like this lady.

PACINA'S STORY

Commentator: "Hopelessness and despair, these are the words that best describe the current situation in Iran. As a result, Iran has one of the highest suicide rates in the world. My name is Dr. Hormoz Shariat, President of Iran Alive Ministries. What you are about to see is an actual story that happened here during the broadcast of Iran Alive. This is the story of a life transformed by the power of the gospel.

'ALLAH IS A DISTANT AND CRUEL GOD, YET MANY IRANIANS ARE READY TO DIE FOR HIM'. Iranian pastor. 'ANYONE WHO CONVERTS FROM ISLAM IS AN APOSTATE. APOSTASY IS PUNISHABLE BY DEATH'. - Islamic law.

Padina lives in Iran. This is her story. As a little girl Padina was taught the beliefs and customs of her religion, Islam. All her life was spent praying to Allah. She truly believed that he was the only god. She says, "As a child I started to recite the daily prayers. Before I would go to school I would memorize the Quran. I hated Christians.

I became very happy when I heard about Christians being persecuted. They always told us if we killed a Christian, we had a one-way ticket to Heaven. I worked very hard to follow every rule of Islam. If I thought I hadn't washed correctly, I would stop n the middle of my prayer, wash correctly and start all over again. This would happen 10 times in one prayer session. I became very depressed and suicidal.

I felt so distant from Allah, and my mom was very sick and dying. I said to my mom, 'I'm going to kill myself.' She said, 'If you are going to kill yourself, you have to kill me as well.' I said, 'I will do this for you, and we both will die.' While she is getting the stuff together to kill both of them her mother turns on the TV. Dr. Shariat comes on and says, 'My brothers and sisters, I am with you tonight. The Lord has a special message for you tonight.

If you feel hopeless, if you feel depressed, if you are planning to commit suicide, the Lord says, 'STOP!', He has hope and a future for you. If you are planning to kill yourself, STOP! And call me. 'My mother spoke to him for half an hour.' I said 'I'm going t do this. Nothing is going to stop me tonight. I saw my mother was repenting and doing the prayer of salvation. I became furious. I yelled, 'Why in the last second of your life did you do this?

Now you are going to Hell.' She said, 'Please Padina, please talk to him about Jesus.' I said, 'Jesus can do nothing! Jesus is nothing! I will not blaspheme Mohammed by speaking to this infidel.' I left my mother crying, holding the phone in her hand. I went back to the phone and said, 'Hello.' Dr. Shariat says, 'When I talked to her, she was cold, she was fighting, and she told me very proudly that she was going to kill herself.

Your Jesus cannot do anything for me. After about an hour of argument with her I couldn't change her mind.' Padina says, 'I just wanted to die.' Dr. Shariat replies, 'You said it yourself, Allah has done nothing for you. Give Jesus just one chance. You can always kill yourself next week.' When he gave me this challenge, I thought, 'This is the best way I can serve Allah. This one last time before I commit suicide.'

Dr. Shariat tells us, 'She was thinking, ok, I will pray and then next week this time I will go live on the air and I will tell everyone I tried Jesus for a week and nothing has changed. I am going to kill myself tonight and I will do it on the air. When I kill myself on this live program, I can say to Allah, even taking my life was for you.'

Early the next morning, I was awakened by a sound. I saw my mother walking. She was walking perfectly. I told her we needed to go to the hospital immediately. The doctors checked the results of the blood work and the MRI. They said, 'It's a miracle. There is no MS in her body.' That is not possible. Something must be wrong.

They say, 'This is a miracle. What Imam did you pray to? What Imam did you pray to?' My mother answered, 'It wasn't an Imam. It was Jesus.' When I said those words, my heart changed. I told Jesus, 'You are the living God. You cleansed me and filled me. I'll give up my life for you.' Today Padina and her mother are apostates. They risk their lives by ministering in Iran's underground church.[11]

That's not only amazing, but when she came here to America and began to help out this ministry that helps Iranian Christians, she was doing a great work but soon went back under threat of persecution, rape, and even death... Because she said, "satan is singing lullabies to the American Church" and she wanted to go back where the power of God was moving. Where people stand in God's Armor, and pray for each other, and where souls get saved by the thousands. This is what Paul is saying. The Christian life is not about you. It's about loving God and other people, including the lost. And whether you realize it or not, when we work together as Christians, and we pray, and pray for each other and pray for each of us to share the Gospel with boldness, we're taking people, like Padina, from the enemy's army and enlisting them into God's Army. We're stealing his troops right from under his nose! No wonder he doesn't want us to pray and work together and share the Gospel. No wonder he doesn't want us to pray and stand in God's mighty power and put on the whole armor of God. He knows that if we do, his days are numbered, and he's doomed! He'll have no army left, if we do what God says to do!

"Put on the full armor of God so that you can take your stand against the devil's schemes." Amen? Let's be those Last Days Warriors for Jesus and have the whole armor on!

How to Receive Jesus Christ:

1. Admit your need (I am a sinner).

2. Be willing to turn from your sins (repent).

3. Believe that Jesus Christ died for you on the Cross and rose from the grave.

4. Through prayer, invite Jesus Christ to come in and control your life through the Holy Spirit. (Receive Him as Lord and Savior.)

What to pray:

Dear Lord Jesus,

I know that I am a sinner and need Your forgiveness. I believe that You died for my sins. I want to turn from my sins. I now invite You to come into my heart and life. I want to trust and follow You as Lord and Savior.

In Jesus' name. Amen.

Notes

Chapter 21   *Protection from satan & demons Part 1*

1. *Shaanxi Earthquake*
(http://en.wikipedia.org/wiki/1556_Shaanxi_earthquake)
2. *Ephesian Position vs Practice Chart*
http://www.preceptaustin.org/ephesians_61-3#6:1
3. *Collision Course*
https://www.gty.org/library/sermons-library/1955
https://www.gty.org/library/sermons-library/1952
4. *War Metaphors*
https://2tim23.wordpress.com/2017/11/25/on-spiritual-warfare-an-exegesis-of-ephesians-610-20/
5. *How Ephesus went down*
https://www.gty.org/library/sermons-library/1952
6. *Pergamum went down*
https://www.gty.org/library/sermons-library/1952
7. *Thyatira west down*
https://www.gty.org/library/sermons-library/1952
8. *Sardis west down*
https://www.gty.org/library/sermons-library/1952
9. *Laodicea west down*
https://www.gty.org/library/sermons-library/1952
10. *MacArthur*
https://www.gty.org/library/sermons-library/1954
11. *Plastic Christianity*
https://www.youtube.com/watch?v=Expao2nWdAU
12. *Mr. Genor*
https://www.youtube.com/watch?v=r8jsUiTuPIA

Chapter 22 *Protection from satan & demons Part 2*

1. *Aids Virus*
   http://bible-prophecy.com/plagues.htm
   http://www.lunarpages.com/stargazers/endworld/signs/pestilenc.htm
   http://news.bbc.co.uk/1/hi/health/2512771.stm
   http://www.aids.org/factSheets/101-what-is-aids.html
   http://www.globalchange.com/ttaa/ttaa%203.htm
2. *Demon forces everywhere*
   https://www.gty.org/library/sermons-library/1954
3. *Interview with the Devil*
   https://video.search.yahoo.com/search/video?fr=tightropetb&p=
   interview+with+the+devil#id=11&vid=5d5dacf294eb4fcdb2bcd2a
   66006650f&action=view
4. *Spoons*
   https://books.google.com/books?id=iBut_sq4fHoC&pg=
   PA112&lpg=PA112&dq=When+the+angels+began+to+serve+
   dinner,+large+platters+of+delicious+food+were+placed+at+the
   +table,+but+before+anyone+was+seated,+another+angel+came+
   along+and+strapped+a+long+iron+spoon+to+each+executive%
   E2%80%99s+arm&source=bl&ots=b1pKfrphUd&sig=K3ah-
   YgXrwLQZhXyVBMs6byguxk&hl=en&sa=X&ved=0ahUKE
   wj-s-G-3sbZAhVP7WMKHRVRCWUQ6AEIJzAA#v=onepage&q=
   When%20the%20angels%20began%20to%20serve%20dinne
   r%2C%20large%20platters%20of%20delicious%20food%20
   were%20placed%20at%20the%20table%2C%20but%20
   before%20anyone%20was%20seated%2C%20another%20
   angel%20came%20along%20and%20strapped%20a%20long
   %20iron%20spoon%20to%20each%20executive%E2%80%99s
   %20arm&f=false
5. *Spiritual Warfare*
   http://www.preceptaustin.org/ephesians_612-13#6:12
6. *Universe Inside and out*
   https://video.search.yahoo.com/search/video;_ylt=AwrSw
   7xGf71ayH8AXk_7w8QF;_ylu=X3oDMTBsOWdjMmRnBHNl
   YwNzZWFyY2gEdnRpZANWSURDMQ--
   ;_ylc=X1MDOTY3ODEzMDcEX3IDMgRhY3RuA2N

sawRiY2sDOXR2bGhyNWRicWZlYSUyNmIlM0QzJTI2
cyUzRGthBGNzcmNwdmlkA2NsYlo5VEV3TGpLZV9ySFp
XcjA5eWdGQ01qQXdNUUFBQUFEX1M3ellEZnIDdGlnaH
Ryb3BldGIEZnIyA3NhLWdwBGdwcmlkA1JuWkU2SWZm
Ui42MWRWSEg3eU9SMEEEbXRlc3RpZANVSTAxJTNE
VklEQzEEbl9yc2x0AzYwBG5fc3VnZwM4BG9yaWdpbgN2a
WRlby5zZWFyY2gueWFob28uY29tBHBvcwM2BHBxc3Ry
A3VuaXZlcnNlIGluc2lkZQRwcXN0cmwDMTUEcXN0cmw
DMjEEcXVlcnkDdW5pdmVyc2UgaW5zaWRlIGNlbGxz
BHRfc3RtcAMxNTIyMzY4NDI4BHZ0ZXN0aWQDVklEQzE-
?gprid=RnZE6IffR.61dVHH7yOR0A&pvid=clcZ9TEwLjKe_
rHZWr09ygFCMjAwMQAAAAD_S7zR&p=universe+inside+
cells&ei=UTF-8&fr2=p%3As%2Cv%3Av%2Cm%3Asa&fr=
tightropetb#id=
9&vid=42241f0d133cd850df091bf638c34916&action=view

Chapter 23

Protection from satan & demons
Part 3

1. *Mt. St. Helens*
   https://en.wikipedia.org/wiki/1980_eruption_of_Mount_St._Helens
2. *You're in Gods Arm now*
   http://www.preceptaustin.org/ephesians_612-13#6:12
3. *Russell Penny*
   Russell L. Penney, *Equipping the Saints Discipleship Manual*,
   (Fort Worth: Tyndale Biblical Institute, 1997, Pg. 80)
4. *Binding and losing*
   (https://www.gotquestions.org/binding-loosing.html)
5. *Deliverance Ministries*
   https://www.charismanews.com/opinion/56705-29-protocols
   -for-engaging-in-deliverance-ministry
6. *Agape Bible Fellowship*
   https://www.youtube.com/watch?v=3Zai8cam29w
7. *Lake Stupid*
   (http://www.ozjokes.com/jokes/miscellaneous/1209-indian-love-
   story)

Chapter 24   *Protection from satan & demons Part 4*

1. *Pepcon*
   https://www.reviewjournal.com/news/5-things-to-know-about-the-pepcon-disaster-28-years-later/
   https://en.wikipedia.org/wiki/PEPCON_disaster
2. *Deaths*
   https://ministrytodaymag.com/leadership40/counseling36/8627-deliverance-malpractice
3. *Roman Belt*
   https://en.wikipedia.org/wiki/Cingulum_militare
   http://www.preceptaustin.org/ephesians_614_by_wayne_barber
4. *Clothe with Truth*
   http://www.preceptaustin.org/ephesians_614_by_wayne_barber
5. *Why must we do it*
   http://www.preceptaustin.org/ephesians_614_by_wayne_barber
6. *Girding the loins*
   http://www.preceptaustin.org/ephesians_614_by_wayne_barber
7. *Girding the loins symbolized*
   http://www.preceptaustin.org/ephesians_614_by_wayne_barber
8. *Cutting Bells*
   (J. Vernon Mcgee, Thru the Bible Vol.4 pg.281)
9. *Belt is Badge of Honor*
   https://en.wikipedia.org/wiki/Cingulum_militare
   https://www.gty.org/library/sermons-library/1955/the-believers-armor-part-1-the-belt-of-truthfulness

Chapter 25   *Protection from satan & demons Part 5*

1. *Chernobyl*
   http://www.world-nuclear.org/information-library/safety-and-security/safety-of-plants/chernobyl-accident.aspx
   http://www.pathlights.com/ce_encyclopedia/Encyclopedia/10mut11.htm#Chernobyl

https://en.wikipedia.org/wiki/Chernobyl_disaster#
Deaths_due_to_radiation_exposure

2. *Breast plate*
https://www.swordsandarmor.com/lorica-segmentata-roman-armor.htm
https://en.wikipedia.org/wiki/Roman_military_personal
_equipment#Torso_armour
https://en.wikipedia.org/wiki/Lorica_segmentata
https://romanmilitary.net/tools/armor/
http://www.freebiblestudyguides.org/bible-teachings/armor-of-god-breasplate-of-righteousness.htm

3. *Satan looks for a crack*
https://www.gty.org/library/sermons-library/90-365/the-armor-of-god-the-belt-of-truthfulness-and-the-breastplate-of-righteousness

4. *Clothe with Righteousness*
http://www.freebiblestudyguides.org/bible-teachings/armor-of-god-breasplate-of-righteousness.htm
https://www.gty.org/library/sermons-library/90-365/the-armor-of-god-the-belt-of-truthfulness-and-the-breastplate-of-righteousness

5. *Positional Righteousness Benefits*
http://www.pulpitpages.com/uploads/9/5/3/2/9532717/the_armor_of_the_christian_part_1_-_eph.613-18.pdf
http://sermonnotebook.org/Ephesians/Ephesians%2047%20-%20Ephesians%206-13-14%20The%20Breastplate%20Of%20Righteousness.htm
https://bible.org/seriespage/lesson-57-protected-truth-and-righteousness-ephesians-614
https://bible.org/seriespage/lesson-57-protected-truth-and-righteousness-ephesians-614

6 *Practical Righteousness*
http://www.pulpitpages.com/uploads/9/5/3/2/9532717/the_armor_of_the_christian_part_1_-_eph.613-18.pdf
http://sermonnotebook.org/Ephesians/Ephesians%2047%20-%20Ephesians%206-13-14%20The%20Breastplate%20Of%20Righteousness.htm
https://bible.org/seriespage/lesson-57-protected-truth-and-righteousness-ephesians-614
https://bible.org/seriespage/lesson-57-protected

-truth-and-righteousness-ephesians-614

7. *Practical Righteousness 2*
http://www.pulpitpages.com/uploads/9/5/3/2/9532717/the_
armor_of_the_christian_part_1_-_eph.613-18.pdf
http://sermonnotebook.org/Ephesians/Ephesians%2047%20-
%20Ephesians%206-13-
14%20The%20Breastplate%20Of%20Righteousness.htm
https://bible.org/seriespage/lesson-57-protected-truth-and-
righteousness-ephesians-614
https://bible.org/seriespage/lesson-57-protected-truth-and-
righteousness-ephesians-614
http://www.alfredplacechurch.org.uk/index.php/sermons
/ephesians/614-the-breastplate-of-righteousness/
https://www.studylight.org/commentaries/dsb/ephesians-6.html
http://www.preceptaustin.org/ephesians_614-15
https://www.sermoncentral.com/illustrations/sermon-illustration-tony-
abram-quotes-world-84083?ref=TextIllustrationSerps

8. *Committed to purity*
http://www.pulpitpages.com/uploads/9/5/3/2/9532717/the_
armor_of_the_christian_part_1_-_eph.613-18.pdf
http://sermonnotebook.org/Ephesians/Ephesians%2047%20-
%20Ephesians%206-13-
14%20The%20Breastplate%20Of%20Righteousness.htm
https://bible.org/seriespage/lesson-57-protected-truth-
and-righteousness-ephesians-614
https://www.gty.org/library/sermons-library/1956

9. *Committed to Christ*
http://www.sermonindex.net/modules/articles/index.php?
view=article&aid=33539
http://www.sermonindex.net/modules/articles/index.php?
view=article&aid=34673

10. *Victories from Righteousness*
https://www.gty.org/library/sermons-library/1956

Chapter 26   *Protection from satan & demons Part 6*

1. *Krakatoa*
   https://www.livescience.com/28186-krakatoa.html
   https://en.wikipedia.org/wiki/Krakatoa
2. *Roman soldiers shoes*
   https://en.wikipedia.org/wiki/Roman_military_personal_equipment
   https://en.wikipedia.org/wiki/Caligae
   http://www.romeacrosseurope.com/?p=2534#sthash.ADd4zsdn.dpbs
3. *Importance of the Caligae*
   http://www.sermonnotebook.org/Ephesians/Ephesians
   %2048%20-%20Ephesians%206-
   15%20The%20Boots%20Of%20Peace.htm
4. *Shoes keep you from stumbling*
   https://www.gty.org/library/sermons-library/1957/the-believers-armor-part-3-the-shoes-of-the-gospel-of-peace
   https://www.studylight.org/commentaries/mpc/ephesians-6.html
5. *A Fathers Choice*
   https://www.facebook.com/LittleStarFoundation/posts/504479166281697
6. *FishlessFishermen*
   https://www.youtube.com/watch?v=aur6-DRTvU0
7. *Rogers Fight*
   https://www.gty.org/library/sermons-library/1957/the-believers-armor-part-3-the-shoes-of-the-gospel-of-peace
8. *Shoes*
   https://www.preachtheword.com/bookstore/holywar.pdf
   https://www.gotquestions.org/gospel-of-peace.html
9. *Duck*
   https://bible.org/illustration/sin-enslaves-forgiveness-frees

Chapter 27 *The Protection from satan & demons*
Part 7

1. *The Great Chinese Famine*
   http://alphahistory.com/chineserevolution/great-chinese-famine/
   https://www.theguardian.com/world/2013/jan/01/china-great-famine-book-tombstone
   https://www.npr.org/2012/11/10/164732497/a-grim-chronicle-of-

chinas-great-famine
https://en.wikipedia.org/wiki/Great_Chinese_Famine
2. *Roman Soldiers Shield*
https://en.wikipedia.org/wiki/Thyreos
https://en.wikipedia.org/wiki/Thyreophoroi
https://ipfs.io/ipfs/QmXoypizjW3WknFiJnKLwHCnL72
vedxjQkDDP1mXWo6uco/wiki/Thureos.html
http://biblehub.com/greek/2375.htm
https://en.wikipedia.org/wiki/Roman_military_personal_equipment
https://www.studylight.org/commentaries/dcc/ephesians-6.html
http://www.baptistbiblebelievers.com/LinkClick.aspx?
fileticket=BlslOnZZ%2b%2bQ%3d&tabid=202&mid=662
3. *Importance of the Shield of Faith*
http://www.preceptaustin.org/ephesians_616-17
4. *Home Insurance*
https://lifehacker.com/how-much-do-you-pay-for-insurance
-1713644359
5. *Monk*
(Email Letter – Source Unknown
6. *Complaining*
http://www.preceptaustin.org/ephesians_616-17
7. *Nail in the Head*
(Email Letter – Source Unknown
8. *Fiery Darts*
https://www.gty.org/library/sermons-library/90-366/the-armor-of-
god-the-shoes-of-the-gospel-of-peace-and-the-shield-of-faith
https://www.gty.org/library/sermons-library/1958/the-believers-
armor-part-4-the-shield-of-faith
http://sermonnotebook.org/Ephesians/Ephesians%2049%20-
%20Ephesians%206-16%20The%20Buckler%20Of%20Faith.htm
https://bible.org/seriespage/lesson-59-essential-shield-ephesians-616
http://www.rondaniel.com/library/49-Ephesians/Ephesians0616.php
https://www.preachtheword.com/sermon/warfare04.shtml
9. *Final Words*
http://www.alfredplacechurch.org.uk/index.php/sermons/ephesians
/616-the-shield-of-faith/

Chapter 28 *The Protection from satan & demons*

Part 8

1. *Haiti Earthquake*
   https://www.cnn.com/2013/12/12/world/haiti-earthquake-fast-facts/index.html
   https://www.britannica.com/event/Haiti-earthquake-of-2010
   https://en.wikipedia.org/wiki/2010_Haiti_earthquake
2. *Roman Soldiers Helmet*
   https://en.wikipedia.org/wiki/Roman_military_personal_equipment
   https://en.wikipedia.org/wiki/Galea_(helmet)
   http://www.sermonindex.net/modules/articles/index.php?view=article&aid=34216
   https://www.studylight.org/commentaries/cgt/ephesians-6.html
   https://www.studylight.org/commentaries/vnt/ephesians-6.html
3. *Importance of Helmet*
   http://www.sermonindex.net/modules/articles/index.php?view=article&aid=34216
   http://www.preceptaustin.org/ephesians_616-17
4. *Concessions*
   https://www.theatlantic.com/news/archive/2016/09/nfl-money-concussions/500060/
5. *Bike Equipment*
   http://www.cyclingweekly.com/news/latest-news/how-much-do-americans-spend-on-cycling-new-study-provides-the-answer-327791#iZPKgUktGYvD8AsW.99
6. *Mind thy Head*
   https://bible.org/seriespage/lesson-60-mind-thy-head-ephesians-617a
7. *Eternal Security*
   https://www.gty.org/library/sermons-library/1960/the-believers-armor-part-6-the-helmet-of-salvation-part-2
   http://www.preceptaustin.org/ephesians_617_by_wayne_barber
   http://www.preceptaustin.org/ephesians_616-17
   http://www.preceptaustin.org/pdf/60214
   https://www.christianity.com/devotionals/sparkling-gems-from-the-greek-rick-renner/sparkling-gems-from-the-greek-week-of-august-8.html
8. *Comma*
   https://storiesforpreaching.com/category/sermonillustrations/forgiveness/

9. *85-year-old Couple*
   Email Letter – Source Unknown
10. *Benefits of Eternal Security*
   https://www.gty.org/library/sermons-library/1959/the-believers-armor-part-5-the-helmet-of-salvation-part-1
   https://www.gty.org/library/sermons-library/1960/the-believers-armor-part-6-the-helmet-of-salvation-part-2
11. *Alligator*
   Email Letter – Source Unknown

Chapter 29   *The Protection from satan & demons Part 9*

1. *The Great Peshtigo Fire*
   https://www.google.com/search?q=worst+disasters+in+history&rlz=1C1CHBD_enUS721US721&oq=worst+disasters&aqs=chrome.0.69i59j69i57j0l4.2746j0j7&sourceid=chrome&ie=UTF-8
   https://en.wikipedia.org/wiki/Peshtigo_fire
   https://www.weather.gov/grb/peshtigofire
   http://www.exploringoffthebeatenpath.com/Parks/PeshtigoFire/index.html
2. *The Roman Soldiers Sword*
   https://en.wikipedia.org/wiki/Roman_military_personal_equipment
   https://redeeminggod.com/sermons/ephesians/ephesians_6_17b/
   https://en.wikipedia.org/wiki/Gladius
   https://lifehopeandtruth.com/change/christian-conversion/armor-of-god/sword-of-the-spirit/
   http://www.freebiblestudyguides.org/bible-teachings/armor-of-god-sword-of-spirit-word.htm
3. *Sword as an Offensive Weapon*
   https://redeeminggod.com/sermons/ephesians/ephesians_6_17b/
4. *Money Spent on Security Systems*
   (https://www.creditdonkey.com/average-cost-home-security-system.html)
5. *Personal Weaponry*
   https://www.csmonitor.com/Business/2013/0103/A-look-at-America-s-gun-industry)
6. *Defense Budget*
   (https://militarybenefits.info/2018-defense-budget-overview/)

7. *Cowboy slap*
   https://www.youtube.com/watch?v=u70GP8K_DO8
8. *Importance of the Sword*
   https://redeeminggod.com/sermons/ephesians/ephesians_6_17b/
9. *Bibleless Christians*
   https://www.gty.org/library/sermons-library/1961/the-believers-armor-part-7-the-sword-of-the-spirit
   https://www.gty.org/library/sermons-library/90-368/the-armor-of-god-the-sword-of-the-spirit
10. *Importance of Rhema*
    https://redeeminggod.com/sermons/ephesians/ephesians_6_17b/
11. *Christian Sword Drills*
    https://redeeminggod.com/sermons/ephesians/ephesians_6_17b/
12. *The Manslater*
    https://www.google.com/search?q=the+manslater&rlz=1C1CHBF_enUS727US727&oq=The+Manslater&aqs=chrome.0.0l5j69i6
    4.13343j0j8&sourceid=chrome&ie=UTF-8
13. *Final Words*
    http://www.preceptaustin.org/ephesians_616-17
    https://bible.org/seriespage/lesson-61-weapon-ephesians-617b
    https://www.fpcjackson.org/resource-library/sermons/god-s-new-family-an-exposition-of-ephesians-lix-the-full-armor-of-god-3-word-and-prayer

Chapter 30 *The Protection from satan & demons Part 10*

1. *Bhola Cyclone*
   https://www.livescience.com/33316-top-10-deadliest-natural-disasters.html
   http://www.hurricanescience.org/history/storms/1970s/greatbhola/
   https://weather.com/storms/hurricane/news/deadliest-cyclone-history-bangladesh-20130605#/1
   https://en.wikipedia.org/wiki/1970_Bhola_cyclone
2. *Roman Soldiers Communication*
   http://www.romanobritain.org/8-military/mil_signalling_systems.htm
   https://www.quora.com/How-did-Roman-legions-communicate-with-each-other-during-the-course-of-battle
3. *Christian Walkie Talkie*

http://www.preceptaustin.org/ephesians_618-20

4. *Pre-Blessed Food*
   https://www.google.com/search?q=pre-blessed+food&rlz=1C1CHBF_enUS727US727&oq=pre-blessed+food&aqs=chrome..69i57j0l4.8663j0j8&sourceid=chrome&ie=UTF-8

5. *How often to Pray*
   http://www.preceptaustin.org/ephesians_618-20

6. *Father Father – Tim Hawkins*
   https://www.google.com/search?q=tim+hawkins+father+father+just+just&rlz=1C1CHBF_enUS727US727&oq=tim+hawkins+father-father&aqs=chrome.1.69i57j0.8831j0j8&sourceid=chrome&ie=UTF-8

7. *Importance of Continuous Prayer*
   https://www.gty.org/library/sermons-library/1962/praying-at-all-times
   http://www.preceptaustin.org/ephesians_618-20
   https://www.gty.org/library/sermons-library/90-369/the-armor-of-god-praying-at-all-times
   https://www.sermoncentral.com/sermons/a-prayer-for-boldness-brian-bill-sermon-on-prayer-how-to-71592?page=1
   https://www.studylight.org/commentaries/dcc/ephesians-6.html

8. *Die you Heretic*
   https://www.gty.org/library/sermons-library/1962/praying-at-all-timeshttp://www.preceptaustin.org/ephesians_618-20https://www.gty.org/library/sermons-library/90-369/the-armor-of-god-praying-at-all-timeshttps://www.sermoncentral.com/sermons/a-prayer-for-boldness-brian-bill-sermon-on-prayer-how-to-71592?page=1https://www.studylight.org/commentaries/dcc/ephesians-6.html

9. *Praying for others for healing*
   http://www.preceptaustin.org/ephesians_618-20
   http://www.preceptaustin.org/ephesians_618
   https://www.gty.org/library/sermons-library/1962/praying-at-all-times
   https://www.gty.org/library/sermons-library/90-369/the-armor-of-god-praying-at-all-times
   http://www.preceptaustin.org/ephesians_618-19_by_wayne_barber

10. *Praying for others for Salvation*
    http://www.preceptaustin.org/ephesians_618-20
    http://www.preceptaustin.org/ephesians_618
    https://www.gty.org/library/sermons-library/1962/praying-at-all-times
    https://www.gty.org/library/sermons-library/90-369/the-armor-of-

god-praying-at-all-times
http://www.preceptaustin.org/ephesians_618-19_by_wayne_barber
https://www.preachtheword.com/sermon/eph32.shtml
https://www.preachtheword.com/sermon/eph33.shtml
https://www.preachtheword.com/sermon/eph34.shtml
https://www.preachtheword.com/sermon/eph35.shtml

11. *Padina*

https://www.youtube.com/watch?v=rVCj26fdJpQ